COLLECTED POEMS

Fleur Adcock was born in New Zealand in 1934. She spent the war years in England, returning with her family to New Zealand in 1947. She emigrated to Britain in 1963, working as a librarian in London until 1979. In 1977-78 she was writer-in-residence at Charlotte Mason College of Education, Ambleside. She was Northern Arts Literary Fellow in 1979-81, living in Newcastle, becoming a freelance writer after her return to London.

Fleur Adcock received an OBE in 1996, and the Queen's Gold Medal for Poetry in 2006 for *Poems 1960-2000* (Bloodaxe Books, 2000). In 2019 she was presented with the New Zealand Prime Minister's Award for Literary Achievement in Poetry 2019 by the Rt Hon Jacinda Ardern, coinciding with the publication of her *Collected Poems* in New Zealand by Victoria University Press under licence from Bloodaxe Books.

She published three pamphlets with Bloodaxe: *Below Loughrigg* (1979), *Hotspur* (1986) and *Meeting the Comet* (1988), as well as her translations of medieval Latin lyrics, *The Virgin & the Nightingale* (1983). She also published two translations of Romanian poets with Oxford University Press, *Orient Express* by Grete Tartler (1989) and *Letters from Darkness* by Daniela Crasnaru (1994). All her other collections were published by Oxford until they shut down their poetry list in 1999, after which Bloodaxe published her *Poems 1960-2000* (2000), followed by *Dragon Talk* (2010), *Glass Wings* (2013), *The Land Ballot* (2015), *Hoard* (2017) and *The Mermaid's Purse* (2021). *Poems 1960-2000* and *Hoard* were Poetry Book Society Special Commendations while *Glass Wings* was a Poetry Book Society Recommendation.

Fleur Adcock's *Collected Poems* was published by Bloodaxe on her 90th birthday in 2024, at the same time an expanded edition of the original New Zealand *Collected Poems* was published by Te Herenga Waka University Press (formerly Victoria University Press of Wellington).

FLEUR ADCOCK

Collected Poems

BLOODAXE BOOKS

ISBN: 978 1 78037 684 4 hardback edition
       978 1 78037 683 7 paperback edition

First published in 2024 by
Bloodaxe Books Ltd,
Eastburn,
South Park,
Hexham,
Northumberland NE46 1BS,
UK

and in New Zealand by Te Herenga Waka University Press.

www.bloodaxebooks.com
For further information about Bloodaxe titles
please visit our website and join our mailing list
or write to the above address for a catalogue.

Supported using public funding by
ARTS COUNCIL
ENGLAND

Cover design: Neil Astley & Pamela Robertson-Pearce.

Printed in Great Britain by Bell & Bain Limited, Glasgow, Scotland, on
acid-free paper sourced from mills with FSC chain of custody certification.

Contents

The Scenic Route (1974)

The Inner Harbour (1979)

Hotspur (1986)

The Incident Book (1986)

Schools

Time-Zones (1991)

Looking Back (1997)

Glass Wings (2013)

Hoard (2017)

THE EYE OF THE HURRICANE

(1964)

AND

TIGERS

(1967)

Note on Propertius

Among the Roman love-poets, possession
is a rare theme. The locked and flower-hung door,
the shivering lover, are allowed. To more
buoyant moods, the canons of expression
gave grudging sanction. Do we, then, assume,
finding Propertius tear-sodden and jealous,
that Cynthia was inexorably callous?
Plenty of moonlight entered that high room
whose doors had met his Alexandrine battles;
and she, so gay a lutanist, was known
to stitch and doze a night away, alone,
until the poet tumbled in with apples
for penitence and for her head his wreath,
brought from a party, of wine-scented roses –
(the garland's aptness lying, one supposes,
less in the flowers than in the thorns beneath:
her waking could, he knew, provide his verses
with less idyllic themes). Onto her bed
he rolled the round fruit, and adorned her head;
then gently roused her sleeping mouth to curses.
Here the conventions reassert their power:
the apples fall and bruise, the roses wither,
touched by a sallowed moon. But there were other
luminous nights – (even the cactus flower
glows briefly golden, fed by spiny flesh) –
and once, as he acknowledged, all was singing:
the moonlight musical, the darkness clinging,
and she compliant to his every wish.

Flight, with Mountains
(in memory of David Herron)

1
Tarmac, take-off: metallic words conduct us
over that substance, black with spilt rain,
to this event. Sealed, we turn and pause.

Engines churn and throb to a climax, then
up: a hard spurt, and the passionate rise
levels out for this gradual incline.

There was something of pleasure in that thrust
from earth into ignorant cloud; but here,
above all tremors of sensation, rest
replaces motion; secretly we enter
the obscurely gliding current, and encased
in vitreous calm inhabit the high air.

Now I see, beneath the plated wing,
cloud edges withdrawing their slow foam
from shoreline, rippling hills, and beyond, the long
crested range of the land's height. I am
carried too far by this blind rocketing:
faced with mountains, I remember him

whose death seems a convention of such a view:
another one for the mountains. Another one
who, climbing to stain the high snow
with his shadow, fell, and briefly caught between
sudden earth and sun, projected below
a flicker of darkness; as, now, this plane.

     2
Only air to hold the wings;
only words to hold the story;
only a frail web of cells
to hold heat in the body.

Breath bleeds from throat and lungs
under the last cold fury;
words wither; meaning fails;
steel wings grow heavy.

     3
Headlines announced it, over a double column of type:
the cabled facts, public regret, and a classified list

of your attainments – degrees, scholarships and positions,
and notable feats of climbing. So the record stands:
no place there for my private annotations. The face
that smiles in some doubt from a fuscous half-tone block
stirs me hardly more than those I have mistaken
daily, about the streets, for yours.
                                        I can refer
to my own pictures; and turning first to the easiest,
least painful, I see Dave the raconteur,
playing a shoal of listeners on a casual line
of dry narration. Other images unreel:
your face in a car, silent, watching the dark road,
or animated and sunburnt from your hard pleasures
of snow and rock-face; again, I see you arguing,
practical and determined, as you draw with awkward puffs
at a rare cigarette.
                        So much, in vivid sequence
memory gives. And then, before I can turn away,
imagination adds the last scene: your eyes bruised,
mouth choked under a murderous weight of snow.

          4
'When you reach the top of a mountain, keep on climbing' –
meaning, we may suppose,
to sketch on space the cool arabesques of birds
in plastic air, or those
exfoliating arcs, upward and outward,
of an aeronautic show.
Easier, such a free fall in reverse,
higher than clogging snow
or clutching gravity, than the awkward local
embrace of rocks. And observe
the planets coursing their elliptical race-tracks,
where each completed curve
cinctures a new dimension. Mark these patterns.
Mark, too, how the high
air thins. The top of any mountain
is a base for the sky.

5

Further by days and oceans than all my flying
you have gone, while here the air insensibly flowing
over a map of mountains drowns my dumbness.
A turn of the earth away, where a crawling dimness
waits now to absorb our light, another
snowscape, named like this one, took you; and neither
rope, nor crumbling ice, nor your unbelieving
uncommitted hands could hold you to living.
Wheels turn; the dissolving air rolls over
an arc of thunder. Gone is gone forever.

Beauty Abroad

Carrying still the dewy rose
for which she's bound to payment, Beauty goes
trembling through the gruesome wood:
small comfort to her that she's meek and good.
A branch cracks, and the beast appears:
she sees the fangs, the eyes, the bristly ears,
stifles a scream, and smooths her dress;
but his concern is for his own distress.
He lays his muzzle on her hand,
says 'Pity me!' and 'Can you understand?
Be kind!' And then goes on to praise
her pretty features and her gentle ways.
Beauty inclines a modest ear,
hears what she has decided she should hear,
and with no thought to ask 'What then?'
follows the creature to his hairy den.
The beast, like any hero, knows
sweet talk can lead him to *la belle chose*.

Knife-play

All my scars are yours. We talk of pledges,
and holding out my hand I show
the faint burn on the palm and the hair-thin
razor-marks at wrist and elbow:

self-inflicted, yes; but your tokens –
made as distraction from a more
inaccessible pain than could have been
caused by cigarette or razor –

and these my slightest marks. In all our meetings
you were the man with the long knives,
piercing the living hopes, cutting connections,
carving and dissecting motives,

and with an expert eye for dagger-throwing:
a showman's aim. Oh, I could dance
and dodge, as often as not, the whistling blades,
turning on a brave performance

to empty stands. I leaned upon a hope
that this might prove to have been less
a gladiatorial show, contrived for murder,
than a formal test of fitness

(initiation rites are always painful)
to bring me ultimately to your
regard. Well, in a sense it was; for now
I have found some kind of favour:

you have learnt softness; I, by your example,
am well-schooled in contempt; and while
you speak of truce I laugh, and to your pleading
turn a cool and guarded profile.

I have now, you might say, the upper hand:
these knives that bristle in my flesh
increase my armoury and lessen yours.
I can pull out, whet and polish

your weapons, and return to the attack,
well-armed. It is a pretty trick,
but one that offers little consolation.
such a victory would be Pyrrhic,

occurring when my strength is almost spent.
No: I would make an end of fighting
and, bleeding as I am from old wounds,
die like the bee upon a sting.

Instructions to Vampires

I would not have you drain
with your sodden lips the flesh that has fed mine,
and leech his bubbling blood to a decline:
not that pain;

nor visit on his mind
that other desiccation, where the wit
shrivels: so to be humbled is not fit
for his kind.

But use acid or flame,
secretly, to brand or cauterise;
and on the soft globes of his mortal eyes
etch my name.

Incident

When you were lying on the white sand,
a rock under your head, and smiling,
(circled by dead shells), I came to you
and you said, reaching to take my hand,
'Lie down.' So for a time we lay
warm on the sand, talking and smoking,
easy; while the grovelling sea behind
sucked at the rocks and measured the day.
Lightly I fell asleep then, and fell
into a cavernous dream of falling.
It was all the cave-myths, it was all
the myths of tunnel or tower or well –
Alice's rabbit-hole into the ground,
or the path of Orpheus: a spiral staircase
to hell, furnished with danger and doubt.
Stumbling, I suddenly woke; and found
water about me. My hair was wet,
and you were lying on the grey sand
waiting for the lapping tide to take me:
watching, and lighting a cigarette.

Unexpected Visit

I have nothing to say about this garden.
I do not want to be here, I can't explain
what happened. I merely opened a usual door
and found this. The rain

has just stopped, and the gravel paths are trickling
with water. Stone lions, on each side,
gleam like wet seals, and the green birds
are stiff with dripping pride.

Not my kind of country. The gracious vistas,
the rose-gardens and terraces, are all wrong –
as comfortless as the weather. But here I am.
I cannot tell how long

I have stood gazing at grass too wet to sit on,
under a sky so dull I cannot read
the sundial, staring along the curving walks
and wondering where they lead;

not really hoping, though, to be enlightened.
It must be morning, I think, but there is no
horizon behind the trees, no sun as clock
or compass. I shall go

and find, somewhere among the formal hedges
or hidden behind a trellis, a toolshed. There
I can sit on a box and wait. Whatever happens
may happen anywhere,

and better, perhaps, among the rakes and flowerpots
and sacks of bulbs than under this pallid sky:
having chosen nothing else, I can at least
choose to be warm and dry.

For Andrew

'Will I die?' you ask. And so I enter on
the dutiful exposition of that which you
would rather not know, and I rather not tell you.
To soften my 'Yes' I offer compensations –
age and fulfilment ('It's so far away;
you will have children and grandchildren by then')
and indifference ('By then you will not care').
No need: you cannot believe me, convinced
that if you always eat plenty of vegetables
and are careful crossing the street you will live for ever.

And so we close the subject, with much unsaid –
this, for instance: Though you and I may die
tomorrow or next year, and nothing remain
of our stock, of the unique, preciously-hoarded
inimitable genes we carry in us,
it is possible that for many generations
there will exist, sprung from whatever seeds,
children straight-limbed, with clear enquiring voices,
bright-eyed as you. Or so I like to think:
sharing in this your childish optimism.

For a Five-Year-Old

A snail is climbing up the window-sill
into your room, after a night of rain.
You call me in to see, and I explain
that it would be unkind to leave it there:
it might crawl to the floor; we must take care
that no one squashes it. You understand,
and carry it outside, with careful hand,
to eat a daffodil.

I see, then, that a kind of faith prevails:
your gentleness is moulded still by words
from me, who have trapped mice and shot wild birds,
from me, who drowned your kittens, who betrayed
your closest relatives, and who purveyed
the harshest kind of truth to many another.
But that is how things are: I am your mother,
and we are kind to snails.

Comment

The four-year-old believes he likes
vermouth; the cat eats cheese;
and you and I, though scarcely more
convincingly than these,
walk in the gardens, hand in hand,
beneath the summer trees.

Miss Hamilton in London

It would not be true to say she was doing nothing:
she visited several bookshops, spent an hour
in the Victoria and Albert Museum (Indian section),
and walked carefully through the streets of Kensington
carrying five mushrooms in a paper bag,
a tin of black pepper, a literary magazine,
and enough money to pay the rent for two weeks.
The sky was cloudy, leaves lay on the pavements.

Nor did she lack human contacts: she spoke
to three shop-assistants and a newsvendor,
and returned the 'Goodnight' of a museum attendant.
Arriving home, she wrote a letter to someone
in Canada, as it might be, or in New Zealand,
listened to the news as she cooked her meal,
and conversed for five minutes with the landlady.
The air was damp with the mist of late autumn.

A full day, and not unrewarding.
Night fell at the usual seasonal hour.
She drew the curtains, switched on the electric fire,
washed her hair and read until it was dry,
then went to bed; where, for the hours of darkness,
she lay pierced by thirty black spears
and felt her limbs numb, her eyes burning,
and dark rust carried along her blood.

The Man Who X-Rayed an Orange

Viewed from the top, he said, it was like a wheel,
the paper-thin spokes raying out from the hub
to the half-transparent circumference of rind,
with small dark ellipses suspended between.
He could see the wood of the table-top through it.
Then he knelt, and with his eye at orange-level
saw it as the globe, its pithy core
upright from pole to flattened pole. Next,
its levitation: sustained (or so he told us)
by a week's diet of nothing but rice-water
he had developed powers, drawing upon which
he raised it to a height of about two feet
above the table, with never a finger near it.
That was all. It descended, gradually opaque,
to rest; while he sat giddy and shivering.
(He shivered telling it.) But surely, we asked,
(and still none of us mentioned self-hypnosis
or hallucinations caused by lack of food),
surely triumphant too? Not quite, he said,
with his little crooked smile. It was not enough:
he should have been able to summon up,
created out of what he had newly learnt,
a perfectly imaginary orange, complete
in every detail; whereupon the real orange
would have vanished. Then came explanations
and his talk of mysticism, occult physics,
alchemy, the Qabalah – all his hobby-horses.
If there was failure, it was only here
in the talking. For surely he had lacked nothing,
neither power nor insight nor imagination,
when he knelt alone in his room, seeing before him
suspended in the air that golden globe,
visible and transparent, light-filled:
his only fruit from the Tree of Life.

Composition for Words and Paint

This darkness has a quality
that poses us in shapes and textures,
one plane behind another,
flatness in depth.

Your face; a fur of hair; a striped
curtain behind, and to one side cushions;
nothing recedes, all lies extended.
I sink upon your image.

I see a soft metallic glint,
a tinsel weave behind the canvas,
aluminium and bronze beneath the ochre.
There is more in this than we know.

I can imagine drawn around you
a white line, in delicate brush-strokes:
emphasis; but you do not need it.
You have completeness.

I am not measuring your gestures;
(I have seen you measure those of others,
know a mind by a hand's trajectory,
the curve of a lip).

But you move, and I move towards you,
draw back your head, and I advance.
I am fixed to the focus of your eyes.
I share your orbit.

Now I discover things about you:
your thin wrists, a tooth missing;
and how I melt and burn before you.
I have known you always.

The greyness from the long windows
reduces visual depth; but tactile
reality defies half-darkness.
My hands prove you solid.

You draw me down upon your body,
hard arms behind my head.
Darkness and soft colours blur.
We have swallowed the light.

Now I dissolve you in my mouth,
catch in the corners of my throat
the sly taste of your love, sliding
into me, singing;

just as the birds have started singing.
Let them come flying through the windows
with chains of opals around their necks.
We are expecting them.

Regression

All the flowers have gone back into the ground.
We fell on them, and they did not lie
crushed and crumpled, waiting to die
on the earth's surface. No: they suddenly wound

the film of their growth backwards. We saw them shrink
from blossom to bud to tiny shoot,
down from the stem and up from the root.
Back to the seed, brothers. It makes you think.

Clearly they do not like us. They've gone away,
given up. And who could blame
anything else for doing the same?
I notice that certain trees look smaller today.

You can't escape the fact: there's a backward trend
from oak to acorn, and from pine
to cone; they all want to resign.
Understandable enough, but where does it end?

Harder, you'd think, for animals; yet the cat
was pregnant, but has not produced.
Her rounded belly is reduced,
somehow, to normal. How to answer that?

Buildings, perhaps, will be the next to go;
imagine it: a tinkle of glass,
a crunch of brick, and a house will pass
through the soil to the protest meeting below.

This whole conspiracy of inverted birth
leaves only us; and how shall we
endure as we deserve to be,
foolish and lost on the naked skin of the earth?

I Ride on My High Bicycle

I ride on my high bicycle
into a sooty Victorian city
of colonnaded bank buildings,
horse-troughs, and green marble fountains.

I glide along, contemplating
the curly lettering on the shop-fronts.
An ebony elephant, ten feet tall,
is wheeled past, advertising something.

When I reach the dark archway
I chain my bicycle to a railing,
nod to a policeman, climb the steps,
and emerge into unexpected sunshine.

There below lies Caroline Bay,
its red roofs and its dazzling water.
Now I am running along the path;
it is four o'clock, there is still just time.

I halt and sit on the sandy grass
to remove my shoes and thick stockings;
but something has caught me; around my shoulders
I feel barbed wire; I am entangled.

It pulls my hair, dragging me downwards;
I am suddenly older than seventeen,
tired, powerless, pessimistic.
I struggle weakly; and wake, of course.

Well, all right. It doesn't matter.
Perhaps I didn't get to the beach:
but I have been there – to all the beaches
(waking or dreaming) and all the cities.

Now it is very early morning
and from my window I see a leopard
tall as a horse, majestic and kindly,
padding over the fallen snow.

Parting Is Such Sweet Sorrow

The room is full of clichés – 'Throw me a crumb'
and 'Now I see the writing on the wall'
and 'Don't take umbrage, dear'. I wish I could.
Instead I stand bedazzled by them all,

longing for shade. Belshazzar's fiery script
glows there, between the prints of tropical birds,
in neon lighting, and the air is full
of crumbs that flash and click about me. Words

glitter in colours like those gaudy prints:
the speech of a computer, metal-based
but feathered like a cloud of darts. All right.
Your signal-system need not go to waste.

Mint me another batch of tokens: say
'I am in your hands; I throw myself upon
your mercy, casting caution to the winds.'
Thank you; there is no need to go on.

Thus authorised by your mechanical
issue, I lift you like a bale of hay,
open the window wide, and toss you out;
and gales of laughter whirl you far away.

Hauntings

Three times I have slept in your house
and this is definitely the last.
I cannot endure the transformations:
nothing stays the same for an hour.

Last time there was a spiral staircase
winding across the high room.
People tramped up and down it all night,
carrying brief-cases, pails of milk, bombs,

pretending not to notice me
as I lay in a bed lousy with dreams.
Couldn't you have kept them away?
After all, they were trespassing.

The time before it was all bathrooms,
full of naked, quarrelling girls –
and you claim to like solitude:
I do not understand your arrangements.

Now the glass doors to the garden
open on rows of stone columns;
beside them stands a golden jeep.
Where are we this time? On what planet?

Every night lasts for a week.
I toss and turn and wander about,
whirring from room to room like a moth,
ignored by those indifferent faces.

At last I think I have woken up.
I lift my head from the pillow, rejoicing.
The alarm-clock is playing Schubert:
I am still asleep. This is too much.

Well, I shall try again in a minute.
I shall wake into this real room
with its shadowy plants and patterned screens
(yes, I remember how it looks).

It will be cool, but I shan't wait
to light the gas-fire. I shall dress
(I know where my clothes are) and slip out.
You needn't think I am here to stay.

Advice to a Discarded Lover

Think, now: if you have found a dead bird,
not only dead, not only fallen,
but full of maggots: what do you feel –
more pity or more revulsion?

Pity is for the moment of death,
and the moments after. It changes
when decay comes, with the creeping stench
and the wriggling, munching scavengers.

Returning later, though, you will see
a shape of clean bone, a few feathers,
an inoffensive symbol of what
once lived. Nothing to make you shudder.

It is clear then. But perhaps you find
the analogy I have chosen
for our dead affair rather gruesome –
too unpleasant a comparison.

It is not accidental. In you
I see maggots close to the surface.
You are eaten up by self-pity,
crawling with unlovable pathos.

If I were to touch you I should feel
against my fingers fat, moist worm-skin.
Do not ask me for charity now:
go away until your bones are clean.

The Water Below

This house is floored with water,
wall to wall, a deep green pit,
still and gleaming, edged with stone.
Over it are built stairways
and railed living-areas
in wrought iron. All rather
impractical; it will be
damp in winter, and we shall
surely drop small objects – keys,
teaspoons, or coins – through the chinks
in the ironwork, to splash
lost into the glimmering
depths (and do we know how deep?).
It will have to be rebuilt:
a solid floor of concrete

over this dark well (perhaps
already full of coins, like
the flooded crypt of that church
in Ravenna). You might say
it could be drained, made into
a useful cellar for coal.
But I am sure the water
would return; would never go.
Under my grandmother's house
in Drury, when I was three,
I always believed there was
water: lift up the floorboards
and you would see it – a lake,
a subterranean sea.
True, I played under the house
and saw only hard-packed earth,
wooden piles, gardening tools,
a place to hunt for lizards.
That was different: below
I saw no water. Above,
I knew it must still be there,
waiting. (For why did we say
'Forgive us our trespasses,
deliver us from evil'?)
Always beneath the safe house
lies the pool, the hidden sea
created before we were.
It is not easy to drain
the waters under the earth.

Think Before You Shoot

Look, children, the wood is full of tigers,
scorching the bluebells with their breath.
You reach for guns. Will you preserve the flowers
at such cost? Will you prefer the death
of prowling stripes to a mush of trampled stalks?

Through the eyes, then – do not spoil the head.
Tigers are easier to shoot than to like.
Sweet necrophiles, you only love them dead.

There now, you've got three – and with such fur, too,
golden and warm and salty. Very good.
Don't expect them to forgive you, though.
There are plenty more of them. This is their wood
(and their bluebells, which you have now forgotten).
They've eaten all the squirrels. They want you,
and it's no excuse to say you're only children.
No one is on your side. What will you do?

The Pangolin

There have been all those tigers, of course,
and a leopard, and a six-legged giraffe,
and a young deer that ran up to my window
before it was killed, and once a blue horse,
and somewhere an impression of massive dogs.
Why do I dream of such large, hot-blooded beasts
covered with sweating fur and full of passions
when there could be dry lizards and cool frogs,
or slow, modest creatures, as a rest
from all those panting, people-sized animals?
Hedgehogs or perhaps tortoises would do,
but I think the pangolin would suit me best:
a vegetable animal, who goes
disguised as an artichoke or asparagus-tip
in a green coat of close-fitting leaves,
with his flat shovel-tail and his pencil-nose:
the scaly anteater. Yes, he would fit
more aptly into a dream than into his cage
in the Small Mammal House; so I invite him
to be dreamt about, if he would care for it.

HIGH TIDE IN THE GARDEN

(1971)

A Game

They are throwing the ball
to and fro between them,
in and out of the picture.
She is in the painting
hung on the wall
in a narrow gold frame.
He stands on the floor
catching and tossing
at the right distance.
She wears a white dress,
black boots and stockings,
and a flowered straw hat.
She moves in silence
but it seems from her face
that she must be laughing.
Behind her is sunlight
and a tree-filled garden;
you might think to hear
birds or running water,
but no, there is nothing.
Once or twice he has spoken
but does so no more,
for she cannot answer.
So he stands smiling,
playing her game
(she is almost a child),
not daring to go,
intent on the ball.
And she is the same.
For what would result
neither wishes to know
if it should fall.

Bogyman

Stepping down from the blackberry bushes
he stands in my path: Bogyman.
He is not as I had remembered him,
though he still wears the broad-brimmed hat,
the rubber-soled shoes and the woollen gloves.
No face; and that soft mooning voice
still spinning its endless distracting yarn.

But this is daylight, a misty autumn
Sunday, not unpopulated
by birds. I can see him in such colours
as he wears – fawn, grey, murky blue –
not all shadow-clothed, as he was that night
when I was ten; he seems less tall
(I have grown) and less muffled in silence.

I have no doubt at all, though, that he is
Bogyman. He is why children
do not sleep all night in their tree-houses.
He is why, when I had pleaded
to spend a night on the common, under
a cosy bush, and my mother
surprisingly said yes, she took no risk.

He was the risk I would not take; better
to make excuses, to lose face,
than to meet the really faceless, the one
whose name was too childish for us
to utter – 'murderers' we talked of, and
'lunatics escaped from Earlswood'.
But I met him, of course, as we all do.

Well, that was then; I survived; and later
survived meetings with his other
forms, bold or pathetic or disguised – the
slummocking figure in a dark
alley, or the lover turned suddenly
icy-faced; fingers at my throat
and ludicrous violence in kitchens.

I am older now, and (I tell myself,
circling carefully around him
at the far edge of the path, pretending
I am not in fact confronted)
can deal with such things. But what, Bogyman,
shall I be at twice my age? (At
your age?) Shall I be grandmotherly, fond

suddenly of gardening, chatty with
neighbours? Or strained, not giving in,
writing for Ambit and hitch-hiking to
Turkey? Or sipping Guinness in
the Bald-Faced Stag, in wrinkled stockings? Or
(and now I look for the first time
straight at you) something like you, Bogyman?

Clarendon Whatmough

Clarendon Whatmough sits in his chair
telling me that I am hollow.
The walls of his study are dark and bare;
he has his back to the window.
Are you priest or psychiatrist, Clarendon Whatmough?
I do not have to believe you.

The priest in the pub kept patting my hand
more times than I thought needful.
I let him think me a Catholic, and
giggled, and felt quite sinful.
You were not present, Clarendon Whatmough:
I couldn't have flirted with you.

Christopher is no longer a saint
but I still carry the medal
with his image on, which my mother sent
to protect me when I travel.
It pleases her – and me: two
unbelievers, Clarendon Whatmough.

But when a friend was likely to die
I wanted to pray, if I could
after so many years, and feeling shy
of churches walked in the wood.
A hypocritical thing to do,
would you say, Clarendon Whatmough?

Or a means of dispelling buried guilt,
a conventional way to ease
my fears? I tell you this: I felt
the sky over the trees
crack open like a nutshell. You
don't believe me, Clarendon Whatmough:

or rather, you would explain that I
induced some kind of reaction
to justify the reversal of my
usual lack of conviction.
No comment from Clarendon Whatmough.
He tells me to continue.

Why lay such critical emphasis
on this other-worldly theme?
I could tell you my sexual fantasies
as revealed in my latest dream.
Do, if you wish, says Clarendon Whatmough:
it's what I expect of you.

Clarendon Whatmough doesn't sneer;
he favours a calm expression,
prefers to look lofty and austere
and let me display an emotion
then anatomise it. Clarendon Whatmough,
shall I analyse you?

No: that would afford me even less
amusement than I provide.
We may both very well be centreless,
but I will not look inside
your shadowy eyes; nor shall you
now, in my open ones, Clarendon Whatmough.

I leave you fixed in your formal chair,
your ambiguous face unseeing,
and go, thankful that I'm aware
at least of my own being.
Who is convinced, though, Clarendon Whatmough,
of your existence? Are you?

A Surprise in the Peninsula

When I came in that night I found
the skin of a dog stretched flat and
nailed upon my wall between the
two windows. It seemed freshly killed –
there was blood at the edges. Not
my dog: I have never owned one,
I rather dislike them. (Perhaps
whoever did it knew that.) It
was a light brown dog, with smooth hair;
no head, but the tail still remained.
On the flat surface of the pelt
was branded the outline of the
peninsula, singed in thick black
strokes into the fur: a coarse map.
The position of the town was
marked by a bullet-hole; it went
right through the wall. I placed my eye
to it, and could see the dark trees
outside the house, flecked with moonlight.
I locked the door then, and sat up
all night, drinking small cups of the
bitter local coffee. A dog
would have been useful, I thought, for
protection. But perhaps the one
I had been given performed that
function; for no one came that night,
nor for three more. On the fourth day
it was time to leave. The dog-skin
still hung on the wall, stiff and dry
by now, the flies and the smell gone.
Could it, I wondered, have been meant
not as a warning, but a gift?
And, scarcely shuddering, I drew
the nails out and took it with me.

Purple Shining Lilies

The events of the *Aeneid* were not enacted
on a porridge-coloured plain; although my
greyish pencilled-over Oxford text
is monochrome, tends to deny
the flaming pyre, that fearful tawny light,
the daily colour-productions in the sky

(dawn variously rosy); Charon's boat
mussel-shell blue on the reedy mud
of Styx; the wolf-twins in a green cave;
huge Triton rising from the flood
to trumpet on his sky-coloured conch;
and everywhere the gleam of gold and blood.

Cybele's priest rode glittering into battle
on a bronze-armoured horse: his great bow
of gold, his cloak saffron, he himself
splendid in *ferrugine et ostro* –
rust and shellfish. (We laugh, but Camilla
for this red and purple gear saw fit to go

to her death.) The names, indeed, are as foreign
in their resonances as the battle-rite:
luteus with its vaguely medical air;
grim *ater*; or the two versions of white:
albus thick and eggy; *candidus*
clear as a candle-flame's transparent light.

It dazzled me, that white, when I was young;
that and *purpureus* – poppy-red,
scarlet, we were firmly taught, not purple
in the given context; but inside my head
the word was both something more than visual
and also exactly what it said.

Poppies and lilies mixed (the mystical
and the moral?) was what I came upon.

53

My eyes leaping across the juxtaposed
adjectives, I saw them both as one,
and brooded secretly upon the image:
purple shining lilies, bright in the sun.

Afterwards

We weave haunted circles about each other,
advance and retreat in turn, like witch-doctors
before a fetish. Yes, you are right to fear
me now, and I you. But love, this ritual
will exhaust us. Come closer. Listen. Be brave.
I am going to talk to you quietly
as sometimes, in the long past (you remember?),
we made love. Let us be intent, and still. Still.
There are ways of approaching it. This is one:
this gentle talk, with no pause for suspicion,
no hesitation, because you do not know
the thing is upon you, until it has come –
now, and you did not even hear it.
                                    Silence
is what I am trying to achieve for us.
A nothingness, a non-relatedness, this
unknowing into which we are sliding now
together: this will have to be our kingdom.

Rain is falling. Listen to the gentle rain.

Happy Ending

After they had not made love
she pulled the sheet up over her eyes
until he was buttoning his shirt:
not shyness for their bodies – those
they had willingly displayed – but a frail
endeavour to apologise.

54

Later, though, drawn together by
a distaste for such 'untidy ends'
they agreed to meet again; whereupon
they giggled, reminisced, held hands
as though what they had made was love –
and not that happier outcome, friends.

Being Blind
(*for Meg Sheffield*)

Listen to that:
it is the sea rushing across the garden
swamping the apple tree, beating against the house,
carrying white petals; the sea from France
coming to us.
     It is the April wind
I tell myself, but cannot rise to look.

You were talking about your blind friend –
how you had to share a room with her once
on holiday, and in the night you woke:
she was staring at you. Was she really blind?
You leaned over her bed for a long time,
watching her, trying to understand,
suppressing unworthy, unendurable
speculations (if she could see
what kind of creature was she?) until
her eyes went swivelling in a dream
as ours do, closed. Yes: blind.

Then I came to bed and, thinking of her
for whom eyelids have no particular purpose,
closed mine. And now there is this sound
of a savage tide rushing towards me.
Do you, in the front of the house, hear it?
I cannot look out. I am blind now.
If I walk downstairs, hand on the banister
(as she did once – admiring, she told us,

our Christmas lights), if I open the door
it will swish and swill over my feet:
the sea. Listen.

Grandma

It was the midnight train; I was tired and edgy.
The advertisement portrayed – I wrote it down – a
'Skull-like young female, licking lips' and I added
'Prefer Grandma, even dead' as she newly was.
I walked home singing one of her Irish ballads.

Death is one thing, necrophilia another.

So I climbed up that ladder in the frescoed barn –
a soft ladder, swaying and collapsing under
my feet (my hands alone hauled me into the loft) –
and found, without surprise, a decomposed lady
who drew me down to her breast, with her disengaged
armbones, saying 'Come, my dearie, don't be afraid,
come to me' into a mess of sweetish decay.

It was a dream. I screamed and woke, put on the light,
dozed, woke again. For half a day I carried that
carcass in my own failing arms. Then remembered:
even the dead want to be loved for their own sake.
She was indeed my grandmother. She did not choose
to be dead and rotten. My blood too (Group A,
Rhesus negative, derived exactly from hers)
will suffer that deterioration; my much
modified version of her nose will fall away,
my longer bones collapse like hers. So let me now
apologise to my sons and their possible
children for the gruesomeness: we do not mean it.

Ngauranga Gorge Hill

The bee in the foxglove, the mouth on the nipple,
the hand between the thighs.
                              Forgive me
these procreative images.
                          Do you remember
that great hill outside Wellington, which we

had to climb, before they built the motorway,
to go north? The engine used to boil
in the old Chev. Straight up the road went
and tipped us over into Johnsonville.

Nothing on the way but rock and gorse, gravel-
pits, and foxgloves; and a tunnel hacked deep,
somewhere, into a cliff. Ah, my burgeoning new
country, I said (being fourteen). Yes, a steep

road to climb. But coming back was better;
a matter for some caution in a car,
but glorious and terrible on a bicycle.
Heart in my pedals, down I would roar

towards the sea; I'd go straight into it
if I didn't brake. No time then to stare
self-consciously at New Zealand vegetation,
at the awkward landscape. I needed all my care

for making the right turn towards the city
at the hill's base, where the paint-hoarding stood
between me and the harbour.
                              For ten years
that city possessed me. In time it bred

two sons for me (little pink mouths tucked
like foxglove-bells over my nipples). Yes,
in this matter Wellington and I have no
quarrel. But I think it was a barren place.

Stewart Island

'But look at all this beauty,'
said the hotel manager's wife
when asked how she could bear to
live there. True: there was a fine bay,
all hills and atmosphere; white
sand, and bush down to the sea's edge;
oyster-boats, too, and Maori
fishermen with Scottish names (she
ran off with one that autumn).
As for me, I walked on the beach;
it was too cold to swim. My
seven-year-old collected shells
and was bitten by sandflies;
my four-year-old paddled, until
a mad seagull jetted down
to jab its claws and beak into
his head. I had already
decided to leave the country.

On a Son Returned to New Zealand

He is my green branch growing in a far plantation.
He is my first invention.

No one can be in two places at once.
So we left Athens on the same morning.
I was in a hot railway carriage, crammed
between Serbian soldiers and peasant
women, on sticky seats, with nothing to
drink but warm mineral water.
                          He was
in a cabin with square windows, sailing
across the Mediterranean, fast,
to Suez.
        Then I was back in London
in the tarnished summer, remembering,

as I folded his bed up, and sent the
television set away. Letters came
from Aden and Singapore, late.
                              He was
already in his father's house, on the
cliff-top, where the winter storms roll across
from Kapiti Island, and the flax bends
before the wind. He could go no further.

He is my bright sea-bird on a rocky beach.

Saturday

I am sitting on the step
drinking coffee and
smoking, listening to jazz.
The smoke separates
two scents: fresh paint in the house
behind me; in front,
buddleia.
              The neighbours cut
back our lilac tree –
it shaded their neat garden.
The buddleia will
be next, no doubt; but bees and
all those butterflies
approve of our shaggy trees.

                              *

I am painting the front door
with such thick juicy
paint I could almost eat it.
People going past
with their shopping stare at my
bare legs and old shirt.
The door will be sea-green.

                    Our
black cat walked across
the painted step and left a
delicate paw-trail.
I swore at her and frightened
two little girls – this
street is given to children.
The other cat is younger,
white and tabby, fat,
with a hoarse voice. In summer
she sleeps all day long
in the rosebay willow-herb,
too lazy to walk
on paint.
            Andrew is upstairs;
having discovered
quick-drying non-drip gloss, he
is old enough now
to paint all his furniture
tangerine and the
woodwork green; he is singing.

                    *

I am lying in the sun,
in the garden. Bees
dive on white clover beside
my ears. The sky is
Greek blue, with a vapour-trail
chalked right across it.
My transistor radio
talks about the moon.

                    *

I am floating in the sky.
Below me the house
crouches among its trees like
a cat in long grass.

60

I want to stroke its roof-ridge
but I think I can
already hear it purring.

Trees

Elm, laburnum, hawthorn, oak:
all the incredible leaves expand
on their dusty branches, like
Japanese paper flowers in water,
like anything one hardly believes
will really work this time; and
I am a stupefied spectator
as usual. What are they all, these
multiverdant, variously-made
soft sudden things, these leaves?
So I walk solemnly in the park
with a copy of *Let's Look at Trees*
from the children's library,
identifying leaf-shapes and bark
while behind my back, at home,
my own garden is turning into a wood.
Before my house the pink may tree
lolls its heavy heads over mine
to grapple my hair as I come
in; at the back door I walk out
under lilac. The two elders
(I let them grow for the wine)
hang vastly over the fence, no doubt
infuriating my tidy neighbours.
In the centre the apple tree
needs pruning. And everywhere,
soaring over the garden shed,
camouflaged by roses, or snaking
up through the grass like vertical worms,
grows every size of sycamore.
Last year we attacked them; I saw
my son, so tender to ants, so sad

over dead caterpillars, hacking
at living roots as thick as his arms,
drenching the stumps with creosote.
No use: they continue to grow.
Under the grass, the ground
must be peppered with winged seeds,
meshed with a tough stringy net
of roots; and the house itself undermined
by wandering wood. Shall we see
the floorboards lifted one morning
by these indomitable weeds,
or find in the airing-cupboard
a rather pale sapling?
And if we do, will it be
worse than cracked pipes or dry rot?
Trees I can tolerate; they are why
I chose this house – for the apple tree,
elder, buddleia, lilac, may;
and outside my bedroom window, higher
every week, its leaves unfurling
pink at the twig-tips (composite
in form) the tallest sycamore.

Country Station

First she made a little garden
of sorrel stalks wedged among
some yellowy-brown moss-cushions

and fenced it with ice-lolly sticks
(there were just enough); then she
set out biscuit-crumbs on a brick

for the ants; now she sits on a
deserted luggage-trolley
to watch them come for their dinner.

It's nice here – cloudy but quite warm.
Five trains have swooshed through, and one
stopped, but at the other platform.

Later, when no one is looking,
she may climb the roof of that
low shed. Her mother is making

another telephone call (she
isn't crying any more).
Perhaps they will stay here all day.

The Three-toed Sloth

The three-toed sloth is the slowest creature we know
for its size. It spends its life hanging upside-down
from a branch, its baby nestling on its breast.
It never cleans itself, but lets fungus grow
on its fur. The grin it wears, like an idiot clown,
proclaims the joys of a life which is one long rest.

The three-toed sloth is content. It doesn't care.
It moves imperceptibly, like the laziest snail
you ever saw blown up to the size of a sheep.
Disguised as a grey-green bough it dangles there
in the steamy Amazon jungle. That long-drawn wail
is its slow-motion sneeze. Then it falls asleep.

One cannot but envy such torpor. Its top speed,
when rushing to save its young, is a dramatic
fourteen feet per minute, in a race with fate.
The puzzle is this, though: how did nature breed
a race so determinedly unenergetic?
What passion ever inspired a sloth to mate?

Against Coupling

I write in praise of the solitary act:
of not feeling a trespassing tongue
forced into one's mouth, one's breath
smothered, nipples crushed against the
ribcage, and that metallic tingling
in the chin set off by a certain odd nerve:

unpleasure. Just to avoid those eyes would help –
such eyes as a young girl draws life from,
listening to the vegetal
rustle within her, as his gaze
stirs polypal fronds in the obscure
sea-bed of her body, and her own eyes blur.

There is much to be said for abandoning
this no longer novel exercise –
for not 'participating in
a total experience' – when
one feels like the lady in Leeds who
had seen *The Sound of Music* eighty-six times;

or more, perhaps, like the school drama mistress
producing *A Midsummer Night's Dream*
for the seventh year running, with
yet another cast from 5B.
Pyramus and Thisbe are dead, but
the hole in the wall can still be troublesome.

I advise you, then, to embrace it without
encumbrance. No need to set the scene,
dress up (or undress), make speeches.
Five minutes of solitude are
enough – in the bath, or to fill
that gap between the Sunday papers and lunch.

Mornings After

The surface dreams are easily remembered:
I wake most often with a comforting sense
of having seen a pleasantly odd film –
nothing too outlandish or too intense;

of having, perhaps, befriended animals,
made love, swum the Channel, flown in the air
without wings, visited Tibet or Chile:
simple childish stuff. Or else the rare

recurrent horror makes its call upon me:
I dream one of my sons is lost or dead,
or that I am trapped in a tunnel underground;
but my scream is enough to recall me to my bed.

Sometimes, indeed, I congratulate myself
on the nice precision of my observation:
on having seen so vividly a certain
colour; having felt the sharp sensation

of cold water on my hands; the exact taste
of wine or peppermints. I take a pride
in finding all my senses operative
even in sleep. So, with nothing to hide,

I amble through my latest entertainment
again, in the bath or going to work,
idly amused at what the night has offered;
unless this is a day when a sick jerk

recalls to me a sudden different vision:
I see myself inspecting the vast slit
of a sagging whore; making love with a hunchbacked
hermaphrodite; eating worms or shit;

or rapt upon necrophily or incest.
And whatever loathsome images I see
are just as vivid as the pleasant others.
I flush and shudder: my God, was that me?

Did I invent so ludicrously revolting
a scene? And if so, how could I forget
until this instant? And why now remember?
Furthermore (and more disturbing yet)

are all my other forgotten dreams like these?
Do I, for hours of my innocent nights,
wallow content and charmed through verminous muck,
rollick in the embraces of such frights?

And are the comic or harmless fantasies
I wake with merely a deceiving guard,
as one might put a Hans Andersen cover
on a volume of the writings of De Sade?

Enough, enough. Bring back those easy pictures,
Tibet or antelopes, a seemly lover,
or even the black tunnel. For the rest,
I do not care to know. Replace the cover.

Gas

1

You recognise a body by its blemishes:
moles and birthmarks, scars, tattoos, oddly formed earlobes.
The present examination must be managed
in darkness, and by touch alone. That should suffice.
Starting at the head, then, there is a small hairless
scar on the left eyebrow; the bridge of the nose flat;
crowded lower teeth, and a chipped upper canine
(the lips part to let my fingers explore); a mole
on the right side of the neck.   No need to go on:
I know it all. But as I draw away, a hand
grips mine: a hand whose thumb bends back as mine does, whose
third finger bears the torn nail I broke in the door
last Thursday; and I feel these fingers check the scar
on my knuckle, measure my wrist's circumference,
move on gently exploring towards my elbow…

2

It was gas, we think.
Insects and reptiles survived it
and most of the birds;
also the larger mammals – grown
cattle, a few sheep,
horses, the landlord's Alsatian
(I shall miss the cats)
and, in this village, about a
fifth of the people.
It culled scientifically
within a fixed range,
sparing the insignificant
and the chosen strong.
It let us sleep for fourteen hours
and wake, not caring
whether we woke or not, in a
soft antiseptic
silence. There was a faint odour

of furniture-wax.
We know now, of course, more or less
what happened, but then
it was rather puzzling: to wake
from a thick dark sleep
lying on the carpeted floor
in the saloon bar
of the Coach and Horses; to sense
others lying near,
very still; and nearest to me
this new second self.

     3
I had one history until today:
now I shall have two.
No matter how nicely she may contrive
to do what I do
there are two hearts now for our identical
blood to pass through.

Nothing can change her. Whether she walks by my side
like a silly twin
or dyes her hair, adopts a new accent,
disguises her skin
with make-up and suntan, she cannot alter
the creature within.

She sees with my imperfect vision, she wears
my fingerprints; she is made
from me. If she should break the bones I gave her,
if disease should invade
her replicas of my limbs and organs,
which of us is betrayed?

     4
How was she torn out of me? Was it the
urgent wrench of birth, a matter of hard
breathless shoving (but there is no blood) or
Eve from Adam's rib, quick and surgical

(but there is no scar) or did I burgeon
with fleshy buds along my limbs, growing
a new substance from that gas I drank in,
to double myself? Did I perform the
amoeba's trick of separating into
two loose amorphous halves, a heart in each?
Or was my skin slipped off like the skin of
a peanut, to reveal two neat sections,
face to face and identical, within?
Yes, we had better say it was like this:
for if it was birth, which was the mother?
Since both have equal rights to our past, she
might justly claim to have created me.

     5

It is the sixth day
now, and nothing much has happened.
Those of us who are
double (all the living ones) go
about our business.
The two Mrs Hudsons bake bread
in the pub kitchen
and contrive meals from what is left –
few shops are open.
The two Patricks serve in the bar
(Bill Hudson is dead).
I and my new sister stay here –
it seems easiest –
and help with the housework; sometimes
we go for walks, or
play darts or chess, finding ourselves
not as evenly
matched as we might have expected:
our capacity
is equal, but our moods vary.
These things occupy
the nights – none of us needs sleep now.
Only the dead sleep
laid out in all the beds upstairs.

They do not decay,
(some effect of the gas) and this
seemed a practical
and not irreverent means of
dealing with them. My
dead friend from London
and a housemaid from the hotel
lie in the bedroom
where we two go to change our clothes.
This evening when we
had done our hair before dinner
we combed and arranged
theirs too.

      6

Saturday night in the bar; eight couples
fill it well enough: twin schoolteachers, two
of the young man from the garage, four girls
from the shop next door, some lads from the farms.
These woodenly try to chat up the girls,
but without heart. There is no sex now, when
each has his undeniable partner,
and no eyes or hands for any other.
Division, not union, is the way we
must reproduce now. Nor can one think with
desire or even curiosity
of one's identical other. How lust
for what is utterly familiar?
How place an auto-erotic hand on
a thigh which matches one's own? So we chat
about local events: the twin calves born,
it seems, on every farm; the corpse
in a well, and the water quite unspoiled;
the Post Office reopened, but with no
telephone links to places further than
the next town – just as there are no programmes
on television or radio, and
the single newspaper that we have seen
(a local one) contained only poems.

No one cares much for communication
outside this circle. I am forgetting
my work in London, my old concerns (we
laugh about the unpaid rent, the office
unmanned, the overdue library books).
They did a good job, whoever they were.

> 7

Two patterns of leaves above me: laurel
rather low, on my right,
and high on my left sycamore; a sky
pale grey: dawn or twilight.

Dew on my face, and on the gravel path
on which I am lying.
That scent of wax in the air, and a few
birds beginning to sing.

My mind is hazed by a long sleep – the first
for days. But I can tell
how it has been: the gas caught us walking
on this path, and we fell.

I feel a crystal, carolling lightness.
Beside me I can see
my newest self. It has happened again:
division, more of me.

Four, perhaps? We two stand up together,
dazed, euphoric, and go
to seek out our matching others, knowing
that they should be two, now.

My partner had been walking, I recall,
a little way ahead.
We find her. But there is only one. I
look upon myself, dead.

8

This is becoming ridiculous:
the gas visits us regularly,
dealing out death or duplication.
I am eight people now – and four dead
(these propped up against the trees in the
gardens, by the gravel walk). We eight
have inherited the pub, and shall,
if we continue to display our
qualities of durability,
inherit the village, God help us.
I see my image everywhere –
feeding the hens, hoeing the spinach,
peeling the potatoes, devising
a clever dish with cabbage and eggs.
I am responsible with and for
all. If B (we go by letters now)
forgets to light the fire, I likewise
have forgotten. If C breaks a cup
we all broke it. I am eight people,
a kind of octopus or spider,
and I cannot say it pleases me.
Sitting through our long sleepless nights, we
no longer play chess or poker (eight
identical hands, in which only
the cards are different). Now, instead,
we plan our death. Not quite suicide,
but a childish game: when the gas comes
(we can predict the time within a
margin of two days) we shall take care
to be in dangerous places. I can
see us all, wading in the river
for hours, taking long baths, finding
ladders and climbing to paint windows
on the third storey. It will be fun –
something, at last, to entertain us.

9

Winter. The village is silent –
no lights in the windows, and
a corpse in every snowdrift.
The electricity failed
months ago. We have chopped down half
the orchard for firewood,
and live on the apples we picked
in autumn. (That was a fine
harvest-day: three of us fell down
from high trees when the gas came.)
One way and another, in fact,
we are reduced now to two –
it can never be one alone,
for the survivor always
wakes with a twin.
                    We have great hopes
of the snow. At this moment
she is standing outside in it
like Socrates. We work shifts,
two hours each. But this evening
when gas-time will be closer
we are going to take blankets
and make up beds in the snow –
as if we were still capable
of sleep. And indeed, it may
come to us there: our only sleep.

10

Come, gentle gas

I lie and look at the night.
The stars look normal enough –
it has nothing to do with them –
and no new satellite
or comet has shown itself.
There is nothing up there to blame.

Come from wherever

She is quiet by my side.
I cannot see her breath
in the frost-purified air.
I would say she had died
if so natural a death
were possible now, here.

Come with what death there is

You have killed almost a score
of the bodies you made
from my basic design.
I offer you two more.
Let the mould be destroyed:
it is no longer mine.

Come, then, secret scented double-dealing gas.
We are cold: come and warm us.
We are tired: come and lull us.
Complete us.
Come. Please.

THE SCENIC ROUTE

(1974)

The Bullaun

'Drink water from the hollow in the stone…'
This was it, then – the cure for madness:
a rock with two round cavities, filled with rain;
a thing I'd read about once, and needed then,
but since forgotten. I didn't expect it here –
not having read the guidebook;
not having planned, even, to be in Antrim.
'There's a round tower, isn't there?' I'd asked.
The friendly woman in the post office
gave me directions: 'Up there past the station,
keep left, on a way further – it's a fair bit –
and have you been to Lough Neagh yet?' I walked –
it wasn't more than a mile – to the stone phallus
rising above its fuzz of beech trees
in the municipal gardens. And beside it,
this. I circled around them,
backing away over wet grass and beechmast,
aiming the camera (since I had it with me,
since I was playing tourist this afternoon)
and saw two little boys pelting across.
'Take our photo! Take our photo! Please!'
We talked it over for a bit –
how I couldn't produce one then and there;
but could I send it to them with the postman?
Well, could they give me their addresses?
Kevin Tierney and Declan McCallion,
Tobergill Gardens. I wrote, they stood and smiled,
I clicked, and waved goodbye, and went.
Two miles away, an hour later,
heading dutifully through the damp golf-course
to Lough Neagh, I thought about the rock,
wanting it. Not for my own salvation;
hardly at all for me: for sick Belfast,
for the gunmen and the slogan-writers,
for the poor crazy girl I met in the station,
for Kevin and Declan, who would soon mistrust
all camera-carrying strangers. But of course

the thing's already theirs: a monument,
a functionless, archaic, pitted stone
and a few mouthfuls of black rainwater.

Please Identify Yourself

British, more or less; Anglican, of a kind.
In Cookstown I dodge the less urgent question
when a friendly Ulsterbus driver raises it;
'You're not a Moneymore girl yourself?' he asks,
deadpan. I make a cowardly retrogression,
slip ten years back. 'No, I'm from New Zealand.'
'Are you now? Well, that's a coincidence:
the priest at Moneymore's a New Zealander.'
And there's the second question, unspoken.
Unanswered.
          I go to Moneymore
anonymously, and stare at all three churches.

In Belfast, though, where sides have to be taken,
I stop compromising – not that you'd guess,
seeing me hatless there among the hatted,
neutral voyeur among the shining faces
in the glossy Martyrs' Memorial Free Church.
The man himself is cheerleader in the pulpit
for crusader choruses: we're laved in blood,
marshalled in ranks. I chant the nursery tunes
and mentally cross myself. You can't stir me
with evangelistic hymns, Dr Paisley:
I know them. Nor with your computer-planned
sermon – Babylon, Revelation, whispers
of popery, slams at the IRA, more blood.
I scrawl incredulous notes under my hymnbook
and burn with Catholicism.
                         Later
hacking along the Lower Falls Road
against a gale, in my clerical black coat,
I meet a bright gust of tinselly children

in beads and lipstick and their mothers' dresses
for Hallowe'en; who chatter and surround me.
Over-reacting once again (a custom
of the country, not mine alone) I give them
all my loose change for their rattling tin
and my blessing – little enough. But now
to my tough Presbyterian ancestors,
Brooks and Hamilton, lying in the graves
I couldn't find at Moneymore and Cookstown
among so many unlabelled bones, I say:
I embrace you also, my dears.

Richey

My great-grandfather Richey Brooks
began in mud: at Moneymore;
'a place of mud and nothing else'
he called it (not the way it looks,
but what lies under those green hills?)
Emigrated in '74;
ended in Drury: mud again –
slipped in the duck-run at ninety-three
(wouldn't give up keeping poultry,
always had to farm something).
Caught pneumonia; died saying
'Do you remember Martha Hamilton
of the Oritor Road?' – still courting
the same girl in his mind. And she
lived after him, fierce widow,
in their daughter's house; watched the plum tree –
the gnarled, sappy branches, the yellow
fruit. Ways of living and dying.

The Voyage Out

The weekly dietary scale
per adult: pork and Indian beef,
three pounds together; one of sugar,
two of potatoes, three and a half
of flour; a gill of vinegar;
salt, pepper, a pint of oatmeal;
coffee, two ounces, likewise tea;
six of butter, suet, treacle,
and, in the tropics, of lime juice;
grudging grants of mustard and pickle;
split peas, raisins, currants, rice,
and half a pound of biscuit a day.
A diet for the young and fit:
monotonous, but not starvation –
and Martha traded half her ration
for extra lime juice from the crew.
Their quarters, also, adequate.
So not the middle passage; no.
But not a pleasure cruise, either.
A hundred days of travelling steerage
under capricious canvas; Martha
newly pregnant, struggling to manage
the first four (Tom, Eliza, Joe,
Annie); to keep them cool and clean
from a two-gallon can of water;
to calm their sleeping; to stay awake,
so heavy, herself; to protect the daughter
she rocked unborn in the swaying hammock
below her ribs (who would be Jane).
True, the family was together.
But who could envy Martha? Sick
with salt meat; thirsty; and gazing on
a sky huge as the whole Atlantic,
storm-waves like Slieve Gallion,
and no more Ireland than went with her.

Train from the Hook of Holland

Not pill-boxes, exactly: blocks
of concrete, octagonal, serrated –
house-sized fancy buttons, roofed
with green turf. 'Hitler's Atlantic wall'
says the man in the corner seat.
On the other side of the train
lambs running, and, yes, a canal.
Then the low sun through a sea-haze
neon-red over – Maassluis, is it?
Some things, once you've got them,
are difficult to get rid of.
But we are happy, going somewhere.

Nelia

She writes to me from a stony island
where they understand none of her languages.
Time has slipped out of its cogwheel:
she walks looking at plants and insects,
thinking without words, forgetting her home
and her work and her callous, temporary young lover.
Her children play like cicadas among the hills
and are safe. She cooks when they are hungry,
sleeps at will, wakes and runs to the sea.
I remember exactly the colour of her daughter's eyes –
glass-green; and the boy's light blue against his tan;
hers less clearly. But I see them now
as blue-black, reflecting an inky sky –
pure, without motes or atmosphere – that extends
uninterrupted from her to the still sun.

Moa Point

At Moa Point that afternoon
two biologists were searching rockpools
for specimens. It was low tide.
I watched. They rolled away a stone,
fossicked in wet weed, described things
rather self-consciously to each other.
Then one of them put into my hands
a cold heavy jelly: my first sea-slug.
I peered gratefully down at it,
turned it over – did nothing, surely?
for them to laugh at. 'See that?'
said the one with freckles (they were both quite young)
'it doesn't seem to worry her.'
'Oh, well,' said the other 'these local kids . . .'
I kept my eyes down for a moment
in solemn, scientific study;
then said in my recently-acquired
almost local accent 'Thank you.'
And firmly but gently (a vet with a kitten)
handed it back.

Briddes

'Briddes' he used to call them,
out of Chaucer – those cool
early-morning creatures
who tinkled in the elm trees.
Briddes talked us awake
and punctuated our childish
medieval loving.
All other birds were birds.

The Famous Traitor

His jailer trod on a rose-petal.
There were others on the stone floor.
His desk tidy; some lines in pencil,
the bible open.
               Years before
he'd lived like a private soldier –
a bag of nuts and the milk ration
for long days' marches. And under
the uniform a mathematician.
Puzzle-maker. After power:
which he got, this pastor's son
turned agnostic.
              The nature
of his 'new kind of treason',
his links with the Nazi high command,
the deals, the sense of mission,
are well-documented; and
beyond every explanation.

He died 'with dignity' some said;
some that he had to wait an hour,
died shivering in the bitter cold.
It looked like fear. It was fear:
or it was not. And he did,
or did not, shake hands before
that moment with the firing-squad.
Authorities let us down here.
His final audience, the 'crowd
of notables', might as well
have been, as he was, blindfold.
We are left with the empty cell
like a film-set; the table
where the man of action/dreamer
made notes on his father's bible
in a litter of roses. Enter
his faithful jailer, to record
just this. The rest remains obscure

like all that made a dictionary word
of his name; like what he did it for.

Script

'Wet the tea, Jinny, the men are back:
I can hear them out there, talking, with the horses,'
my mother's grandmother said. They both heard it,
she and her daughter – the wagon bumpily halted,
a rattle of harness, two familiar voices
in sentences to be identified later
and quoted endlessly. But the tea was cold
when the men came in. They'd been six miles away,
pausing to rest on Manurewa Hill
in a grove of trees – whence 'Fetch the nosebags, Dickie'
came clearly over. A freak wind, maybe:
soundwaves carrying, their words lifted up
and dropped on Drury. Eighty years ago,
long before the wireless was invented,
Grandma told us. It made a good story:
baffling. But then, so was the real thing –
radio.
        My father understood it.
Out on the bush farm at Te Rau a Moa
as a teenager he patiently constructed
little fiddly devices, sat for hours
every day adjusting a cat's whisker,
filtering morse through headphones. Later came
loudspeakers, and the whole family could gather
to hear the creaky music of 1YA.
So my father's people were technicians, is that it?
And my mother's were communicators, yes? –
Who worked as a barber in the evenings
for the talking's sake? Who became a teacher –
and who was in love with tractors? No prizes.
Don't classify. Leave the air-waves open.

We each extract what we most need. My sons
rig out their rooms with stereo equipment.
I walk dozily through the house
in the mornings with a neat black box,
audible newspaper, time-keeper and saver,
sufficient for days like that.
                              On days like this
I sit in my own high borrowed grove
and let the leafy air clear my mind
for reception. The slow pigeon-flight,
the scraped-wire pipping of some bird,
the loamy scent, offer themselves to me
as little presents, part of an exchange
to be continued and continually
(is this a rondo? that professor asked)
perpetuated. It is not like music,
though the effects can strike as music does:
it is more like agriculture, a nourishing
of the growth-mechanisms, a taking-in
of food for what will flower and seed and sprout.

On a path in the wood two white-haired women
are marching arm in arm, singing a hymn.
A girl stops me to ask where I bought my sandals.
I say 'In Italy, I think' and we laugh.
I am astonished several times a day.
When I get home I shall make tea or coffee
for whoever is there, talk and listen to talk,
share food and living-space. There will always
be time to reassemble the frail components
of this afternoon, to winnow the scattered sounds
dropped into my range, and rescue from them
a seed-hoard for transmission. There will be
always the taking-in and the sending-out.

In Memoriam: James K. Baxter

Dear Jim, I'm using a Shakespearian form
to write you what I'll call a farewell letter.
Rhyming iambics have become the norm
for verse epistles, and I'm no trendsetter.
Perhaps you'll think it's going back a bit,
but as a craftsman you'll approve of it.

What better model have we, after all?
Dylan the Welshman, long your youthful passion,
doesn't quite do now, and the dying fall
of Eliot was never in your fashion.
Of North Americans the one you'd favour
is Lowell. But his salt has the wrong savour:

our ocean's called Pacific, not Atlantic –
which doesn't mean to say Neruda meets
the case. As for the classically romantic –
well, maybe it was easier for Keats:
I'd write with more conviction about death
if it were clutching at my every breath.

And now we've come to it. The subject's out:
the ineluctable, the all-pervasive.
Your death is what this letter's all about;
and if so far I've seemed a bit evasive
it's not from cowardice or phoney tact –
it's simply that I can't believe the fact.

I'd put you, with New Zealand, in cold storage
to wait for my return (should I so choose).
News of destruction can't delete an image:
what isn't seen to go, one doesn't lose.
The bulldozed streets, the buildings they've torn down
remain untouched until I'm back in town.

And so with you, framed in that sepia vision
a hemisphere away from me, and half

the twenty years I've known you. Such division
converts a face into a photograph:
a little blurred perhaps, the outlines dim,
but fixed, enduring, permanently Jim.

I saw you first when I was seventeen,
a word-struck student, ripe for dazzling. You
held unassuming court in the canteen –
the famous poet in the coffee-queue.
I watched with awe. But soon, as spheres are apt
to do in Wellington, ours overlapped.

I married, you might say, into the art.
You were my husband's friend; you'd wander in
on your way home from teaching, at the start,
for literary shop-talk over gin.
And then those fabled parties of one's youth:
home-brew and hot-lines to poetic truth.

Later the drinks were tea and lemonade,
the visits family ones, the talk less vatic;
and later still, down south, after I'd made
my getaway, came idiosyncratic
letters, your generous comments on my verse,
and poems of your own. But why rehearse

matters which you, acute observer, wise
recorder, don't forget? And now I falter,
knowing your present case: those tolerant eyes
will register no more. But I can't alter
this message to a dirge; the public attitude
isn't my style: I write in simple gratitude.

To think of elegies is to recall
several of yours. I find, when I look through
your varied, eloquent poems, nearly all
frosted with hints at death. What can I do
now, when it has become your own condition,
but praise all that you gave to the tradition?

St John's School

When I went back the school was rather small
but not unexpectedly or oddly so.
I peered in at the windows of the hall
where we sang *O God Our Help* thirty years ago
for D-Day, the Normandy landings. It was all
as I'd pictured it. Outside, they'd cut the row

of dusty laurels, laid a lawn instead,
and the prefab classroom at the end was new;
but there were the lavatories, there was the shed
where we sat on rainy days with nothing to do,
giggling; and the beech trees overhead
whose fallen husks we used to riffle through

for triangular nuts. Yes, all as it should be –
no false images to negotiate,
no shocks. I wandered off contentedly
across the playground, out through the north gate,
down the still knee-straining slope, to see
what sprang up suddenly across the street:

the church, that had hardly existed in my past,
that had lurked behind a tree or two, unknown –
and uncensorious of me as I chased
squirrels over the graves – the church had grown:
high on its huge mound it soared, vast;
and God glared out from behind a tombstone.

Pupation

Books, music, the garden, cats:
I have cocooned myself
in solitude, fatly silken.
Settled?

       I flatter myself.
Things buzz under my ribs;
there are ticklings, dim blunderings.
Ichneumon flies have got in.

The Drought Breaks

That wet gravelly sound is rain.
Soil that was bumpy and crumbled
flattens under it, somewhere;
splatters into mud. Spiked grass
grows soft with it and bends like hair.
You lean over me, smiling at last.

Kilpeck

We are dried and brittle this morning,
fragile with continence, quiet.
You have brought me to see a church.
I stare at a Norman arch in red sandstone
carved like a Mayan temple-gate;
at serpents writhing up the doorposts
and squat saints with South-American features
who stare back over our heads
from a panel of beasts and fishes.
The gargoyles jutting from under the eaves
are the colour of newborn children.

Last night you asked me
if poetry was the most important thing.

We walk on around the building
craning our heads back to look up
at lions, griffins, fat-faced bears.
The Victorians broke some of these figures
as being too obscene for a church;
but they missed the Whore of Kilpeck.
She leans out under the roof
holding her pink stony cleft agape
with her ancient little hands.
There was always witchcraft here, you say.

The sheep-track up to the fragments
of castle-wall is fringed with bright bushes.

We clamber awkwardly, separate.
Hawthorn and dog-rose offer hips and haws,
orange and crimson capsules, pretending
harvest. I taste a blackberry.
The soil here is coloured like brick-dust,
like the warm sandstone. A fruitful county.
We regard it uneasily.

There is little left to say
after all the talk we had last night
instead of going to bed –
fearful for our originality,
avoiding the sweet obvious act
as if it were the only kind of indulgence.
Silly perhaps.
                    We have our reward.
We are languorous now, heavy
with whatever we were conserving,
carrying each a delicate burden
of choices made or about to be made.
Words whisper hopefully in our heads.

Slithering down the track we hold hands
to keep a necessary balance.
The gargoyles extend their feral faces,
rosy, less lined than ours.
We are wearing out our identities.

Feverish

Only a slight fever:
I was not quite out of my mind;
enough to forget my name
and the number and sex of my children
(while clinging to their existence –
three daughters, could it be?)
but not to forget my language
with Words for Music Perhaps,
Crazy Jane and the bishop,
galloping through my head.
As for my body, not
quite out of that either:
curled in an S-bend somewhere,
conscious of knees and skull
pressing against a wall
(if I was on my side)
or against a heavy lid
(if I was on my back);
or I could have been face downward
kneeling crouched on a raft,
castaway animal, drifting;
or shrivelled over a desk
head down asleep on it
like Harold, our wasted Orion,
who slept on the bare sand
all those nights in the desert
lightly, head on his briefcase;
who carried the new Peace
to chief after chief, winning
their difficult signatures

by wit and a cool head
under fire and public school charm;
who has now forgotten his Arabic
and the names of his brother's children
and what he did last week;
dozes over an ashtray
or shuffles through Who Was Who.
Crazy Jane I can take –
the withered breasts that she flaunted,
her fierce remembering tongue;
but spare me his forgetting.
Age is a sad fever.

Folie à Deux

They call it pica,
this ranging after alien tastes:
acorns (a good fresh country food,
better than I'd remembered)
that morning in the wood,

and moonlit roses –
perfumed lettuce, rather unpleasant:
we rinsed them from our teeth with wine.
It seems a shared perversion,
not just a kink of mine –

you were the one
who nibbled the chrysanthemums.
All right: we are avoiding something.
Tonight you are here early.
We seem to lack nothing.

We are alone,
quiet, unhurried. The whisky has
a smoky tang, like dark chocolate.
You speak of ceremony, of
something to celebrate.

I hear the church bells
and suddenly fear blasphemy,
even name it. The word's unusual
between us. But you don't laugh.
We postpone our ritual

and act another:
sit face to face across a table,
talk about places we have known
and friends who are still alive
and poems (not our own).

It works. We are altered
from that fey couple who talked out
fountains of images, a spray
of loves, deaths, dramas, jokes:
their histories; who lay

manic with words,
fingers twined in each other's hair
(no closer) wasting nights and hours;
who chewed, as dry placebos,
those bitter seeds and flowers.

It is the moment.
We rise, and touch at last. And now
without pretence or argument,
fasting, and in our right minds,
go to our sacrament.

Acris Hiems

A letter from that pale city
I escaped from ten years ago
and no good news.
I carry it with me
devising comfortable answers
(the sickness, shall I say?
is not peculiarly yours),
as I walk along Beech Drive,
Church Vale, Ringwood Avenue
at eleven on a Tuesday morning
going nowhere.
A bony day, an invisible wind,
the sky white as an ambulance,
and no one in sight.
Friend, I will say in my letter –
since you call me a friend still,
whatever I have been – forgive me.
Rounding the next corner
I see a van that crawls along
beside the birch-trunks and pink pavements.
A handbell rings from the driver's window:
he has paraffin for sale
and ought to do good business
now that we have power-cuts.
But the painted doors do not open.
The wind in the ornamental hedges
rustles. Nobody comes.
The bell rings. The houses listen.
Bring out your dead.

December Morning

I raise the blind and sit by the window
dry-mouthed, waiting for light.
One needs a modest goal,
something safely attainable.
An hour before sunrise
(due at seven fifty-three)
I go out into the cold new morning
for a proper view of that performance;
walk greedily towards the heath
gulping the blanched air
and come in good time to Kenwood.
They have just opened the gates.
There is a kind of world here, too:
on the grassy slopes above the lake
in the white early Sunday
I see with something like affection
people I do not know
walking their unlovable dogs.

Showcase

Looking through the glass showcase right into the glass of the shelf,
your eye level with it, not swerving above it or below,
you see neither the reflected image nor the object itself.

There is only a swimming horizon, a watery prison for the sight,
acres of shadowy green jelly, and no way yet to know
what they support, what stands in the carefully angled light.

You take a breath, raise your head, and see whether the case reveals
Dutch goblet, carved reliquary, the Pope's elaborately-petalled rose
of gold leaf, or the bronze Cretan balanced on his neat heels,

and you look, drowning or perhaps rescued from drowning, and your eyes close.

Over the Edge

All my dead people
seeping through the riverbank where they are buried
colouring the stream pale brown
are why I swim in the river,
feeling now rather closer to them
than when the water was clear,
when I could walk barefoot on the gravel
seeing only the flicker of minnows
possessing nothing but balance.

The Net

She keeps the memory-game
as a charm against falling in love
and each night she climbs out of the same window
into the same garden with the arch for roses –
no roses, though; and the white snake dead too;
nothing but evergreen shrubs, and grass, and water,
and the wire trellis that will trap her in the end.

An Illustration to Dante

Here are Paolo and Francesca
whirled around in the circle of Hell
clipped serenely together
her dead face raised against his.
I can feel the pressure of his arms
like yours about me, locking.

They float in a sea of whitish blobs –
fire, is it? It could have been
hail, said Ruskin, but Rossetti
'didn't know how to do hail'.
Well, he could do tenderness.
My spine trickles with little white flames.

Tokens

The sheets have been laundered clean
of our joint essence – a compound,
not a mixture; but here are still

your forgotten pipe and tobacco,
your books open on my table,
your voice speaking in my poems.

Naxal

The concrete road from the palace to the cinema
bruises the feet. At the Chinese Embassy
I turn past high new walls on to padded mud.
A road is intended – men with trowels and baskets
work on it daily, dreamy Nepali girls
tilt little pots of water on to cement –
but it's gentle walking now. It leads 'inside'.
The tall pine at the end – still notable
though it lost its lingam top for winter firewood –
begins the village: a couple of streets, a temple,
an open space with the pond and the peepul tree,
rows of brick houses, little businesses
proceeding under their doll's-house-level beams;
rice being pounded, charcoal fires in pots,
rickshaws for people like me who don't want them.
The children wave and call 'Bye-bye! Paisa?'
holding out their perfect hands for my coins.
These houses may be eighteenth-century:
I covet their fretted lattice window-frames
and stare slightly too long into back rooms.
There are no screens at the carved windows, no filters
for the water they splash and drink at the common pump;
and no mosquitoes now, in the early spring.
But finally, stepping over the warm threshold
of the temple courtyard, I feel a tentative itch;
passing the scummy tank, a little sickness;
touching an infant's head, a little pain.

Bodnath

I have made my pilgrimage a day early:
Ash Wednesday is tomorrow; this week is Losar.
Pacing clockwise around the chaitya
I twirl the prayerwheels, my foreign fingers
polishing their bronze by a fraction more.
The courtyard is crowded with Tibetans,
incredibly jewelled and furred and hatted –
colour-plates from the *National Geographic*.
The beggar-woman with her monstrous leg
and the snuffling children are genuine too.
I toss them paisa; then go to spend
thirty rupees on a turquoise-studded
silver spoon for the Watkins' baby.

High on his whitewashed mound, Lord Buddha
overlooks the blossom of kite-tails
fluttering from his solid neck.
Om Mani Padme Hum.
His four painted square faces
turn twelve coloured eyes on the globe.
In the shrine below I see him again:
dim bronze, made of curves and surfaces,
shadowed, vulnerable, retiring.
Filmy scarves of white muslin
veil him; rice-grains lie at his feet;
in copper bowls arranged before him
smouldering incense crumbles to ash.

External Service

Already I know my way around the bazaar,
can use half a dozen words of basic Nepali,
and recognise several incarnations of Shiva.
If I stay here much longer I shall learn to identify
more trees besides those in our compound,
other birds than the rock-dove and the crow.
That plink-plink rhythm in the distance is a rice-mill.
The cannon is fired at noon, or to mark a death –
an echoing gesture. Now on the foreign news
I hear that the serious thunder-makers from Ireland
have crossed the channel. A pall of thick black smoke,
says the tidy English voice, hangs over London.
Here the sky is crystal. It is time to go.

Flying Back

They give us moistened BOAC towels
and I scrub my forehead. Red powder
for Holi: a trace of Delhi, an assault
met there in the wild streets this morning.
Without compunction I obliterate it –
India's not my country, let it go.
But crumpling the vermilion-stained napkin
(I shan't read it: some priest may do that)
I think of the stone foreheads in their hundreds:
Ganesh and Hanuman, who made me smile,
and Vishnu, and the four faces of Buddha,
reddened with genuine devotions;
and of the wooden cleft in a twisted tree
which I saw a beggar-woman sign scarlet
before she pressed her face down on to it;
and here's Nepal again. Sacred places
don't travel. The gods are stronger at home.
But if my tentative western brow may wear
this reluctant blush, these grains at the hair-roots,

I claim the right also to an image
as guardian; and choose winged Garuda.
His bland archaic countenance beams out
that serenity to which I journey.

Near Creeslough

I am in a foreign country.
There are heron and cormorant on the lake.
Young men in T-shirts against an Atlantic gale
are wheeling gravel, renewing the paths
in a stone shell chalked with their own history:

something to fear and covet.
We are the only visitors.
Notices tell us in two old languages
(one mine) that this is Caisleán na dTúath,
Doe Castle. A castle for everyman.

It has ramparts, towers, a dungeon –
we step over gridded emptiness.
The floors have rotted away in seventy years;
the spiral stair endures, a little chipped,
after four hundred. Here is my phobia.

And for you, at the top of it,
yours: a wind-racked vacancy,
a savage drop, a view with no holds –
to which you climb; and if you do, I do:
going up, after all, is the lesser challenge.

The high ledge receives us.
We stand there half a minute longer
than honour and simple vanity require;
then I follow you down the stone gullet,
feet on the splintering treads, eyes inward,

and we step on springy grass
once again; there have been no lapses.
Now ravens ferrying food up to a nest
make their easy ascents. Pleased with our own
we stroll away to eat oranges in the car.

Kilmacrenan

The hailstorm was in my head.
It drove us out into the blind lanes
to stumble over gravel and bog,
teeter on the skidding riverbank
together, stare down and consider.
But we drew back. When the real hail
began its pounding upon us
we were already half recovered.
Walking under that pouring icefall
hand in hand, towards lighted rooms,
we became patchworks of cold and hot,
glowing, streaming with water,
dissolving whatever dared to touch us.

Glenshane

Abandoning all my principles
I travel by car with you for days,
eat meat from tins, drink pints of Guinness,
smoke too much, and now on this pass
higher than all our settled landscapes
feed salted peanuts into your mouth
as you drive at eighty miles an hour.

THE INNER HARBOUR

(1979)

Beginnings

Future Work

'Please send future work.'
– editor's note on a rejection slip

It is going to be a splendid summer.
The apple tree will be thick with golden russets
expanding weightily in the soft air.
I shall finish the brick wall beside the terrace
and plant out all the geranium cuttings.
Pinks and carnations will be everywhere.

She will come out to me in the garden,
her bare feet pale on the cut grass,
bringing jasmine tea and strawberries on a tray.
I shall be correcting the proofs of my novel
(third in a trilogy – simultaneous publication
in four continents); and my latest play

will be in production at the Aldwych
starring Glenda Jackson and Paul Scofield
with Olivier brilliant in a minor part.
I shall probably have finished my translations
of Persian creation myths and the Pre-Socratics
(drawing new parallels) and be ready to start

on Lucretius. But first I'll take a break
at the chess championships in Manila –
on present form, I'm fairly likely to win.
And poems? Yes, there will certainly be poems:
they sing in my head, they tingle along my nerves.
It is all magnificently about to begin.

Our Trip to the Federation

We went to Malaya for an afternoon,
driving over the long dull roads
in Bill's Toyota, the two boys in the back.
It was rubber plantations mostly
and villages like all Asian villages,
brown with dust and wood, bright with marketing.

Before we had to turn back we stopped
at a Chinese roadside cemetery
and visited among the long grass
the complicated coloured graves,
patchwork semi-circles of painted stone:
one mustn't set a foot on the wrong bit.

Across the road were rubber trees again
and a kampong behind: we looked in
at thatched houses, flowering shrubs, melons,
unusual speckled poultry, and the usual
beautiful children. We observed
how the bark was slashed for rubber-tapping.

Does it sound like a geography lesson
or a dream? Rubber-seeds are mottled,
smooth, like nuts. I picked up three
and have smuggled them absent-mindedly
in and out of several countries.
Shall I plant them and see what grows?

Mr Morrison

Goslings dive in the lake,
leaves dazzle on the trees;
on the warm grass two ducks are parked neatly
together like a pair of shoes.

A coot plays beaks with its chick;
children laugh and exclaim.
Mr Morrison saunters past, smiling at them,
humming a Sunday-school hymn.

He wonders about his mood,
irredeemably content:
he should worry more about poverty, oppression,
injustice; but he can't, he can't.

He is not too callous to care
but is satisfied in his work,
well-fed, well-housed, tolerably married,
and enjoying a walk in the park.

Then the sun sticks in the sky,
the tune sticks in his throat,
a burning hand with razors for fingernails
reaches inside his coat

and hotly claws at his heart.
He stands very quiet and still,
seeing if he dares to breathe just a fraction;
sweating; afraid he'll fall.

With stiff little wooden steps
he edges his way to a bench
and lowers his body with its secret fiery
tenant down, inch by inch.

He orders himself to be calm:
no doubt it will soon pass.
He resolves to smoke less, watch his cholesterol,
walk more, use the car less.

And it passes: he is released,
the stabbing fingers depart.
Tentatively at first, then easily,
he fills his lungs without hurt.

He is safe; and he is absolved:
it was not just pain, after all;
it enrolled him among the sufferers, allotted him
a stake in the world's ill.

Doors open inside his head;
once again he begins to hum:
he's been granted one small occasion for worry
and the promise of more to come.

Things

There are worse things than having behaved foolishly in public.
There are worse things than these miniature betrayals,
committed or endured or suspected; there are worse things
than not being able to sleep for thinking about them.
It is 5 a.m. All the worse things come stalking in
and stand icily about the bed looking worse and worse and worse.

A Way Out

The other option's to become a bird.
That's kindly done, to guess from how they sing,
decently independent of the word
as we are not; and how they use the air
to sail as we might soaring on a swing
higher and higher; but the rope's not there,

it's free fall upward, out into the sky;
or if the arc veer downward, then it's planned:
a bird can loiter, skimming just as high
as lets him supervise the hazel copse,
the turnip field, the orchard, and then land
on just the twig he's chosen. Down he drops

to feed, if so it be: a pretty killer,
a keen-eyed stomach weighted like a dart.
He feels no pity for the caterpillar,
that moistly munching hoop of innocent green.
It is such tender lapses twist the heart.
A bird's heart is a tight little red bean,

untwistable. His beak is made of bone,
his feet apparently of stainless wire;
his coat's impermeable; his nest's his own.
The clogging multiplicity of things
amongst which other creatures, battling, tire
can be evaded by a pair of wings.

The point is, most of it occurs below,
earthed at the levels of the grovelling wood
and gritty buildings. Up's the way to go.
If it's escapist, if it's like a dream
the dream's prolonged until it ends for good.
I see no disadvantage in the scheme.

Prelude

Is it the long dry grass that is so erotic,
waving about us with hair-fine fronds of straw,
with feathery flourishes of seed, inviting us
to cling together, fall, roll into it
blind and gasping, smothered by stalks and hair,
pollen and each other's tongues on our hot faces?
Then imagine if the summer rain were to come,
heavy drops hissing through the warm air,
a sluice on our wet bodies, plastering us
with strands of delicious grass; a hum in our ears.

We walk a yard apart, talking
of literature and of botany.
We have known each other, remotely, for nineteen years.

Accidental

We awakened facing each other
across the white counterpane.
I prefer to be alone in the mornings.
The waiter offered us
melon, papaya, orange juice or fresh raspberries.
We did not discuss it.

All those years of looking but not touching:
at most a kiss in a taxi.
And now this accident,
this blind unstoppable robot walk
into a conspiracy of our bodies.
Had we ruined the whole thing?

The waiter waited:
it was his business to appear composed.
Perhaps we should make it ours also?
We moved an inch or two closer together.
Our toes touched. We looked. We had decided.
Papaya then; and coffee and rolls. Of course.

A Message

Discreet, not cryptic. I write to you from the garden
in tawny, provoking August; summer is just
on the turn. The lawn is hayseeds and grassy dust.

There are brilliant yellow daisies, though, and fuchsia
(you'll know why) and that mauve and silvery-grey
creeper under the apple tree where we lay.

There have been storms. The apples are few, but heavy,
heavy. And where blossom was, the tree
surges with bright pink flowers – the sweet pea

has taken it over again. Things operate
oddly here. Remember how I found
the buddleia dead, and cut it back to the ground?

That was in April. Now it's ten feet high:
thick straight branches – they've never been so strong –
leaves like a new species, half a yard long,

and spikes of flowers, airily late for their season
but gigantic. A mutation, is it? Well,
summers to come will test it. Let time tell.

Gardens are rife with sermon-fodder. I delve
among blossoming accidents for their designs
but make no statement. Read between these lines.

Proposal for a Survey

Another poem about a Norfolk church,
a neolithic circle, Hadrian's Wall?
Histories and prehistories: indexes
and bibliographies can't list them all.
A map of Poets' England from the air
could show not only who and when but where.

Aerial photogrammetry's the thing,
using some form of infra-red technique.
Stones that have been so fervently described
surely retain some heat. They needn't speak:
the cunning camera ranging in its flight
will chart their higher temperatures as light.

We'll see the favoured regions all lit up –
the Thames a fiery vein, Cornwall a glow,
Tintagel like an incandescent stud,
most of East Anglia sparkling like Heathrow;
and Shropshire luminous among the best,
with Offa's Dyke in diamonds to the west.

The Lake District will be itself a lake
of patchy brilliance poured along the vales,
with somewhat lesser splashes to the east
across Northumbria and the Yorkshire dales.
Cities and churches, villages and lanes,
will gleam in sparks and streaks and radiant stains.

The lens, of course, will not discriminate
between the venerable and the new;
Stonehenge and Avebury may catch the eye
but Liverpool will have its aura too.
As well as Canterbury there'll be Leeds
and Hull criss-crossed with nets of glittering beads.

Nor will the cool machine be influenced
by literary fashion to reject
any on grounds of quality or taste:
intensity is all it will detect,
mapping in light, for better or for worse,
whatever has been written of in verse.

The dreariness of eighteenth-century odes
will not disqualify a crag, a park,
a country residence; nor will the rant
of satirists leave London in the dark.
All will shine forth. But limits there must be:
borders will not be crossed, nor will the sea.

Let Scotland, Wales and Ireland chart themselves,
as they'd prefer. For us, there's just one doubt:
that medieval England may be dimmed
by age, and all that's earlier blotted out.
X-rays might help. But surely ardent rhyme
will, as it's always claimed, outshine mere time?

By its own power the influence will rise
from sites and settlements deep underground
of those who sang about them while they stood.
Pale phosphorescent glimmers will be found

of epics chanted to pre-Roman tunes
and poems in, instead of about, runes.

Fairy-tale

This is a story. Dear Clive
(a name unmet among my acquaintance)
you landed on my island: Mauritius
I'll call it – it was not unlike.
The Governor came to meet your plane.
I stood on the grass by the summerhouse.
It was dark, I think. And next morning
we walked in the ripples of the sea
watching the green and purple creatures
flashing in and out of the waves
about our ankles. Seabirds, were they?
Or air-fishes, a flying shoal
of sea-parrots, finned and feathered?
Even they were less of a marvel,
pretty things, than that you'd returned
after a year and such distraction
to walk with me on the splashy strand.

At the Creative Writing Course

Slightly frightened of the bullocks
as we walk into their mud towards them
she arms herself by naming them for me:
'Friesian, Aberdeen, Devon, South Devon…'
A mixed herd. I was nervous too,
but no longer. 'Devon, Friesian, Aberdeen…'
the light young voice chants at them
faster as the long heavy heads
lift and lurch towards us. And pause,
turn away to let us pass. I am learning
to show confidence before large cattle.
She is learning to be a poet.

Endings

The Ex-Queen Among the Astronomers

They serve revolving saucer eyes,
dishes of stars; they wait upon
huge lenses hung aloft to frame
the slow procession of the skies.

They calculate, adjust, record,
watch transits, measure distances.
They carry pocket telescopes
to spy through when they walk abroad.

Spectra possess their eyes; they face
upwards, alert for meteorites,
cherishing little glassy worlds:
receptacles for outer space.

But she, exile, expelled, ex-queen,
swishes among the men of science
waiting for cloudy skies, for nights
when constellations can't be seen.

She wears the rings he let her keep;
she walks as she was taught to walk
for his approval, years ago.
His bitter features taunt her sleep.

And so when these have laid aside
their telescopes, when lids are closed
between machine and sky, she seeks
terrestrial bodies to bestride.

She plucks this one or that among
the astronomers, and is become
his canopy, his occultation;
she sucks at earlobe, penis, tongue

114

mouthing the tubes of flesh; her hair
crackles, her eyes are comet-sparks.
She brings the distant briefly close
above his dreamy abstract stare.

Off the Track

Our busy springtime has corrupted
into a green indolence of summer,
static, swollen, invisibly devoured.
Too many leaves have grown between us.
Almost without choosing I have turned
from wherever we were towards this thicket
It is not the refuge I had hoped for.
Walking away from you I walk
into a trailing mist of caterpillars:
they swing at my face, tinily suspended,
half-blinding; and my hands are smudged
with a syrup of crushed aphids.

You must be miles away by now
in open country, climbing steadily,
head down, looking for larks' eggs.

Beaux Yeux

Arranging for my due ration of terror
involves me in such lunacies
as recently demanding to be shown
the broad blue ovals of your eyes.

Yes: quite as alarming as you'd promised,
those lapidary iris discs
level in your dark small face.
Still, for an hour or two I held them

until you laughed, replaced your tinted glasses,
switched accents once again
and went away, looking faintly uncertain
in the sunlight (but in charge, no doubt of it)

and leaving me this round baby sparrow
modelled in feather-coloured clay,
a small snug handful; hardly apt
unless in being cooler than a pebble.

Send-off

Half an hour before my flight was called
he walked across the airport bar towards me
carrying what was left of our future
together: two drinks on a tray.

In Focus

Inside my closed eyelids, printed out
from some dying braincell as I awakened,
was this close-up of granular earthy dust,
fragments of chaff and grit, a triangular
splinter of glass, a rusty metal washer
on rough concrete under a wooden step.

Not a memory. But the caption told me
I was at Grange Farm, seven years old,
in the back yard, kneeling outside the shed
with some obscure seven-year-old's motive,
seeing as once, I must believe, I saw:
sharply; concentrating as once I did.

Glad to be there again I relaxed the focus
(eyes still shut); let the whole scene open out
to the pump and separator under the porch,
the strolling chickens, the pear trees next to the yard,

116

the barn full of white cats, the loaded haycart,
the spinney... I saw it rolling on and on.

As it couldn't, of course. That I had faced
when I made my compulsive return visit
after more than twenty years. 'Your aunt's not well,'
said Uncle George – little and gnarled himself –
'You'll find she doesn't talk.' They'd sold the farm,
retired to Melton Mowbray with their daughter.

'Premature senility,' she whispered.
But we all went out together in the car
to see the old place, Auntie sitting
straight-backed, dignified, mute,
perhaps a little puzzled as we churned
through splattering clay lanes, between wet hedges

to Grange Farm again: to a square house,
small, bleak, and surrounded by mud;
to be greeted, shown to the parlour, given tea,
with Auntie's affliction gently signalled –
'Her mouth hurts.' Not my real aunt,
nor my real uncle. Both dead now.

I find it easiest to imagine dying
as like the gradual running down of a film,
the brain still flickering when the heart and blood
have halted, and the last few frames
lingering. Then where the projector jams
is where we go, or are, or are no longer.

If that comes anywhere near it, then I hope
that for those two an after-image glowed
in death of something better than mud and silence
or than my minute study of a patch of ground;
unless, like that for me, it spread before them
sunny ploughland, pastures, the scented orchard.

Letter from Highgate Wood

Your 'wedge of stubborn particles':

that silver birch, thin as a bent flagpole,
drives up through elm and oak and hornbeam
to sky-level, catching the late sunlight.

There's woodsmoke, a stack of cut billets
from some thick trunk they've had to hack;
and of course a replacement programme under way –
saplings fenced off against marauders.

'We have seasons' your poem says;
and your letter tells me the black invader
has moved into the lymph; is not defeated.

'He's lucky to be still around,' said your friend –
himself still around, still travelling
after a near-axing as severe,
it yet may prove, as yours at present.

I have come here to think, not for comfort;
to confront these matters, to imagine
the proliferating ungentle cells.

But the place won't let me be fearful;
the green things work their usual trick –
'Choose life' – and I remember instead
our own most verdant season.

My dear, after more than a dozen years
light sings in the leaves of it still.

Poem Ended by a Death

They will wash all my kisses and fingerprints off you
and my tearstains – I was more inclined to weep

in those wild-garlicky days – and our happier stains,
thin scales of papery silk . . . Fuck that for a cheap
opener; and false too – any such traces
you pumiced away yourself, those years ago
when you sent my letters back, in the week I married
that anecdotal ape. So start again. So:

They will remove the tubes and drips and dressings
which I censor from my dreams. They will, it is true,
wash you; and they will put you into a box.
After which whatever else they may do
won't matter. This is my laconic style.
You praised it, as I praised your intricate pearled
embroideries; these links laced us together,
plain and purl across the ribs of the world . . .

Having No Mind for the Same Poem

Nor for the same conversation again and again.
But the power of meditation to cure an allergy,
that I will discuss
cross-legged on the lawn at evening
midges flittering, a tree beside us
none of us can name;
and rocks; a scent of syringa;
certain Japanese questions; the journey . . .

Nor for parody.

Nor, if we come to it, for the same letter:
'hard to believe . . . I remember best his laugh . . .
such a vigorous man . . . please tell . . .'
and running, almost running to stuff coins
into the box for cancer research.

The others.

Nor for the same hopeless prayer.

Syringa

The syringa's out. That's nice for me:
all along Charing Cross Embankment
the sweet dragging scent reinventing
one of my childhood gardens.
Nice for the drunks and drop-outs too,
if they like it. I'm walking to work:
they'll be here all day under the blossom
with their cider and their British sherry
and their carrier-bags of secrets.
There's been a change in the population:
the ones I had names for – Fat Billy,
the Happy Couple, the Lady with the Dog –
have moved on or been moved off.
But it doesn't do to wonder:
staring hurts in two directions. Once
a tall man chased me here, and I ran
for no good reason: afraid, perhaps,
of turning into Mrs Toothless
with her ankle-socks and her pony-tailed skull
whose eyes avoided mine so many mornings.
And she's gone too. The place has been,
as whatever office will have termed it,
cleaned up. Except that it's not clean
and not really a place: a hesitation
between the traffic fumes and a fragrance,
where this evening I shall walk again.

Dry Spell

It is not one thing, but more one thing than others:
the carved spoon broken in its case, a slate split on the roof,
dead leaves falling upon dead grass littered
with feathers, and the berries ripe too soon.

All of a piece and all in pieces, the dry mouth failing
to say it. I am sick with symbols.
Here is the thing itself: it is a drought.
I must learn it and live it drably through.

Visited

This truth-telling is well enough
looking into the slaty eyes of the visitants
acknowledging the messages they bring

but they plod past so familiarly
mouldy faces droning about acceptance
that one almost looks for a real monster

spiny and gaping as the fine mad fish
in the corner of that old shipwreck painting
rearing its red gullet out of the foam.

The Soho Hospital for Women

1

Strange room, from this angle:
white door open before me,
strange bed, mechanical hum, white lights.
There will be stranger rooms to come.

As I almost slept I saw the deep flower opening
and leaned over into it, gratefully.
It swimmingly closed in my face. I was not ready.
It was not death, it was acceptance.

*

Our thin patient cat died purring,
her small triangular head tilted back,
the nurse's fingers caressing her throat,
my hand on her shrunken spine; the quick needle.

That was the second death by cancer.
The first is not for me to speak of.
It was telephone calls and brave letters
and a friend's hand bleeding under the coffin.

*

Doctor, I am not afraid of a word.
But neither do I wish to embrace that visitor,
to engulf it as Hine-Nui-te-Po
engulfed Maui; that would be the way of it.

And she was the winner there: her womb crushed him.
Goddesses can do these things.
But I have admitted the gloved hands and the speculum
and must part my ordinary legs to the surgeon's knife.

    2
Nellie has only one breast
ample enough to make several.
Her quilted dressing-gown softens
to semi-doubtful this imbalance
and there's no starched vanity
in our abundant ward-mother:
her silvery hair's in braids, her slippers
loll, her weathered smile holds true.
When she dresses up in her black

with her glittering marcasite brooch on
to go for the weekly radium treatment
she's the bright star of the taxi-party –
whatever may be growing under her ribs.

*

Doris hardly smokes in the ward –
and hardly eats more than a dreamy spoonful –
but the corridors and bathrooms
reek of her Players Number 10,
and the drug-trolley pauses
for long minutes by her bed.
Each week for the taxi-outing
she puts on her skirt again
and has to pin the slack waistband
more tightly over her scarlet sweater.
Her face, a white shadow through smoked glass,
lets Soho display itself unregarded.

*

Third in the car is Mrs Golding
who never smiles. And why should she?

    3
The senior consultant on his rounds
murmurs in so subdued a voice
to the students marshalled behind
that they gather in, forming a cell,
a cluster, a rosette around him
as he stands at the foot of my bed
going through my notes with them,
half-audibly instructive, grave.

The slight ache as I strain forward
to listen still seems imagined.

Then he turns his practised smile on me:
'How are you this morning?' 'Fine,
very well, thank you.' I smile too.

And possibly all that murmurs within me
is the slow dissolving of stitches.

4

I am out in the supermarket choosing –
this very afternoon, this day –
picking up tomatoes, cheese, bread,

things I want and shall be using
to make myself a meal, while they
eat their stodgy suppers in bed:

Janet with her big freckled breasts,
her prim Scots voice, her one friend,
and never in hospital before,

who came in to have a few tests
and now can't see where they'll end;
and Coral in the bed by the door

who whimpered and gasped behind a screen
with nurses to and fro all night
and far too much of the day;

pallid, bewildered, nineteen.
And Mary, who will be all right
but gradually. And Alice, who may.

Whereas I stand almost intact,
giddy with freedom, not with pain.
I lift my light basket, observing

how little I needed in fact;
and move to the checkout, to the rain,
to the lights and the long street curving.

Variations on a Theme of Horace

Clear is the man and of a cold life
who needn't fear the slings and arrows;
cold is the man, and perhaps the moorish bows
will avoid him and the wolf turn tail.

*

Sitting in the crypt under bare arches
at a quite ordinary table with a neat cloth,
a glass of wine before him, 'I'm never sure,'
he said, 'that I'll wake up tomorrow morning.'

Upstairs musicians were stretching their bows
for a late quartet which would also save us from nothing.
This ex-church was bombed to rubble,
rebuilt. It is not of that he was thinking.

And policemen decorate the underground stations
to protect us from the impure of heart;
the traveller must learn to suspect his neighbour,
each man his own watchdog. Nor of that.

Of a certain high felicity, perhaps,
imagining its absence; of the chances.
(If echoes fall into the likeness of music
that, like symmetry, may be accidental.)

'Avoid archaism for its own sake –
viols, rebecks: what is important
is simply that the instruments should be able
to play the notes.' A hard-learnt compromise.

But using what we have while we have it
seems, at times, enough or more than enough.
And here were old and newer things for our pleasure –
the sweet curves of the arches; music to come.

Which this one set before him with his own death –
far from probably imminent, not soon likely –
ticking contrapuntally like a pace-maker
inside him. Were we, then, lighter, colder?

Had we ignored a central insistent theme?
Possibly even the birds aren't happy:
it may be that they twitter from rage or fear.
So many tones; one can't be sure of one's reading.

Just as one can't quite despise Horace
on whom the dreaded tree never did quite fall;
timid enjoyer that he was, he died
in due course of something or other. And meanwhile

sang of his Lalage in public measures,
enjoyed his farm and his dinners rather more,
had as much, no doubt, as any of us to lose.
And the black cypress stalks after us all.

A Walk in the Snow

Neighbours lent her a tall feathery dog
to make her expedition seem natural.
She couldn't really fancy a walk alone,
drawn though she was to the shawled whiteness,
the flung drifts of wool. She was not a walker.
Her winter pleasures were in firelit rooms –
entertaining friends with inventive dishes
or with sherry, conversation, palm-reading:
'You've suffered,' she'd say. 'Of course, life is suffering . . .'
holding a wrist with her little puffy hand
older than her face. She was writing a novel.
But today there was the common smothered in snow,
blanked-out, white as meringue, the paths gone:
a few mounds of bracken spikily veiled
and the rest smooth succulence. They pocked it,
she and the dog; they wrote on it with their feet –

her suede boots, his bright flurrying paws.
It was their snow, and they took it.
                                    That evening
the poltergeist, the switcher-on of lights
and conjuror with ashtrays, was absent.
The house lay mute. She hesitated a moment
at bedtime before the Valium bottle;
then, to be on the safe side, took her usual;
and swam into a deep snowy sleep
where a lodge (was it?) and men in fur hats,
and the galloping . . . and something about . . .

A Day in October

1.30 p.m.
Outside the National Gallery
a man checks bags for bombs or weapons –
not thoroughly enough: he'd have missed
a tiny hand-grenade in my make-up purse,
a cigarette packet of gelignite.
I walk in gently to Room III
not to disturb them: Piero's angels,
serene and cheerful, whom surely nothing could frighten,
and St Michael in his red boots
armed against all comers.
Brave images. But under my heart
an explosive bubble of tenderness gathers
and I shiver before the chalky Christ:
what must we do to save
the white limbs, pale tree, trusting verticals?
Playing the old bargaining game
I juggle with prices, offer a finger
for this or that painting, a hand or an eye
for the room's contents. What for the whole building?
And shouldn't I jump aside if the bomb flew,
cowardly as instinct makes us?
'Goodbye' I tell the angels, just in case.

4 p.m.
It's a day for pictures:
this afternoon, in the course of duty,
I open a book of black-and-white photographs,
rather smudgy, the text quaintly translated
from the Japanese: Atomic Bomb Injuries.
All the familiar shots are here:
the shadow blast-printed on to a wall,
the seared or bloated faces of children.
I am managing not to react to them.
Then this soldier, who died from merely helping,
several slow weeks afterwards.
His body is a Scarfe cartoon –
skinny trunk, enormous toes and fingers,
joints huge with lymphatic nodes.
My throat swells with tears at last.
Almost I fall into that inheritance,
long resisted and never my own doctrine,
a body I would not be part of.
I all but say it: 'What have we done?
How shall we pay for this?'
But having a job to do I swallow
tears, guilt, these pallid secretions;
close the book; and carry it away
to answer someone's factual enquiry.

7 p.m.
In the desert the biggest tank battle
since World War II smashes on.
My friends are not sure whether their brothers
in Israel are still alive.
All day the skies roar with jets.
And I do not write political poems.

House-talk

Through my pillow, through mattress, carpet, floor and ceiling,
sounds ooze up from the room below:
footsteps, chinking crockery, hot-water pipes groaning,
the muffled clunk of the refrigerator door,
and voices. They are trying to be quiet,
my son and his friends, home late in the evening.

Tones come softly filtered through the layers of padding.
I hear the words but not what the words are,
as on my radio when the batteries are fading.
Voices are reduced to a muted music:
Andrew's bass, his friend's tenor, the indistinguishable
light murmurs of the girls; occasional giggling.

Surely wood and plaster retain something
in their grain of all the essences they absorb?
This house has been lived in for ninety years,
nine by us. It has heard all manner of talking.
Its porous fabric must be saturated
with words. I offer it my peaceful breathing.

Foreigner

These winds bully me:

I am to lie down in a ditch
quiet under the thrashing nettles
and pull the mud up to my chin.

Not that I would submit so
to one voice only;
but by the voices of these several winds
merged into a flowing fringe of tones
that swirl and comb over the hills
I am compelled.

I shall lie sound-proofed in the mud,
a huge caddis-fly larva,
a face floating upon Egyptian unguents
in a runnel at the bottom of England.

In the Dingle Peninsula

We give ten pence to the old woman
and climb through nettles to the beehive hut.
You've been before. You're showing me prehistory,
ushering me into a stone cocoon.
I finger the corbelled wall and squat against it
bowing my back in submission to its curves.

The floor's washed rock: not even a scorchmark
as trace of the once-dwellers. But they're here,
closer than you, and trying to seduce me:
the arched stones burn against my shoulders,
my knees tingle, the cool air buzzes . . .
I drag my eyelids open and sleep-walk out.

'We're skeletons underneath' I've heard you say,
looking into coffins at neat arrangements
laid out in museums. We're skeletons.
I take the bones of your hand lightly in mine
through the dry flesh and walk unresisting,
willing to share it, over the peopled soil.

In the Terai

Our throats full of dust, teeth harsh with it,
plastery sweat in our hair and nostrils,
we slam the flaps of the Landrover down
and think we choke on these roads.
Well, they will be better in time:
all along the dry riverbed
just as when we drove past this morning

men and women squatting under umbrellas
or cloth stretched over sticks, or nothing,
are splitting chipped stones to make smaller chips,
picking the fingernail-sized fragments
into graded heaps: roads by the handful.
We stop at the village and buy glasses of tea,
stewed and sweet; swallow dust with it
and are glad enough. The sun tilts lower.
Somewhere, surely, in this valley
under cool thatch mothers are feeding children
with steamy rice, leaning over them
to pour milk or water; the cups
tasting of earthenware, neutral, clean,
the young heads smelling only of hair.

River

*'. . . I saw with infinite pleasure the great object of my mission; the long
sought for, majestic Niger, glittering to the morning sun, as broad as
the Thames at Westminster, and flowing slowly to the eastward.'*

MUNGO PARK
Travels in the Interior Districts of Africa

The strong image is always the river
was a line for the poem I never wrote
twenty years ago and never have written
of the green Wanganui under its willows
or the ice-blue milky-foaming Clutha
stopping my tremulous teenage heart.

But now when I cross Westminster Bridge
all that comes to mind is the Niger
a river Mungo Park invented for me
as he invented all those African villages
and a certain kind of astonishing silence –
the explorer having done the poet's job
and the poet feeling gratefully redundant.

To and Fro

The Inner Harbour

Paua-Shell

Spilt petrol
oil on a puddle
the sea's colour-chart
porcelain, tie-dyed.
Tap the shell:
glazed calcium.

Cat's-Eye

Boss-eye, wall-eye, squinty lid
stony door for a sea-snail's tunnel

the long beach littered with them
domes of shell, discarded virginities

where the green girl wanders, willing
to lose hers to the right man

or to the wrong man, if he should raise
his frolic head above a sand dune

glossy-black-haired, and that smile on him

Sea-Lives

Under the sand at low tide
are whispers, hisses, long slithers,
bubbles, the suck of ingestion, a soft
snap: mysteries and exclusions.

Things grow on the dunes too –
pale straggle of lupin-bushes,
cutty-grass, evening primroses
puckering in the low light.

But the sea knows better.
Walk at the edge of its rich waves:
on the surface nothing shows;
underneath it is fat and fecund.

Shrimping-Net

Standing just under the boatshed
knee-deep in dappled water
sand-coloured legs and the sand itself
greenish in the lit ripples
watching the shrimps avoid her net
little flexible glass rockets
and the lifted mesh always empty
gauze and wire dripping sunlight

She is too tall to stand under
this house. It is a fantasy

And moving in from the bright outskirts
further under the shadowy floor
hearing a footstep creak above
her head brushing the rough timber
edging further bending her knees
creosote beams grazing her shoulder
the ground higher the roof lower
sand sifting on to her hair

She kneels in dark shallow water,
palms pressed upon shells and weed.

Immigrant

November '63: eight months in London.
I pause on the low bridge to watch the pelicans:
they float swanlike, arching their white necks
over only slightly ruffled bundles of wings,
burying awkward beaks in the lake's water.

I clench cold fists in my Marks and Spencer's jacket
and secretly test my accent once again:
St James's Park; St James's Park; St James's Park.

Settlers

First there is the hill   wooden houses
warm branches close against the face

Bamboo was in it somewhere
or another tall reed   and pines

Let it shift a little
settle into its own place

When we lived on the mountain
she said   But it was not
a mountain   nor they placed so high
nor where they came from a mountain
Manchester   and then the slow seas
hatches battened   a typhoon
so that all in the end became
mountains
            Steps to the venture
vehicles luggage bits of paper
all their people fallen away
shrunken into framed wedding groups
One knows at the time it can't be happening

Neighbours helped them build a house
what neighbours there were   and to farm
she and the boy much alone
her husband away in the town working
clipping hair   Her heart was weak
they said   ninety years with a weak heart
and such grotesque accidents
burns wrenches caustic soda
conspired against she had to believe

The waterfall   that was real
but she never mentioned the waterfall

After twelve years the slow reverse
from green wetness   cattle   weather
to somewhere at least   a township
air lower than the mountain's   calmer
a house with an orchard   peach and plum trees
tomato plants   their bruised scented leaves
and a third life   grandchildren
even the trip back to England at last

Then calmer still and closer in
suburbs   retraction into a city

We took her a cake for her birthday
going together   it was easier
Separately would have been kinder
and twice   For the same stories
rain cold now on the southerly harbour
wondering she must have been why
alone in the house or whether alone
her son in Europe   but someone
a man she thought in the locked room
where their things were stored   her things
about her   china the boxwood cabinet
photographs   Them's your Grandpa's people
and the noises in the room   a face

Hard to tell if she was frightened

Not simple   no   Much neglected
and much here omitted   Footnotes
Alice and her children gone ahead
the black sheep brother   the money
the whole slow long knotted tangle

And her fine straight profile too
her giggle   Eee   her dark eyes

Going Back

There were always the places I couldn't spell, or couldn't find on maps –
too small, but swollen in family legend:
famous for bush-fires, near-drownings, or just the standard pioneer
grimness – twenty cows to milk by hand
before breakfast, and then a five-mile walk to school.
(Do I exaggerate? Perhaps; but hardly at all.)

They were my father's, mostly. One or two, until I was five,
rolled in and out of my own vision:
a wall with blackboards; a gate where I swung, the wind bleak in the
        telegraph wires;
Mother in this or that schoolhouse kitchen,
singing. And, in between, back to familiar bases:
Drury again, Christmas Days in grandparents' houses.

Suddenly no more New Zealand except in receding pictures
for years. And then we had it again, but different:
a city, big schools, my father a university teacher now.
But, being a nostalgic family, we went
in a newish car, along better roads, where once we'd rattled
in the Baby Austin over metal or clay surfaces, unsealed.

And we got most of it – nearly all the places that seemed to matter:
'Do you remember this path?' and 'There's the harbour
we had to cross in the launch when you were a new baby
and a storm came up, and we thought we'd go under.'
Here and there a known vista or the familiar angle
of a room to a garden made my own memories tingle.

But nostalgia-time ran out as I grew older and more busy
and became a parent myself, and left the country
for longer than they had left it; with certain things undone:
among them, two holes in the map empty.
Now I've stitched them in. I have the fabric complete,
the whole of the North Island pinned out flat.

First my own most haunting obsession, the school at Tokorangi.
It was I who spotted the turning off the road,
identified the trees, the mound, the contours programmed into my system
when I was five, and the L-shaped shed
echoing for two of us with voices; for the rest
an object of polite historical interest.

And a week later, one for my father, smaller and more remote,
a square wooden box on a little hill.
The door creaked rustily open. He stood in the entrance porch, he touched
the tap he'd so often turned, the very nail
where sixty years ago the barometer had hung
to be read at the start of each patterned morning.

Two bits of the back-blocks, then, two differently rural settings
for schools, were they? Schools no longer.
Left idle by the motorised successors of the pioneers
each had the same still mask to offer:
broken windows, grassy silence, all the children gone away,
and classrooms turned into barns for storing hay.

Instead of an Interview

The hills, I told them; and water, and the clear air
(not yielding to more journalistic probings);
and a river or two, I could say, and certain bays
and ah, those various and incredible hills . . .

And all my family still in the one city
within walking distances of each other
through streets I could follow blind. My school was gone
and half my Thorndon smashed for the motorway
but every corner revealed familiar settings
for the dreams I'd not bothered to remember –
ingrained; ingrown; incestuous: like the country.

And another city offering me a lover
and quite enough friends to be going on with;
bookshops; galleries; gardens; fish in the sea;
lemons and passionfruit growing free as the bush.
Then the bush itself; and the wild grand south;
and wooden houses in occasional special towns.

And not a town or a city I could live in.
Home, as I explained to a weeping niece,
home is London; and England, Ireland, Europe.
I have come home with a suitcase full of stones –
of shells and pebbles, pottery, pieces of bark:
here they lie around the floor of my study
as I telephone a cable 'Safely home'

and moments later, thinking of my dears,
wish the over-resonant word cancelled:
'Arrived safely' would have been clear enough,
neutral, kinder. But another loaded word
creeps up now to interrogate me.
By going back to look, after thirteen years,
have I made myself for the first time an exile?

Londoner

Scarcely two hours back in the country
and I'm shopping in East Finchley High Road
in a cotton skirt, a cardigan, jandals –
or flipflops as people call them here,
where February's winter. Aren't I cold?
The neighbours in their overcoats are smiling
at my smiles and not at my bare toes:
they know me here.
                            I hardly know myself,
yet. It takes me until Monday evening,
walking from the office after dark
to Westminster Bridge. It's cold, it's foggy,
the traffic's as abominable as ever,
and there across the Thames is County Hall,
that uninspired stone body, floodlit.
It makes me laugh. In fact, it makes me sing.

To Marilyn from London

You did London early, at nineteen:
the basement room, the geriatric nursing,
cinema queues, modish fall-apart dresses,
and marriage at Stoke Newington Registry Office,
Spring 1955, on the rebound.

Marrying was what we did in those days.
And soon enough you were back in Wellington
with your eye-shadow and your Edith Piaf records
buying kitchen furniture on hire-purchase
and writing novels when the babies were asleep.

Somehow you're still there, I'm here; and now
Sarah arrives: baby-faced like you then,
second of your four blonde Christmas-tree fairies,
nineteen; competent; with her one suitcase
and her two passports. It begins again.

BELOW LOUGHRIGG

(1979)

Below Loughrigg

The power speaks only out of sleep and blackness
no use looking for the sun
what is not present cannot be illumined

Katherine's lungs, remember, eaten by disease
but Mary's fingers too
devoured and she goes on writing

The water speaks from the rocks, the cavern speaks,
where water halloos through it
this happens also in darkness

A steep bit here, up from the valley
to the terraces, the path eroded by water
Now listen for the voice

These things wane with the vital forces
he said, little having waned in him
except faith, and anger had replaced it

One force can be as good as another
we may not think so; but channelled
in ways it has eaten out; issuing

into neither a pool nor the sea
but a shapely lake afloat with wooded islands
a real water and multiplied on maps

which can be read in the sunlight; for the sun
will not be stopped from visiting
and the lake exists and the wind sings over it.

Three Rainbows in One Morning

It is not only the eye that is astonished.

Predictable enough in rainbow weather,
the drenched air saturated with colours,
that over each valley should hang an arc
and over this long lake the longest.
Knowing how it happens is no defence.
They stop the car and are delighted.

But some centre of gravity is upset,
some internal gauge or indicator
fed once again with the routine question
'This place, now: would it be possible
to live here?' buzzes, rolls
and registers 'Yes. Yes; perhaps.'

Binoculars

'What are you looking at?' 'Looking.'
High screed sides; possibly a raven,
he thought. Bracken a fuzz of rust
on the iron slopes of the fell
(off the edge of their map, nameless)
and the sky clean after rain.
At last he put the binoculars down,
drove on further to the north.

It was a good day in the end:
the cold lake lapping against pines,
and the square-built northern town idle
in sunlight. It seemed they had crossed borders.
Driving south became a return
to nests of trees in ornamental colours.
Leaving, he left her the binoculars
to watch her wrens and robins until spring.

Paths

I am the dotted lines on the map:
footpaths exist only when they are walked on.
I am gravel tracks through woodland; I am
field paths, the muddy ledge by the stream,
the stepping-stones. I am the grassy lane
open between waist-high bracken where sheep
fidget. I am the track to the top
skirting and scaling rocks. I am the cairn.

Here on the brow of the world I stop,
set my stone face to the wind, and turn
to each wide quarter. I am that I am.

Mid-point

Finding I've walked halfway around Loughrigg
I wonder: do I still want to go on?
Normally, yes. But now, hardly recovered
from 'flu, and feeling slightly faint in the sun,
dazzled by early spring, I hesitate.
How far is it around this sprawling fell?
I've come perhaps three miles. Will it be four,
or less, the Grasmere way? It's hard to tell.
The ups and downs undo one's feel for distance;
the soaring views distract from what's at hand.
But here's the tarn, spangled with quick refractions
of sunlight, to remind me where I stand.
There's no way on or back except by walking
and whichever route I choose involves a climb.
On, then, no question: if I find myself
lacking in energy, at least I've time.
It will be cooler when I'm facing north –
frost often lingers there – and I'll take heart
from gazing down again on Rydal Water.
The point of no return was at the start.

The Spirit of the Place

Mist like evaporating stone
smudges the bracken. Not much further now.
Below on the other side of the village
Windermere tilts its pewter face
over towards me as I move downhill.
I've walked my boots clean in gravelly streams;
picking twigs of glittering holly
to take home I've lacerated my fingers
(it serves me right: holly belongs on trees).
Now as the early dusk descends behind me
dogs in the kennels above Nook Lane
are barking, growling, hysterical at something;
and from the housing estate below
a deep mad voice bellows 'Wordsworth! Wordsworth!'

The Vale of Grasmere

These coloured slopes ought to inspire,
as much as anything, discretion:
think of the egotisms laid bare,
the shy campaigns of self-projection
tricked out as visits to Dove Cottage
tellingly rendered. Every year
some poet comes on pilgrimage
along these valleys. Read his verses:
each bud of delicate perception
sprouts from a blossoming neurosis
too well watered by Grasmere –
in which he sees his own reflection.
He sits beside a tarn or ghyll
sensitively eating chocolate
and eyes Helm Crag or Rydal Fell
plotting some novel way to use it.
Most of the rocks are wreathed by now
with faded rags of fluttering soul.
But the body finds another function

146

for crags and fells, as Wordsworth knew
himself: they offer hands and feet
their own creative work to do.
'I climb because I can't write,'
one honest man said. Better so.

Letter to Alistair Campbell

Those thorn trees in your poems, Alistair,
we have them here. Also the white cauldron,
the basin of your waterfall. I stare
at Stock Ghyll Force and can't escape your words.
You'd love this place: it's your Central Otago
in English dress – the bony land's the same;
and if the Cromwell Gorge is doomed to go
under a lake, submerging its brave orchards
for cheap electric power, this is where
you'd find a subtly altered image of it,
its cousin in another hemisphere:
the rivers gentler, hills more widely splayed
but craggy enough. Well. Some year you'll manage
to travel north, as I two years ago
went south. Meanwhile our sons are of an age
to do it for us: Andrew's been with you
in Wellington. Now I'm about to welcome
our firstborn Gregory to England. Soon,
if Andrew will surrender him, he'll come
from grimy fetid London – still my base,
I grant you, still my centre, but with air
that chokes me now each time I enter it –
to this pure valley where no haze but weather
obscures the peaks from time to time, clean rain
or tender mist (forgive my lyrical
effusiveness: Wordsworthian locutions
are carried on the winds in what I call
my this year's home. You've had such fits yourself.)
So: Gregory will come to Ambleside
and see the lakes, the Rothay, all these waters.

Two years ago he sat with me beside
the Clutha, on those rocks where you and I
did our first timid courting. Symmetry
pleases me; correspondences and chimes
are not just ornament. And if I try
too hard to emphasise the visual echoes
between a place of mine and one of yours
it's not only for art's sake but for friendship:
five years of marriage, twenty of divorce
are our foundation. It occurred to me
in August, round about the twenty-third,
that we'd deprived ourselves of cake, champagne,
a silver tea-service, the family gathered –
I almost felt I ought to send a card.
Well, that can wait: it won't be long before
you have my blessings on your twentieth year
with Meg; but let this, in the meantime, be for
our older link through places and your poems.

Declensions

Snow on the tops: half the day I've sat at the window
    staring at fells made suddenly remote
by whiteness that disguises them as high mountains
    reared behind the bracken-covered slopes
of others whose colour yesterday was theirs.
    In the middle distance, half-stripped trees
have shed pink stains on the grass beneath them.
    That other pinkness over Windermere
is the setting sun through cloud. And in the foreground
    birds act out their various natures
around the food I've set on the terrace wall:
    the plump chaffinch eats on steadily
even in a hail-shower; tits return when it's over
    to swing on their bacon-rind; a dunnock hops
picking stray seeds; and the territorial robin,
    brisk, beady-eyed, sees them all off.

I am not at all sure that this is the real world
      but I am looking at it very closely.
Is landscape serious? Are birds? But they are fading
      in dusk, in the crawling darkness. Enough.
Knowing no way to record what is famous
      precisely for being unrecordable,
I draw the curtains and settle to my book:
      Dr William Smith's First Greek Course,
Exercise Fourteen: third declension nouns.
      My letters, awkward from years of non-use,
sprinkle over the page like birds' footprints,
      quaint thorny symbols, pecked with accents:
as I turn the antique model sentences:
      The vines are praised by the husbandmen.
The citizens delight in strife and faction.
      The harbour has a difficult entrance.

Weathering

Literally thin-skinned, I suppose, my face
catches the wind off the snow-line and flushes
with a flush that will never wholly settle. Well:
that was a metropolitan vanity,
wanting to look young for ever, to pass.

I was never a Pre-Raphaelite beauty,
nor anything but pretty enough to satisfy
men who need to be seen with passable women.
But now that I am in love with a place
which doesn't care how I look, or if I'm happy,

happy is how I look, and that's all.
My hair will turn grey in any case,
my nails chip and flake, my waist thicken,
and the years work all their usual changes.
If my face is to be weather-beaten as well

that's little enough lost, a fair bargain
for a year among lakes and fells, when simply
to look out of my window at the high pass
makes me indifferent to mirrors and to what
my soul may wear over its new complexion.

Going out from Ambleside

1

He is lying on his back watching a kestrel,
his head on the turf, hands under his neck,
warm air washing over his face,
and the sky clear blue where the kestrel hovers.

A person comes with a thermometer.
He watches a ceiling for three minutes.
The person leaves. He watches the kestrel again
his head pressed back among the harebells.

2

Today he will go over to Langdale.
He springs lightly in his seven-league boots
around the side of Loughrigg
bouncing from rock to rock in the water-courses
evading slithery clumps of weed, skipping
like a sheep among the rushes
coursing along the curved path upward
through bracken, over turf to a knoll
and across it, around and on again
higher and higher, glowing with exaltation
up to where it all opens out.
That was easy. And it was just the beginning.

3

They bring him tea or soup.
He does not notice it. He is busy
identifying fungi in Skelghyll Wood,
comparing them with the pictures in his mind:

Purple Blewit, Yellow Prickle Fungus,
Puffball, Russula, two kinds of Boletus –
the right weather for them.
And what are these little pearly knobs
pressing up among the leaf-mould?
He treads carefully over damp grass,
patches of brilliant moss, pine-needles,
hoping for a Fly Agaric.
Scarlet catches his eye. But it was only
reddening leaves on a bramble.
And here's bracken, fully brown,
and acorns. It must be October.

4

What is this high wind coming,
leaves leaping from the trees to bite his face?
A storm. He should have noticed the signs.
But it doesn't matter. Ah, turn into it,
let the rain bite on the warm skin too.

5

Cold. Suddenly cold. Or hot.
A pain under his breastbone;
and his feet are bare. This is curious.

Someone comes with an injection.

6

They have brought Kurt Schwitters to see him,
a clumsy-looking man in a beret
asking for bits of stuff to make a collage.
Here, take my stamp-collection
and the letters my children wrote from school
and this photograph of my wife. She's dead now.
You are dead too, Kurt Schwitters.

7

This is a day for sailing, perhaps,
coming down from the fells to lake-level;

or for something gentler: for idling
with a fishing-line and listening to water;
or just for lying in a boat
on a summer evening in the lee of a shore
letting the wind steer, leaving the hull
to its own course, the waves to lap it along.

8

But where now suddenly? Dawn light,
peaks around him, shadowy and familiar,
tufts of mist over a tarn below.
Somehow he is higher than he intended;
and careless, giddy, running to the edge
and over it, straight down on splintery scree
leaning back on his boots, a ski-run
scattering chips of slate, a skid with no stopping
down through the brief mist and into the tarn.

9

Tomorrow perhaps he will think about Helvellyn . . .

SELECTED POEMS

(1983)

In the Unicorn, Ambleside

I want to have ice-skates and a hoop
and to have lived all my life in the same house
above Stock; and to skate on Lily Tarn
every winter, because it always freezes –
or always did freeze when you were a girl.

I want to believe your tales about Wordsworth –
'Listen to what the locals say,' you tell me:
'He drank in every pub from here to Ullswater,
and had half the girls. We all know that.'
I want not to know better, out of books.

I sit in the pub with my posh friends, talking
literature and publishing as usual.
Some of them really do admire Wordsworth.
But they won't listen to you. I listen:
how can I get you to listen to me?

I can't help not being local;
but I'm here, aren't I? And this afternoon
Jane and I sat beside Lily Tarn
watching the bright wind attack the ice.
None of you were up there skating.

Downstream

Last I became a raft of green bubbles
meshed into the miniature leaves
of that small pondweed (has it a name?)
that lies green-black on the stream's face:
a sprinkle of round seeds, if you mistake it,
or of seed-hulls holding air among them.

I was those globules; there they floated –
all there was to do was to float
on the degenerate stream, suburbanised,

the mill-stream where it is lost among houses
and hardly moving, swilling just a little
to and fro if the wind blows it.

But it did move, and I moved on, drifting
until I entered the river
where I was comported upon a tear's fashion
blending into the long water
until you would not see that there had been
tear or bubble or any round thing ever.

The Hillside

Tawny-white as a ripe hayfield.
But it is heavy with frost, not seed.

It frames him for you as he sits by the window,
his hair white also, a switch of silver.

He pours you another glass of wine,
laughs at your shy anecdotes, quietly caps them,

is witty as always; glows as hardly ever,
his back to the rectangles of glass.

The snow holds off. Clouds neither pass nor lower
their flakes on to the hill's pale surface.

Tell him there is green beneath it still:
he will almost, for this afternoon, believe you.

This Ungentle Music

Angry Mozart: the only kind for now.
Tinkling would appal on such an evening,
summer, when the possible things to do
are: rip all weeds out of the garden,

butcher the soft redundancy of the hedge
in public; and go, when the light slackens,
to stamp sharp echoes along the street
mouthing futilities: 'A world where . . .'
as if there were a choice of other worlds
than this one in which it is the case
that nothing can stamp out leukaemia.
So Malcolm has had to die at twenty,
humming off on a low blue flame
of heroin, a terminal kindness.

Wild rock howls on someone's record.
Fog sifts over the young moon.

The Ring

Then in the end she didn't marry him
and go to Guyana; the politics of the thing
had to be considered, and her daughter,
too English by now. But she found the ring,

her mourned and glittering hoop of diamonds,
not lost in a drain after all
but wrenched and twisted into a painful oblong
jammed between the divan-bed and the wall.

Corrosion

It was going to be a novel
about his friend, the seventeen-year-old
with the pale hair ('younger brother';
that day on the river-bank).
                              Until
he thought perhaps a sonnet-sequence:
more stripped-down, more crystalline.

Or just one sonnet even, one
imaging of the slight bones
almost visible through that skin,
a fine articulation of golden wire.
The bones were what he most held to,
talking about them often: of how
if David (we could call him)
were to have been drenched with acid
and his skin burnt off, the luminous flesh
burnt, it would make no difference.

The slow acid of age
with its lesser burning
he may also have touched on.

4 May 1979

Doom and sunshine stream over the garden.
The mindless daffodils are nodding
bright primped heads at the Tory sky:
such blue elation of spring air!
Such freshness! – the oxides and pollutants
hardly yet more than a sweet dust.
Honesty, that mistaken plant,
has opened several dozen purple buds,
about which the bees are confident.
It might be 1970; it might be 1914.

Madmen

Odd how the seemingly maddest of men –
sheer loonies, the classically paranoid,
violently possessive about their secrets,
whispered after from corners, terrified
of poison in their coffee, driven frantic
(whether for or against him) by discussion of God,
peculiar, to say the least, about their mothers –

return to their gentle senses in bed.
Suddenly straightforward, they perform
with routine confidence, neither afraid
that their partner will turn and bite their balls off
nor groping under the pillow for a razor-blade;
eccentric only in their conversation,
which rambles on about the meaning of a word
they used in an argument in 1969,
they leave their women grateful, relieved, and bored.

Shakespeare's Hotspur

He gurgled beautifully on television,
playing your death, that Shakespearian actor.
Blood glugged under his tongue, he gagged on
words, as you did. Hotspur, Hotspur:
it was an arrow killed you, not a prince,
not Hal clashing over you in his armour,
stabbing featly for the cameras, and your face
unmaimed. You fell into the hands of Shakespeare,
were given a lovely fluency,
undone, redone, made his creature.
In life you never found it easy
to volley phrases off into the future.
And as for your death-scene, that hot day
at Shrewsbury you lifted your visor:
a random arrow smashed into your eye
and mummed your tongue-tied mouth for ever.

Nature Table

The tadpoles won't keep still in the aquarium;
Ben's tried seven times to count them –
thirty-two, thirty-three, wriggle, wriggle –
all right, he's got better things to do.

Heidi stares into the tank, wearing
a snail on her knuckle like a ring.
She can see purple clouds in the water,
a sky for the tadpoles in their world.

Matthew's drawing a worm. Yesterday
he put one down Elizabeth's neck.
But these are safely locked in the wormery
eating their mud; he's tried that too.

Laura sways with her nose in a daffodil,
drunk on pollen, her eyes tight shut.
The whole inside of her head is filling
with a slow hum of fizzy yellow.

Tom squashes his nose against the window.
He hopes it may look like a snail's belly
to the thrush outside. But is not attacked:
the thrush is happy on the bird-table.

The wind ruffles a chaffinch's crest
and gives the sparrows frilly grey knickers
as they squabble over their seeds and bread.
The sun swings in and out of clouds.

Ben's constructing a wigwam of leaves
for the snails. Heidi whispers to the tadpoles
'Promise you won't start eating each other!'
Matthew's rather hoping they will.

A wash of sun sluices the window,
bleaches Tom's hair blonder, separates
Laura from her daffodil with a sneeze,
and sends the tadpoles briefly frantic;

until the clouds flop down again
grey as wet canvas. The wind quickens,
birds go flying, window-glass rattles,
pellets of hail are among the birdseed.

Revision

It has to be learned afresh
every new start or every season,
revised like the languages that faltered
after I left school or when I stopped
going every year to Italy. Or
like how to float on my back, swimming,
not swimming, ears full of sea-water;
like the taste of the wine at first communion
(because each communion is the first);
like dancing and how to ride a horse –
can I still? Do I still want to?

The sun is on the leaves again;
birds are making rather special noises;
and I can see for miles and miles
even with my eyes closed.

So yes: teach it to me again.

Influenza

Dreamy with illness
we are Siamese twins
fused at the groin
too languid to stir.

We sprawl transfixed
remote from the day.
The window is open.
The curtain flutters.

Epics of sound-effects
ripple timelessly:
a dog is barking
in vague slow bursts;

cars drone; someone
is felling a tree.
Forests could topple
between the axe-blows.

Draughts idle over
our burning faces
and my fingers over
the drum in your ribs.

You lick my eyelid:
the fever grips us.
We shake in its hands
until it lets go.

Then you gulp cold water
and make of your mouth
a wet cool tunnel.
I slake my lips at it.

Crab

Late at night we wrench open a crab;
flesh bursts out of its cup

in pastel colours. The dark fronds attract me:
Poison, you say, Dead Men's Fingers –

don't put them in your mouth, stop!
They brush over my tongue, limp and mossy,

until you snatch them from me, as you snatch
yourself, gently, if I come too close.

Here are the permitted parts of the crab,
wholesome on their nests of lettuce

and we are safe again in words.
All day the kitchen will smell of sea.

Eclipse

Today the Dog of Heaven swallowed the sun.
Birds twanged for the dusk and fell silent,
one puzzled flock after another –
African egrets; parakeets; Chinese crows.

But firecrackers fended the beast off:
he spat it out, his hot glorious gobful.
Now it will be ours again tomorrow
for the birds here to rediscover at dawn.

What they chirrup to it will ring like praise
from blackbirds, thrushes, eleven kinds of finches,
that certain tribesmen in the south of China
have not unlearnt their pre-republican ways.

On the Border

Dear posterity, it's 2 a.m.
and I can't sleep for the smothering heat,
or under mosquito nets. The others
are swathed in theirs, humid and sweating,
long white packets on rows of chairs
(no bunks. The building isn't finished).

I prowled in the dark back room for water
and came outside for a cigarette
and a pee in waist-high leafy scrub.
The moon is brilliant: the same moon,
I have to believe, as mine in England
or theirs in the places where I'm not.

Knobbly trees mark the horizon,
black and angular, with no leaves:
blossoming flame trees; and behind them
soft throbbings come from the village.
Birds or animals croak and howl;
the river rustles; there could be snakes.

I don't care. I am standing here,
posterity, on the face of the earth,
letting the breeze blow up my nightdress,
writing in English, as I do,
in all this tropical non-silence.
Now let me tell you about the elephants.

The Prize-winning Poem

It will be typed, of course, and not all in capitals: it will use upper and lower
        case
in the normal way; and where a space is usual it will have a space.
It will probably be on white paper, or possibly blue, but almost certainly not
        pink.
It will not be decorated with ornamental scroll-work in coloured ink,
nor will a photograph of the poet be glued above his or her name,
and still less a snap of the poet's children frolicking in a jolly game.
The poem will not be about feeling lonely and being fifteen
and unless the occasion of the competition is a royal jubilee it will not be
        about the queen.
It will not be the first poem the author has written in his life
and will probably not be about the death of his daughter, son or wife
because although to write such elegies fulfils a therapeutic need
in large numbers they are deeply depressing for the judges to read.
The title will not be 'Thoughts' or 'Life' or 'I Wonder Why'
or 'The Bunny-Rabbit's Birthday Party' or 'In Days of Long Gone By'.
'Tis and 'twas, o'er and e'er, and such poetical contractions will not be found
in the chosen poem. Similarly clichés will not abound:
dawn will not herald another bright new day, nor dew sparkle like
        diamonds in a dell,
nor trees their arms upstretch. Also the poet will be able to spell.

Large meaningless concepts will not be viewed with favour: myriad is out;
infinity is becoming suspect; aeons and galaxies are in some doubt.
Archaisms and inversions will not occur; nymphs will not their fate
      bemoan.
Apart from this there will be no restrictions upon the style or tone.
What is required is simply the masterpiece we'd all write if we could.
There is only one prescription for it: it's got to be good.

An Emblem

Someone has nailed a lucky horse-shoe
beside my door while I was out –
or is it a loop of rubber? No:
it's in two sections. They glide about,
silently undulating: two
slugs in a circle, tail to snout.

The ends link up: it's a shiny quoit
of rippling slug-flesh, thick as a snake,
liquorice-black against the white
paint; a pair of wetly-nak-
ed tubes. It doesn't seem quite right
to watch what kind of love they'll make.

But who could resist? I'll compromise
and give them a little time alone
to nuzzle each other, slide and ooze
into conjunction on their own;
surely they're experts, with such bodies,
each a complete erogenous zone –

self-lubricating, swelling smooth
and boneless under grainy skin.
Ten minutes, then, for them to writhe
in privacy, to slither in-
to position, to arrange each lithe
tapered hose-pipe around its twin.

All right, now, slugs, I'm back; time's up.
And what a pretty coupling I find!
They're swinging from the wall by a rope
of glue, spun out of their combined
mucus and anchored at the top.
It lets them dangle, intertwined,

formally perfect, like some emblem:
heraldic serpents coiled in a twist.
But just in case their pose may seem
immodest or exhibitionist
they've dressed themselves in a cloud of foam,
a frothy veil for love-in-a-mist.

Piano Concerto in E Flat Major

In her 1930s bob or even, perhaps,
if she saw something quainter as her fashion,
long thick hair in a plait, the music student
showed her composition to her tutor;
and she aroused, or this enhanced, his passion.

He quoted from it in his new concerto,
offering back to her as homage
those several bars of hers the pianist plays
in the second movement: part of what she dreamed
re-translated, marked more with his image.

But the seven steady notes of the main theme
are his alone. Did the romance go well?
Whether he married her's recorded somewhere
in books. The wistful strings, the determined
percussion, the English cadences, don't tell.

Villa Isola Bella

'You will find Isola Bella in pokerwork on my heart'
KATHERINE MANSFIELD TO JOHN MIDDLETON MURRY
10 November 1920 (inscribed outside the
Katherine Mansfield memorial room in Menton)

Your villa, Katherine, but not your room,
and not much of your garden. Goods trains boom
all night, a dozen metres from the bed
where tinier tremors hurtle through my head.
The ghost of your hot flat-iron burns my lung;
my throat's all scorching lumps. I grope among
black laurels and the shadowy date-palm, made
like fans of steel, each rustling frond a blade,
across the gravel to the outside loo
whose light won't wake my sleeping sister. You
smoked shameless Turkish all through your TB.
I drag at Silk Cut filters, duty-free,
then gargle sensibly with Oraldene
and spit pink froth. Not blood: it doesn't mean,
like your spat scarlet, that I'll soon be dead –
merely that pharmacists are fond of red.
I'm hardly sick at all. There's just this fuzz
that blurs and syncopates the singing buzz
of crickets, frogs, and traffic in my ears:
a nameless fever, atavistic fears.
Disease is portable: my bare half-week
down here's hatched no maladie exotique;
I brought my tinglings with me, just as you
brought ragged lungs and work you burned to do,
and, as its fuel, your ecstasy-prone heart.
Whatever haunts my bloodstream didn't start
below your villa, in our genteel den
(till lately a pissoir for passing men).
But your harsh breathing and impatient face,
bright with consumption, must have left a trace
held in the air. Well, Katherine, Goodnight:
let's try to sleep. I'm switching out the light.

Watch me through tepid darkness, wavering back
past leaves and stucco and their reverent plaque
to open what was not in fact your door
and find my narrow mattress on the floor.

Lantern Slides

1

'You'll have to put the little girl down.'
Is it a little girl who's bundled
in both our coats against my shoulder,
buried among the trailing cloth?

It's a big haul up to the quay,
my other arm heavy with luggage,
the ship lurching. Who's my burden?
She had a man's voice this morning.

2

Floods everywhere. Monsoon rain
syphoning down into the valley.
When it stops you see the fungus
hugely coiling out of the grass.

Really, in such a derelict lane
you wouldn't expect so many cars,
black and square, driving jerkily.
It's not as if we were near a village.

3

Now here's the bridal procession:
the groom pale and slender in black
and his hair black under his hat-brim;
is that a frock-coat he's wearing?

The bride's as tall as his trouser pocket;
she hoists her arm to hold his hand,

and rucks her veil askew. Don't,
for your peace of mind, look under it.

     4
The ceremony will be in a cavern,
a deep deserted underground station
built like a theatre; and so it is:
ochre-painted, proscenium-arched.

The men have ribbons on their hatbands;
there they are, behind the grille,
receding with her, minute by minute,
shrivelling down the empty track.

Dreaming

'Oblivion, that's all. I never dream,' he said –
proud of it, another immunity,
another removal from the standard frame which she
inhabited, dreaming beside him of a dead
woman tucked neatly into a small bed,
a cot or a child's bunk, unexpectedly
victim of some friend or lover. 'Comfort me,'
said the dreamer, 'I need to be comforted.'
He did that, not bothering to comprehend,
and she returned to her story: a doctor came
to identify the placid corpse in her dream.
It was obscure; but glancing towards the end
she guessed that killer and lover and doctor were the same;
proving that things are ultimately what they seem.

Street Song

Pink Lane, Strawberry Lane, Pudding Chare:
someone is waiting, I don't know where;
hiding among the nursery names,
he wants to play peculiar games.

In Leazes Terrace or Leazes Park
someone is loitering in the dark,
feeling the giggles rise in his throat
and fingering something under his coat.

He could be sidling along Forth Lane
to stop some girl from catching her train,
or stalking the grounds of the RVI
to see if a student nurse goes by.

In Belle Grove Terrace or Fountain Row
or Hunter's Road he's raring to go –
unless he's the quiet shape you'll meet
on the cobbles in Back Stowell Street.

Monk Street, Friars Street, Gallowgate
are better avoided when it's late.
Even in Sandhill and the Side
there are shadows where a man could hide.

So don't go lightly along Darn Crook
because the Ripper's been brought to book.
Wear flat shoes, and be ready to run:
remember, sisters, there's more than one.

Across the Moor

He had followed her across the moor,
taking shortcuts, light and silent
on the grass where the fair had been –
and in such weather, the clouds dazzling
in a loud warm wind, who'd hear?

He was almost up with her
at the far side, near the road,
when a man with a blotched skin
brought his ugly dogs towards them.
It could have been an interruption.

And as she closed the cattle-gate
in his face almost, he saw
that she was not the one, and let her go.

There had been something. It was
not quite clear yet, he thought.
So he loitered on the bridge,
idle now, the wind in his hair,
gazing over into the stream
of traffic; and for a moment
it seemed to him he saw it there.

Bethan and Bethany

Bethan and Bethany sleep in real linen –
avert your covetous eyes, you starers;
their counterpanes are of handmade lace:
this is a civilised country.

If it is all just one big suburb
gliding behind its freezing mist
it is a decorated one;
it is of brick, and it is tidy.

Above the court-house portico
Justice holds her scales in balance;
the seventeenth-century church is locked
but the plaque outside has been regilded.

Bethan and Bethany, twelve and eleven,
bared their eyes to the television
rose-red-neon-lit, and whispered
in their related languages.

Guess now, through the frilled net curtains,
which belongs here and which doesn't.
Each of them owns the same records;
this is an international culture.

The yobs in the street hoot like all yobs,
hawk and whistle and use no language.
Bethan and Bethany stir in their sleep.
The brindled cat walks on their stomachs.

Blue Glass

The underworld of children becomes the overworld
when Janey or Sharon shuts the attic door
on a sunny afternoon and tiptoes in sandals
that softly waffle-print the dusty floor

to the cluttered bed below the skylight,
managing not to sneeze as she lifts
newspapers, boxes, gap-stringed tennis-racquets
and a hamster's cage to the floor, and shifts

the tasselled cover to make a clean surface
and a pillow to be tidy under her head
before she straightens, mouths the dark sentence,
and lays herself out like a mummy on the bed.

Her wrists are crossed. The pads of her fingertips
trace the cold glass emblem where it lies
like a chain of hailstones melting in the dips
above her collarbones. She needs no eyes

to see it: the blue bead necklace, of sapphire
or lapis, or of other words she knows
which might mean blueness: amethyst, azure,
chalcedony can hardly say how it glows.

She stole it. She tells herself that she found it.
It's hers now. It owns her. She slithers among
its globular teeth, skidding on blue pellets.
Ice-beads flare and blossom on her tongue,

turn into flowers, populate the spaces
around and below her. The attic has become
her bluebell wood. Among their sappy grasses
the light-fringed gas-flames of bluebells hum.

They lift her body like a cloud of petals.
High now, floating, this is what she sees:
granular bark six inches from her eyeballs;
the wood of rafters is the wood of trees.

Her breathing moistens the branches' undersides;
the sunlight in an interrupted shaft
warms her legs and lulls her as she rides
on air, a slender and impossible raft

of bones and flesh; and whether it is knowledge
or a limpid innocence on which she feeds
for power hasn't mattered. She turns the necklace
kindly in her fingers, and soothes the beads.

Mary Magdalene and the Birds

1

Tricks and tumbles are my trade; I'm
all birds to all men.
I switch voices, adapt my features,
do whatever turn you fancy.
All that is constant is my hair:

plumage, darlings, beware of it.

2

Blackbird: that's the one to watch –
or he is, with his gloss and weapon.
Not a profession for a female,
his brown shadow. Thrush is better,
cunning rehearser among the leaves,
and speckle-breasted, maculate.

3

A wound of some kind. All that talk
of the pelican, self-wounding,
feeding his brood from an ever-bleeding
bosom turns me slightly sick.

But seriousness can light upon
the flightiest. This tingling ache,
nicer than pain, is a blade-stroke:
not my own, but I let it happen.

4

What is balsam? What is nard?
Sweetnesses from the sweet life,
obsolete, fit only for wasting.

I groom you with this essence. Wash it
down the drain with tears and water.
We are too human. Let it pass.

5

With my body I thee worship:
breast on stone lies the rockdove
cold on that bare nest, cooing
its low call, unlulled,
restless for the calling to cease.

6

Mary Magdalene sang in the garden.
It was a swansong, said the women,
for his downdrift on the river.

It sounded more of the spring curlew
or a dawn sky full of larks,
watery trillings you could drown in.

HOTSPUR

(1986)

a ballad for music by
GILLIAN WHITEHEAD

I

There is no safety
there is no shelter
the dark dream
will drag us under.

*

I married a man of metal and fire,
quick as a cat, and wild:
Harry Percy the Hotspur,
the Earl of Northumberland's child.

He rode to battle at fourteen years.
He won his prickly name.
His talking is a halting spate,
his temper a trembling flame.

He has three castles to his use,
north of the Roman Wall:
Alnwick, Berwick, Warkworth –
and bowers for me in them all.

I may dance and carol and sing;
I may go sweetly dressed
in silks that suit the lady I am;
I may lie on his breast;

and peace may perch like a hawk on my wrist
but can never come tame to hand,
wed as I am to a warrior
in a wild warring land.

*

High is his prowess
in works of chivalry,
noble his largesse,

franchyse and courtesy.

All this wilderness
owes him loyalty;
and deathly rashness
bears him company.

II

The Earl of Douglas clattered south
with Scottish lords and men at arms.
He smudged our tall Northumberland skies
black with the smoke of burning farms.

My Hotspur hurried to halt his course;
Newcastle was their meeting-place.
Douglas camped on the Castle Leazes;
they met in combat, face to face.

It was as fair as any fight,
but Douglas drew the lucky chance:
he hurled my husband from his saddle,
stunned on the earth, and snatched his lance.

I weep to think what Harry saw
as soon as he had strength to stand:
the silken pennon of the Percies
flaunted in a foreign hand.

'Sir, I shall bear this token off
and set it high on my castle gate.'
'Sir, you shall not pass the bounds
of the county till you meet your fate.'

The city held against the siege;
the Scots were tired and forced to turn.
They tramped away with all their gear
to wait my lord at Otterburn.

III

I sit with my ladies in the turret-room
late in the day, and watch them sewing.
Their fingers flicker over the linen;
mine lie idle with remembering.

Last night the moon travelled through cloud
growing and shrinking minute by minute,
one day from fullness, a pewter cup
of white milk with white froth on it.

These August days are long to pass.
I have watched the berries on the rowan
creeping from green towards vermilion,
slow as my own body to ripen.

I was eight years old when we married,
a child-bride for a boy warrior.
Eight more years dragged past before
they thought me fit for the bridal chamber.

Now I am a woman, and proved to be so:
I carry the tender crop of our future;
while he pursues what he cannot leave,
drawn to danger by his lion's nature.

Daylight fades in the turret-slit;
my ladies lay aside their needles.
They murmur and yawn and fold away
the fine-worked linen to dress a cradle.

And I should rest before the harvest moon
rises to dazzle me. But now
I stitch and cannot think of sleep.
What should I be sewing for tomorrow?

IV

It fell about the Lammastide –
the people put it in a song –
the famous fray at Otterburn,
fought by moonlight, hard and long.

The Percies wore the silver crescent;
the moon was a full moon overhead.
Harry and his brother were taken,
but first they'd left the Douglas dead.

Who was the victor on that field
the Scots and the English won't agree;
but which force won as songs will tell it
matters little that I can see:

it surges on from year to year,
one more battle and still one more:
one in defence, one in aggression,
another to balance out the score.

*

Crows flap
fretting for blood.
The field of battle
is a ravening flood.

There is no safety
there is no shelter
the fell tide
will suck him under.

V

He did not fall at Otterburn;
he did not fall at Humbledowne;

he fell on the field at Shrewsbury,
a rebel against the crown.

He might have been a king himself;
he put one king upon the throne,
then turned against him, and sought to make
a king of my brother's son.

Families undo families;
kings go up and kings go down.
My man fell; but they propped him up
dead in Shrewsbury Town.

They tied his corpse in the marketplace,
jammed for their jeers between two stones;
then hacked him apart: a heavy price
he paid for juggling with thrones.

Four fair cities received his limbs,
far apart as the four winds are,
and his head stared north from the walls of York
fixed on Micklegate Bar.

                    *

Now let forgetfulness wash over
his bones and the land's bones,
the long snaky spine of the wall,
earthworks and standing stones,
rock and castle and tower and all.

                    *

There is no safety
there is no shelter
the fell flood
has drawn him under.

Notes

Henry Percy, known as Hotspur, eldest son of the first Earl of Northumberland, was born on 20 May 1364. The Percies were of Norman descent; they controlled the north of England with something like kingly power for several centuries, first as feudal lords and then as Barons of Alnwick and later Earls of Northumberland. They have been described as 'the hereditary guardians of the north and the scourge of Scotland'.

Accounts of Hotspur's life appear in the *Dictionary of National Biography* and the *Complete Peerage* and, in a fictionalised form, in Shakespeare's *Richard II* and *Henry IV, Part I.* He was a valiant and precocious warrior, and soon became a favourite with the people. He held such positions as were consistent with his rank and descent – Governor of Berwick and Warden of the Marches – but his chief pleasures were warfare (against the Scots or the French or anyone else) and, as an incidental sideline to this, political intrigue. It proved his undoing. He was killed at the Battle of Shrewsbury on 12 July 1403 in an unsuccessful rebellion against Henry IV, whom he had conspired to put on the throne.

His character was not entirely admirable, to modern eyes: he had a tendency to change sides and to choose his allies according to their usefulness, disregarding former loyalties; and he was as brutal as any of his opponents when he chose: his fate of being quartered after his death was one which he had himself ordered to be performed on a defeated enemy. However, his personal courage and his even then slightly anachronistic devotion to the ideals of chivalry made him a natural focus for the legends which have clung to his name.

The ballad is sung in the person of his wife Elizabeth Mortimer (not Kate, as Shakespeare calls her). She was born at Usk on 12 February 1371 and was the daughter of the Earl of March and the granddaughter, through her mother, of Edward III. She married Hotspur in 1379 and they had a daughter (whose date of birth is not recorded) and a son, born in 1393 and named after his father.

I

A halting spate: Hotspur was said to have some kind of impediment in his speech, which at times delayed his fiery utterances.

High is his prowess: This section quotes the traditional elements of the ideal of chivalry.

II

Castle Leazes: The pasture-lands north of the city wall.

182

'Sir, I shall bear this token off...': The two speeches are taken from the version quoted by Froissart.

IV

Otterburn: The battle was probably fought on the night of 19 August 1388, by moonlight.

Silver crescent: This was the cap-badge of the Percies; their coat of arms bore a blue lion rampant.

His brother: Ralph Percy.

V

Humbledowne (or Humbleton, or Homildon Hill): The battle fought here on 13 September 1402 was Hotspur's revenge for Otterburn. The English won, capturing the 3rd Earl of Douglas (Archibald, successor to James, the 2nd Earl, who fell at Otterburn) and many other Scots.

He might have been a king himself: Not by legal succession; but if Elizabeth's nephew, the young Earl of March, had been set on the throne, Hotspur would very probably have been regent. In any case his popularity was such that the people could well have seen him as a possible king.

Four fair cities: After his body had been displayed in the marketplace at Shrewsbury it was buried; but a rumour arose that he was still alive, and his corpse was therefore disinterred and dismembered, and the four limbs sent to London, Bristol, Chester and Newcastle to be shown as evidence of his death.

THE INCIDENT BOOK

(1986)

Uniunea Scriitorilor

Caterpillars are falling on the Writers' Union.
The writers are indifferent to the caterpillars.
They sit over their wine at the metal tables
wearing animated expressions and eating fried eggs
with pickled gherkins, or (the dish of the day),
extremely small sausages: two each.

Meanwhile here and there an inch of grey bristles,
a miniature bottle-brush, twitches along a sleeve
or clings to a shoulder. The stone-paved courtyard
is dappled with desperate clumps of whiskers,
launched from the sunlit mulberry trees
to take their chance among literary furniture.

A poet ignores a fluffy intruder
in his bread-basket (the bread's all finished)
but flicks another from the velvet hat
(which surely she must have designed herself –
such elegance never appears in the shop-windows)
of his pretty companion, who looks like an actress.

The writers are talking more and more rapidly.
Not all are writers. One is a painter;
many are translators. Even those who are not
are adaptable and resourceful linguists.
'Pardon!' says one to the foreign visitor.
'Permit me! You have a worm on your back.'

Leaving the Tate

Coming out with your clutch of postcards
in a Tate Gallery bag and another clutch
of images packed into your head you pause
on the steps to look across the river

and there's a new one: light bright buildings,
a streak of brown water, and such a sky
you wonder who painted it – Constable? No:
too brilliant. Crome? No: too ecstatic –

a madly pure Pre-Raphaelite sky,
perhaps, sheer blue apart from the white plumes
rushing up it (today, that is,
April. Another day would be different

but it wouldn't matter. All skies work.)
Cut to the lower right for a detail:
seagulls pecking on mud, below
two office blocks and a Georgian terrace.

Now swing to the left, and take in plane trees
bobbled with seeds, and that brick building,
and a red bus . . . Cut it off just there,
by the lamp-post. Leave the scaffolding in.

That's your next one. Curious how
these outdoor pictures didn't exist
before you'd looked at the indoor pictures,
the ones on the walls. But here they are now,

marching out of their panorama
and queuing up for the viewfinder
your eye's become. You can isolate them
by holding your optic muscles still.

You can zoom in on figure studies
(that boy with the rucksack), or still lives,
abstracts, townscapes. No one made them.
The light painted them. You're in charge

of the hanging committee. Put what space
you like around the ones you fix on,
and gloat. Art multiplies itself.
Art's whatever you choose to frame.

The Bedroom Window

A small dazzle of stained glass which
I did not choose but might have, hanging
in front of the branches of a pine tree
which I do not own but covet; beyond them
a view of crinkly hills which I do not
etc and did not etc but might have
in another life, or the same life earlier.

The cat is fed, the plants are watered,
the milkman will call; the pine tree smells like
childhood. I am pretending to live here.
Out beyond the coloured glass and
the window-glass and the gully tall with
pine trees I dive back to wherever
I got my appetite for hills from.

The Chiffonier

You're glad I like the chiffonier. But I
feel suddenly uneasy, scenting why
you're pleased I like this pretty thing you've bought,
the twin of one that stood beside your cot
when you were small: you've marked it down for me;
it's not too heavy to be sent by sea
when the time comes, and it's got space inside
to pack some other things you've set aside,
things that are small enough to go by water
twelve thousand miles to me, your English daughter.
I know your habits – writing all our names
in books and on the backs of picture-frames,
allotting antique glass and porcelain dishes
to granddaughters according to their wishes,
promising me the tinted photograph
of my great-grandmother. We used to laugh,
seeing how each occasional acquisition
was less for you than for later disposition:

'You know how Marilyn likes blue and white
china? I've seen some plates I thought I might
indulge in.' Bless you, Mother! But we're not
quite so inclined to laugh now that you've got
something that's new to you but not a part
of your estate: that weakness in your heart.
It makes my distance from you, when I go
back home next week, suddenly swell and grow
from thirty hours' flying to a vast
galactic space between present and past.
How many more times can I hope to come
to Wellington and find you still at home?
We've talked about it, as one has to, trying
to see the lighter aspects of your dying:
'You've got another twenty years or more,'
I said, 'but when you think you're at death's door
just let me know. I'll come and hang about
for however long it takes to see you out.'
'I don't think it'll be like that,' you said:
'I'll pop off suddenly one night in bed.'
How secretive! How satisfying! You'll
sneak off, a kid running away from school –
well, that at least's the only way I find
I can bring myself to see it in my mind.
But now I see you in your Indian skirt
and casual cornflower-blue linen shirt
in the garden, under your feijoa tree,
looking about as old or young as me.
Dear little Mother! Naturally I'm glad
you found a piece of furniture that had
happy associations with your youth;
and yes, I do admire it – that's the truth:
its polished wood and touch of Art Nouveau
appeal to me. But surely you must know
I value this or any other treasure
of yours chiefly because it gives you pleasure.
I have to write this now, while you're still here:
I want my mother, not her chiffonier.

Tadpoles

(for Oliver)

Their little black thread legs, their threads of arms,
their mini-miniature shoulders, elbows, knees –
this piquant angularity, delicious
after that rippling smoothness, after nothing
but a flow of curves and roundnesses in water;
and their little hands, the size of their hands, the fingers
like hair-stubble, and their clumps-of-eyelashes feet . . .

Taddies, accept me as your grandmother,
a hugely gloating grand-maternal frog,
almost as entranced by other people's
tadpoles as I once was by my own,
that year when Oliver was still a tadpole
in Elizabeth's womb, and I a grandmother
only prospectively, and at long distance.

All this glory from globes of slithery glup!
Well, slithery glup was all right, with its cloudy
compacted spheres, its polka dots of blackness.
Then dots evolved into commas; the commas hatched.
When they were nothing but animated match-heads
with tails, a flickering flock of magnified
spermatazoa, they were already my darlings.

And Oliver lay lodged in his dreamy sphere,
a pink tadpole, a promise of limbs and language,
while my avatars of infancy grew up
into ribbon-tailed blackcurrants, fluttery-smooth,
and then into soaked brown raisins, a little venous,
with touches of transparency at the sides
where limbs minutely hinted at themselves.

It is the transformation that enchants.
As a mother reads her child's form in the womb,
imaging eyes and fingers, radar-sensing
a thumb in a blind mouth, so tadpole-watchers

can stare at the cunning shapes beneath the skin
and await the tiny, magnificent effloration.
It is a lesson for a grandmother.

My tadpoles grew to frogs in their generation;
they may have been the grandparents of these
about-to-be frogs. And Oliver's a boy,
hopping and bouncing in his bright green tracksuit,
my true darling; but too far away now
for me to call him across the world and say
'Oliver, look at what's happening to the tadpoles!'

For Heidi with Blue Hair

When you dyed your hair blue
(or, at least, ultramarine
for the clipped sides, with a crest
of jet-black spikes on top)
you were sent home from school

because, as the headmistress put it,
although dyed hair was not
specifically forbidden, yours
was, apart from anything else,
not done in the school colours.

Tears in the kitchen, telephone calls
to school from your freedom-loving father:
'She's not a punk in her behaviour;
it's just a style.' (You wiped your eyes,
also not in a school colour.)

'She discussed it with me first –
we checked the rules.' 'And anyway, Dad,
it cost twenty-five dollars.
Tell them it won't wash out –
not even if I wanted to try.'

It would have been unfair to mention
your mother's death, but that
shimmered behind the arguments.
The school had nothing else against you;
the teachers twittered and gave in.

Next day your black friend had hers done
in grey, white and flaxen yellow –
the school colours precisely:
an act of solidarity, a witty
tease. The battle was already won.

The Keepsake

(*in memory of Pete Laver*)

'To Fleur from Pete, on loan perpetual.'
It's written on the flyleaf of the book
I wouldn't let you give away outright:
'Just make it permanent loan,' I said – a joke
between librarians, professional
jargon. It seemed quite witty, on a night

when most things passed for wit. We were all hoarse
by then, from laughing at the bits you'd read
aloud – the heaving bosoms, blushing sighs,
demoniac lips. 'Listen to this!' you said:
' "Thus rendered bold by frequent intercourse
I dared to take her hand." ' We wiped our eyes.

' "Colonel, what mean these stains upon your dress?" '
We howled. And then there was Lord Ravenstone
faced with Augusta's dutiful rejection
in anguished prose; or, for a change of tone,
a touch of Gothic: Madame la Comtesse
's walled-up lover. An inspired collection:

The Keepsake, 1835; the standard
drawing-room annual, useful as a means
for luring ladies into chaste flirtation
in early 19th century courtship scenes.
I'd never seen a copy; often wondered.
Well, here it was – a pretty compilation

of tales and verses: stanzas by Lord Blank
and Countess This and Mrs That; demure
engravings, all white shoulders, corkscrew hair
and swelling bosoms; stories full of pure
sentiments, in which gentlemen of rank
urged suits upon the nobly-minded fair.

You passed the volume round, and poured more wine.
Outside your cottage lightning flashed again:
a Grasmere storm, theatrically right
for stories of romance and terror. Then
somehow, quite suddenly, the book was mine.
The date in it's five weeks ago tonight.

'On loan perpetual.' If that implied
some dark finality, some hint of 'nox
perpetua', something desolate and bleak,
we didn't see it then, among the jokes.
Yesterday, walking on the fells, you died.
I'm left with this, a trifling, quaint antique.

You'll not reclaim it now; it's mine to keep:
a keepsake, nothing more. You've changed the 'loan
perpetual' to a bequest by dying.
Augusta, Lady Blanche, Lord Ravenstone –
I've read the lot, trying to get to sleep.
The jokes have all gone flat. I can't stop crying.

England's Glory

Red-tipped, explosive, self-complete:
one you can strike on the coal-face, or
the sole of your boot. Not for the south, where
soft men with soft hands rub effete
brown-capped sticks on a toning strip
chequered with coffee-grounds, the only
match for the matches, and any lonely
stray (if they let them stray) picked up
from a table or found loose in a pocket
can't, without its container, flare
fire at a stroke: is not a pure-
ly self-contained ignition unit.

'Security' proclaims the craven
yellow box with its Noah's ark,
'Brymay' Special Safety's trade-mark
for southern consumption. That's all right, then:
bankers can take them home to Surrey
for their cigars, and scatter the odd
match-head, whether or not it's dead,
on their parquet floors, without the worry
of subsequent arson. Not like here
where a match is a man's match, an object
to be handled with as much respect
but as casually as a man's beer.

You can't mistake the England's Glory
box: its crimson, blue and white
front's a miniature banner, fit
for the Durham Miners' Gala, gaudy
enough to march ahead of a band.
Forget that placid ark: the vessel
this one's adorned with has two funnels
gushing fat blue smoke to the wind.
The side's of sandpaper. The back
label's functional, printed with either
holiday vouchers, a special offer

on World Cup tickets, or this month's joke.

Somewhere across England's broad
midriff, wanderingly drawn
from west to east, there exists a line
to the north of which the shops provide
(catering for a sudden switch
of taste) superior fried fish, runnier
yogurt, blouses cut for the fuller
northern figure; and the northern match.
Here England's Glory begins; through all
the vigorous north it reigns unrivalled
until its truce with Scottish Bluebell
round about Berwick and Carlisle.

The Genius of Surrey

The landscape of my middle childhood
lacked factories. There had been no
industrial revolution in Surrey,
was the message. Woods and shops and houses,
churches, allotments, pubs and schools
and loonie-bins were all we had.

Except, of course, the sewerage works,
on 'Surridge Hill', as we used to call it.
How sweetly rural the name sounds!
Wordsworth's genius, said Walter Pater,
would have found its true test
had he become the poet of Surrey.

Yorkshire had a talent for mills
and placed them to set off its contours;
Westmorland could also have worn
a few more factories with an air.
As for Surrey's genius, that
was found to be for the suburban.

Loving Hitler

There they were around the wireless
waiting to listen to Lord Haw-Haw.
'Quiet now, children!' they said as usual:
'Ssh, be quiet! We're trying to listen.'
'Germany calling!' said Lord Haw-Haw.

I came out with it: 'I love Hitler.'
They turned on me: 'You can't love Hitler !
Dreadful, wicked – ' (mutter, mutter,
the shocked voices buzzing together) –
'Don't be silly. You don't mean it.'

I held out for perhaps five minutes,
a mini-proto-neo-Nazi,
six years old and wanting attention.
Hitler always got their attention;
now I had it, for five minutes.

Everyone at school loved someone,
and it had to be a boy or a man
if you were a girl. So why not Hitler?
Of course, you couldn't love Lord Haw-Haw;
but Hitler – well, he was so famous!

It might be easier to love Albert,
the boy who came to help with the milking,
but Albert laughed at me. Hitler wouldn't:
one thing you could say for Hitler,
you never heard him laugh at people.

All the same, I settled for Albert.

Schools

Halfway Street, Sidcup

'We did sums at school, Mummy –
you do them like this: look.' I showed her.

It turned out she knew already.

St Gertrude's, Sidcup

Nuns, now: ladies in black hoods
for teachers – surely that was surprising?

It seems not. It was just England:
like houses made of brick, with stairs,

and dark skies, and Christmas coming
in winter, and there being a war on.

I was five, and unsurprisable –
except by nasty dogs, or the time

when I ran to catch the bus from school
and my knickers fell down in the snow.

Scalford School

The French boy was sick on the floor at prayers.
For years his name made me feel sick too:
Maurice. The teachers said it the English way,
but he was French, or French-speaking –
Belgian, perhaps; at any rate from some
country where things were wrong in 1940.
Until I grew up, 'Maurice' meant
his narrow pale face, pointed chin,
bony legs, and the wet pink sick.

But we were foreign too, of course,
my sister and I, in spite of our
unthinkingly acquired Leicestershire accents.
An older girl was struck one day
by our, to us, quite ordinary noses;
made an anthropological deduction:
'Have all the other people in New Zealand
got silly little noses too?'
I couldn't remember. Firmly I said 'Yes.'

Salfords, Surrey

Forget about the school – there was one,
which I've near enough forgotten.

But look at this – and you still can,
on the corner of Honeycrock Lane –

this tiny tin-roofed shed of brick,
once the smallest possible Public

Library. I used to lie
flat on the floor, and work my way

along the shelves, trying to choose
between Rose Fyleman's fairy verse

and *Tales of Sir Benjamin Bulbous, Bart.*
The book that really stuck in my heart

I can't identify: a saga
about a talking horse, the Pooka,

and Kathleen, and the quest they both
made through tunnels under the earth

for – something. Herbs and flowers came
into it, spangled through a dream

of eyebright, speedwell, Kathleen's bare
legs blotched blue with cold. Well; there

were other stories. When I'd read
all mine I'd see what Mummy had.

Of Mice and Men: that sounded nice.
I'd just got far enough to notice

it wasn't much like *Peter Rabbit*
when she took it away and hid it.

No loss, I'd say. But where shall I find
the Pooka's travels underground?

Outwood

Milkmaids, buttercups, ox-eye daisies,
white and yellow in the tall grass:
I fought my way to school through flowers –
bird's-foot trefoil, clover, vetch –
my sandals all smudged with pollen,
seedy grass-heads caught in my socks.

At school I used to read, mostly,
and hide in the shed at dinnertime,
writing poems in my notebook.
'Little fairies dancing,' I wrote,
and 'Peter and I, we watch the birds fly,
high in the sky, in the evening.'

Then home across the warm common
to tease my little sister again:
'I suppose you thought I'd been to school:
I've been to work in a bicycle shop.'
Mummy went to a real job
every day, on a real bicycle;

Doris used to look after us.
She took us for a walk with a soldier,
through the damp ferns in the wood
into a clearing like a garden,
rosy-pink with beds of campion,
herb-robert, lady's smock.

The blackberry briars were pale with blossom.
I snagged my tussore dress on a thorn;
Doris didn't even notice.
She and the soldier lay on the grass;
he leaned over her pink blouse
and their voices went soft and round, like petals.

On the School Bus

The little girls in the velvet collars
(twins, we thought) had lost their mother:
the ambulance men had had to scrape her
off the road, said the sickening whispers.

Horror's catching. The safe procedure
to ward it off, or so we gathered,
was a homeopathic dose of torture.
So we pulled their hair, like all the others.

Earlswood

Air-raid shelters at school were damp tunnels
where you sang 'Ten Green Bottles' yet again
and might as well have been doing decimals.

At home, though, it was cosier and more fun:
cocoa and toast inside the Table Shelter,
our iron-panelled bunker, our new den.

By day we ate off it; at night you'd find us
under it, the floor plump with mattresses
and the wire grilles neatly latched around us.

You had to be careful not to bump your head;
we padded the hard metal bits with pillows,
then giggled in our glorious social bed.

What could be safer? What could be more romantic
than playing cards by torchlight in a raid?
Odd that it made our mother so neurotic

to hear the sirens; we were quite content –
but slightly cramped once there were four of us,
after we'd taken in old Mrs Brent

from down by the Nag's Head, who'd been bombed out.
She had her arm in plaster, but she managed
to dress herself, and smiled, and seemed all right.

Perhaps I just imagined hearing her
moaning a little in the night, and shaking
splinters of glass out of her long grey hair.

The next week we were sent to Leicestershire.

Scalford Again

Being in Mr Wood's class this time,
and understanding, when he explained it clearly,
about the outside of a bicycle wheel
travelling around faster than the centre;
and not minding his warts; and liking Scripture
because of the Psalms: I basked in all this
no less than in the Infants the time before,
with tambourines and Milly-Molly-Mandy.
Although I'd enjoyed Milly-Molly-Mandy:
it had something to do with apricots, I thought,
or marigolds; or some warm orange glow.

Neston

Just visiting: another village school
with a desk for me to fill, while Chippenham
decided whether it wanted me – too young
for there, too over-qualified for here.

I knew it all – except, of course, geography.
Here was a map; I vaguely scratched in towns.
Ah, but here was a job: the infant teacher
was called away for half an hour. Would I . . . ?

Marooned there in a tide of little bodies
alive with Wiltshire voices, I was dumb.
They skipped about my feet, a flock of lambs
bleating around a daft young heifer.

Chippenham

The maths master was eight feet tall.
He jabbed his clothes-prop arm at me
halfway across the classroom, stretched
his knobbly finger, shouted 'You!

You're only here one day in three,
and when you are you might as well
not be, for all the work you do!
What do you think you're playing at?'

What did I think? I shrank into
my grubby blouse. Who did I think
I was, among these blazered boys,
these tidy girls in olive serge?

My green skirt wasn't uniform:
clothes were on coupons, after all.
I'd get a gymslip – blue, not green –
for Redhill Grammar, some time soon

when we went home. But, just for now,
what did I think? I thought I was
betrayed. I thought of how I'd stood
an hour waiting for the bus

that morning, by a flooded field,
watching the grass-blades drift and sway
beneath the water like wet hair;
hoping for Mrs Johnson's call:

'Jean, are you there? The clock was wrong.
You've missed the bus.' And back I'd run
to change my clothes, be Jean again,
play with the baby, carry pails

of water from the village tap,
go to the shop, eat toast and jam,
and then, if she could shake enough
pennies and farthings from her bag,

we might get to the pictures. But
the clock was fast, it seemed, not slow;
the bus arrived; and as I slid
anonymously into it

an elegant male prefect said
'Let Fleur sit down, she's got bad feet.'
I felt my impetigo scabs
blaze through my shoes. How did he know?

Tunbridge Wells

My turn for Audrey Pomegranate,
all-purpose friend for newcomers;
the rest had had enough of her –
her too-much hair, her too-much flesh,
her moles, her sideways-gliding mouth,
her smirking knowledge about rabbits.

Better a gluey friend than none,
and who was I to pick and choose?
She nearly stuck; but just in time
I met a girl called Mary Button,
a neat Dutch doll as clean as soap,
and Audrey P. was back on offer.

The High Tree

There was a tree higher than clouds or lightning,
higher than any plane could fly.

England huddled under its roots; leaves from it
fluttered on Europe out of the sky.

The weather missed it: it was higher than weather,
up in the sunshine, always dry.

It was a refuge. When you sat in its branches
threatening strangers passed you by.

Nothing could find you. Even friendly people,
if you invited them to try,

couldn't climb very far. It made them dizzy:
they'd shiver and shut their eyes and cry,

and you'd have to guide them down again, backwards,
wishing they hadn't climbed so high.

So it wasn't a social tree. It was perfect
for someone solitary and shy

who liked gazing out over miles of history,
watching it happen, like a spy,

and was casual about heights, but didn't fancy
coming down again to defy

the powers below. Odd that they didn't notice
all this climbing on the sly,

and odder still, if they knew, that they didn't ban it.
Knowing them now, you'd wonder why.

Drowning

'Si qua mulier maritum suum, cui legitime est iuncta, dimiserit, necetur in luto.'
[*If any woman has killed her lawfully married husband let her be drowned in mud.*]
LEX BURGUND., 34, I.

Death by drowning drowns the soul:
bubbles cannot carry it;
frail pops of air, farts
loosed in water are no vessels
for the immortal part of us.
And in a pit of mud, what bubbles?
There she lies, her last breath with her,
her soul rotting in her breast.

*

Is the sea better, then?
Will the salty brine preserve
pickled souls for the Day of Judgement?
Are we herrings to be trawled
in long nets by Saint Peter?
Ocean is a heavy load:
My soul flies up to thee, O God –
but not through mud, not through water.

And so, Bishop Synesius,
how can you wonder that we stand
with drawn swords on this bucking deck,
choosing to fall on friendly steel
and squirt our souls into the heavens
rather than choke them fathoms deep?
One more lash of the storm and it's done:
self-murder, but not soul-murder.

Then let the fishes feast on us
and slurp our blood after we're finished:

207

they'll find no souls to suck from us.
Yours, perhaps, has a safe-conduct:
you're a bishop, and subtle, and Greek.
Well, sir, pray and ponder. But our
language has no word for dilemma.
Drowning's the strongest word for death.

'Personal Poem'

It's the old story of the personal;
or of the Person – 'Al', we could call him –
with his oneness, his centrality,
fingers tapping to the band music,
and his eyes glowing like that
as if he had invented the guitar;
or coming around the corner on his tractor
calling out some comment you just missed.

The radios begin at 6 a.m.
It is really a very crowded city.
You're lucky to find two rooms, one for sleeping,
and a patch of allotment for potatoes.

Here we are on the hills, and it's no better.
Of course the birds are singing, but they would.
All you get is contempt, didn't they say so?
All right, contemn us.
We asked for nothing but a few gestures –
that kiss inside his open collar,
between the neck and shoulder, shockingly
personal to watch.

It's Al again, laughing in his teeth,
telling us about his Jamaican childhood
and the time his friend had crabs
from making love to the teacher's maid.
'It gave me a funny feeling,' he says
'to see them crawling there, little animals.

I hadn't even grown hair on mine.
In a way I was jealous –
imagine!' We imagine.

All these people running about in tracksuits
for nothing. And one standing at the gate
with a paper bag of bananas. 'Hi,' he says,
'How are you?' Nobody answers.

So at the May Day rally there they are.
Surely that's his jacket she's wearing?
And the face under the hair is his,
the way she wrinkles her nose.
How people give themselves away!
Yet all we have is hearsay.

Too late to take a boat out;
and anyway, the lake's crowded,
kids and oars together, and all their voices.
But really no one in particular,
unless you say so. Unless we say so.

An Epitaph

I wish to apologise for being mangled.
It was the romantic temperament
that did for me. I could stand rejection –
so grand, 'the stone the builders rejected . . .' –
but not acceptance. 'Alas,' I said
(a word I use), 'alas, I am taken
up, or in, or out of myself :
shall I never be solitary?'
Acceptance fell on me like a sandbag.
My bones crack. It squelches out of them.
Ah, acceptance! Leave me under this stone.

Being Taken from the Place

Less like an aircraft than a kettle,
this van, the way the floor buzzes
tinnily over its boiling wheels,
rolling me south.
                          Sounds flick backwards
in a travelling cauldron of noise. I lie
on the metal floor, hearing their voices
whirring like mechanical flies
over the seething burr of the engine.

They won't hear if I talk to myself;
whatever I say they can't hear me.
I say 'Illness is a kind of failure.'
I say 'Northumbrian rose quartz.'

Accidents

The accidents are never happening:
they are too imaginable to be true.
The driver knows his car is still on the road,
heading for Durham in the rain.
The mother knows her baby is just asleep,
curled up with his cuddly blanket, waiting
to be lifted and fed: there's no such thing as cot-death.
The rescue party digging all night in the dunes
can't believe the tunnel has really collapsed:
the children have somehow gone to their Auntie's house;
she has lent them their cousins' pyjamas, they are sitting
giggling together in the big spare room,
pretending to try and spill each other's cocoa.

On the Land

I'm still too young to remember how
I learned to mind a team of horses,
to plough and harrow: not a knack
you'd lose easily, once you had it.

It was in the Great War, that much
remembered age. I was a landgirl
in my puttees and boots and breeches
and a round hat like a felt halo.

We didn't mind the lads laughing:
let them while they could, we thought,
they hadn't long. But it seemed long –
hay-making, and apple-picking,

and storing all those scented things
in sneezy dimness in the barn.
Then Jack turned seventeen and went,
and I knew Ted would go soon.

He went the week of Candlemas.
After that it was all weather:
frosts and rains and spring and summer,
and the long days growing longer.

It rained for the potato harvest.
The front of my smock hung heavy
with claggy mud, from kneeling in it
mining for strays. Round segments

chopped clean off by the blade
flashed white as severed kneecaps.
I grubbed for whole ones, baby skulls
to fill my sack again and again.

When the pain came, it wouldn't
stop. I couldn't stand. I dropped
the sack and sank into a trench.
Ethel found me doubled up.

Mr Gregson took me home,
jolting on the back of the wagon.
I tossed and writhed on my hard bed,
my head hunched into the bolster,

dreaming of how if just for once,
for half an hour, the knobbly mattress
could turn into a billow of clouds
I might be able to get to sleep.

Icon

In the interests of economy
I am not going to tell you
what happened between the time
when they checked into the hotel

with its acres of tiled bathrooms
(but the bidet in theirs was cracked)
and the morning two days later
when he awoke to find her gone.

After he had read her note
and done the brief things he could do
he found himself crossing the square
to the Orthodox Cathedral.

The dark icon by the door
was patched with lumpy silver islands
nailed to the Virgin's robes; they looked
like flattened-out Monopoly tokens,

he thought: a boot, and something like
a heart, and a pair of wings, and something
oblong. They were hard to see
in the brown light, but he peered at them

for several minutes, leaning over
the scarved head of an old woman
on her knees there, blocking his view;
who prayed and prayed and wouldn't move.

Drawings

The ones not in the catalogue:
little sketches, done in her garden – this
head of a child (the same child
we saw in the picnic scene, remember?)
And trees, of course, and grasses,
and a study of hawthorn berries.
Doodles, unfinished drafts: look
at this chestnut leaf, abandoned in mid-
stroke – a telephone call, perhaps;
a visitor; some interruption.

She may have been happier,
or happy longer, or at least more often . . .
but that's presumption. Let's move on:
grasses again; a group of stones
from her rockery, done in charcoal; and this
not quite completed pencil sketch of
a tiger lily, the springy crown
of petals curved back on itself
right to the stem, the long electric
stamens almost still vibrating.

The Telephone Call

They asked me 'Are you sitting down?
Right? This is Universal Lotteries,'
they said. 'You've won the top prize,
the Ultra-super Global Special.
What would you do with a million pounds?
Or, actually, with more than a million –
not that it makes a lot of difference
once you're a millionaire.' And they laughed.

'Are you OK?' they asked – 'Still there?
Come on, now, tell us, how does it feel?'
I said 'I just . . . I can't believe it! '
They said 'That's what they all say.
What else? Go on, tell us about it.'
I said 'I feel the top of my head
has floated off, out through the window,
revolving like a flying saucer.'

'That's unusual,' they said. 'Go on.'
I said 'I'm finding it hard to talk.
My throat's gone dry, my nose is tingling.
I think I'm going to sneeze – or cry.'
'That's right,' they said, 'don't be ashamed
of giving way to your emotions.
It isn't every day you hear
you're going to get a million pounds.

Relax, now, have a little cry;
we'll give you a moment . . .' 'Hang on!' I said.
'I haven't bought a lottery ticket
for years and years. And what did you say
the company's called?' They laughed again.
'Not to worry about a ticket.
We're Universal. We operate
a Retrospective Chances Module.

Nearly everyone's bought a ticket
in some lottery or another,
once at least. We buy up the files,
feed the names into our computer,
and see who the lucky person is.'
'Well, that's incredible,' I said.
'It's marvellous. I still can't quite . . .
I'll believe it when I see the cheque.'

'Oh,' they said, 'there's no cheque.'
'But the money?' 'We don't deal in money.
Experiences are what we deal in.
You've had a great experience, right?
Exciting? Something you'll remember?
That's your prize. So congratulations
from all of us at Universal.
Have a nice day!' And the line went dead.

Incidentals

Excavations

Here is a hole full of men shouting
'I don't love you. I loved you once
but I don't now. I went off you,
or I was frightened, or my wife was pregnant,
or I found I preferred men instead.'

What can I say to that kind of talk?
'Thank you for being honest, you
who were so shifty when it happened,
pretending you were suddenly busy
with your new job or your new conscience.'

I chuck them a shovelful of earth
to make them blink for a bit, to smirch
their green eyes and their long lashes
or their brown eyes . . . Pretty bastards:
the rain will wash their bawling faces

and I bear them little enough ill will.
Now on to the next hole,
covered and fairly well stamped down,
full of the men whom I stopped loving
and didn't always tell at the time –

being, I found, rather busy
with my new man or my new freedom.
These are quiet and unaccusing,
cuddled up with their subsequent ladies,
hardly unsettling the bumpy ground.

Pastoral

Eat their own hair, sheep do,
nibbling away under the snow, under their bellies –
calling it wool makes it no more palatable.

What else is there to do in the big drifts,
forced against a wall of wet stone?
But let me have your hair to nibble

before we are in winter; and the thong
of dark seeds you wear at your neck;
and for my tongue the salt on your skin to gobble.

Kissing

The young are walking on the riverbank,
arms around each other's waists and shoulders,
pretending to be looking at the waterlilies
and what might be a nest of some kind, over
there, which two who are clamped together
mouth to mouth have forgotten about.
The others, making courteous detours
around them, talk, stop talking, kiss.
They can see no one older than themselves.
It's their river. They've got all day.

Seeing's not everything. At this very
moment the middle-aged are kissing
in the backs of taxis, on the way
to airports and stations. Their mouths and tongues
are soft and powerful and as moist as ever.
Their hands are not inside each other's clothes
(because of the driver) but locked so tightly
together that it hurts: it may leave marks
on their not of course youthful skin, which they won't
notice. They too may have futures.

Double-take

You see your nextdoor neighbour from above,
from an upstairs window, and he reminds you
of your ex-lover, who is bald on top,
which you had forgotten. At ground level
there is no resemblance. Next time you chat
with your nextdoor neighbour, you are relieved
to find that you don't fancy him.

A week later you meet your ex-lover
at a party, after more than a year.
He reminds you (although only slightly)
of your nextdoor neighbour. He has a paunch
like your neighbour's before he went on that diet.
You remember how much you despise him.

He behaves as if he's pleased to see you.
When you leave (a little earlier
than you'd intended, to get away)
he gives you a kiss which is more than neighbourly
and says he'll ring you. He seems to mean it.
How odd! But you are quite relieved
to find that you don't fancy him.

Unless you do? Or why that sudden
something, once you get outside
in the air? Why are your legs prancing
so cheerfully along the pavement?
And what exactly have you just remembered?
You go home cursing chemistry.

Choices

There was never just one book for the desert island,
one perfectly tissue-typed aesthetic match,
that wouldn't drive you crazy within six months;
just as there was never one all-purpose
ideal outfit, unquestionably right
for wearing at the ball on the Titanic
and also in the lifeboat afterwards.

And never, a fortiori, just one man;
if it's not their conversation or their habits
(more irritating, even, than your own –
and who would you wish those on?) it's their bodies:
two-thirds of them get fatter by the minute,
the bony ones turn out to be psychopaths,
and the few in the middle range go bald.

Somehow you'll end up there, on the island,
in your old jeans and that comic dressing-gown
one of the fast-fatteners always laughed at,
with a blank notebook (all you've brought to read)
and a sea-and-sun-proof crate of cigarettes;
but with nobody, thank God, to lecture you
on how he managed to give them up.

Street Scene, London N2

This is the front door. You can just see
the number on it, there behind the piano,
between the young man with the fierce expression
and the one with the axe, who's trying not to laugh.

Those furry-headed plants beside the step
are Michaelmas daisies, as perhaps you've guessed,
although they're not in colour; and the path
is tiled in red and black, like a Dutch interior.

But the photograph, of course, is black and white.
The piano also sported black and white
when it was whole (look, you can see its ribcage,
the wiry harp inside it, a spread wing).

The young men are playing Laurel and Hardy
(though both are tall, and neither of them is fat,
and one of them is actually a pianist):
they are committing a pianocide.

It wasn't really much of a piano:
warped and fungoid, grossly out of tune –
facts they have not imparted to the wincing
passers-by, whom you will have to imagine.

You will also have to imagine, if you dare,
the jangling chords of axe-blow, saw-stroke, screeching
timber, wires twanged in a terminal
appassionato. This is a silent picture.

Laurel and Hardy will complete their show:
the wires, released from their frame, will thrash and tangle
and be tamed into a ball; the varnished panels
will be sawn stacks of boards and blocks and kindling.

Later the mother will come home for Christmas.
The fire will purr and tinkle in the grate,
a chromatic harmony of tones; and somewhere
there'll be a muffled sack of snarling keys.

Gentlemen's Hairdressers

The barbers' shop has gone anonymous:
white paint, glossy as Brilliantine
('The Perfect Hairdressing') has covered
Jim's and Alfred's friendly monickers.

GENTLEMENS HAIRD in chaste blue Roman
glorifies pure form. The man
on the ladder lays a scarlet slash
of marking-tape for the next upright.

Below him Jim and Alfred are still
in business. Alfred munches a pie
and dusts the crumbs from his grey moustache
over the racing-page. A gentleman

tilts his head under Jim's clippers.
In the window the Durex poster,
the one with the motorbike, has faded
to pale northern shades of sea.

An hour later the ladder's gone
and purity's been deposed: the lettering's
denser now, the Roman caps
blocked in with three-dimensional grey.

The word 'Styling' in shapeless cursive
wriggles above the open door.
Swaddled and perched on Alfred's chair
a tiny Greek boy squeals and squeals.

Post Office

The queue's right out through the glass doors
to the street: Thursday, pension day.
They built this Post Office too small.
Of course, the previous one was smaller –
a tiny prefab, next to the betting-shop,
says the man who's just arrived;
and the present one, at which we're queuing,
was cherry trees in front of a church.
The church was where the supermarket is:
'My wife and I got married in that church,'
the man says. 'We hold hands sometimes
when we're standing waiting at the checkout –
have a little moment together!' He laughs.
The queue shuffles forward a step.
Three members of it silently vow
never to grow old in this suburb;
one vows never to grow old at all.
'I first met her over there,' the man says,
'on that corner where the bank is now.
The other corner was Williams Brothers –
remember Williams Brothers? They gave you tokens,
tin money, like, for your dividend.'
The woman in front of him remembers.
She nods, and swivels her loose lower denture,
remembering Williams Brothers' metal tokens,
and the marble slab on the cheese-counter,
and the carved mahogany booth where you went to pay.
The boy in front of her is chewing gum;
his jaws rotate with the same motion
as hers: to and fro, to and fro.

Demonstration

'YOU ARE NOW WALKING IN THE ROAD.
The lines marked out with sticky tape
are where the kerb is going to be
under the traffic-scheme proposals.
This tree will go. The flower-beds
and seats outside the supermarket
will go. The pavements will be narrowed
to make room for six lanes of traffic.'

We are now walking in the road
with a few banners and some leaflets
and forms to sign for a petition.
The Council will ignore them all.
The Council wants a monster junction
with traffic-islands, metal railings,
computer-managed lights and crossings,
and lots and lots of lanes of traffic.

We are still walking in the road.
It seems a long time since we started,
and most of us are getting older
(the ones who aren't, of course, are dead).
This borough has the highest number
of pensioners in Greater London.
Perhaps the junction, with its modern
split-second lights, will cut them down.

But while we're walking in the road
others are driving. At our backs
we hear the roar of heavy traffic
churning from Finchley to Westminster;
and over it, from a loudspeaker,
a stern, conceited female voice
with artificial vowels exhorts us:
'Come with us into the nineties!'

Witnesses

We three in our dark decent clothes,
unlike ourselves, more like the three
witches, we say, crouched over the only
ashtray, smoke floating into our hair,

wait. An hour; another hour.
If you stand up and walk ten steps
to the glass doors you can see her there
in the witness box, a Joan of Arc,

straight, still, her neck slender,
her lips moving from time to time
in reply to voices we can't hear:
'I put it to you . . . I should like to suggest . . .'

It's her small child who is at stake.
His future hangs from these black-clad
proceedings, these ferretings under her sober
dress, under our skirts and dresses

to sniff out corruption: 'I put it to you
that in fact your husband . . . that my client . . .
that you yourself initiated the violence . . .
that your hysteria . . .' She sits like marble.

We pace the corridors, peep at the distance
from door to witness box (two steps up,
remember, be careful not to trip
when the time comes) and imagine them there,

the ones we can't see. A man in a wig
and black robes. Two other men
in lesser wigs and gowns. More men
in dark suits. We sit down together,

shake the smoke from our hair, pass round
more cigarettes (to be held carefully
so as not to smirch our own meek versions
of their clothing), and wait to be called.

Last Song

Goodbye, sweet symmetry. Goodbye, sweet world
of mirror-images and matching halves,
where animals have usually four legs
and people nearly always two;
where birds and bats and butterflies and bees
have balanced wings, and even flies
can fly straight if they try. Goodbye
to one-a-side for eyes and ears and arms
and breasts and balls and shoulder-blades
and hands; goodbye to the straight line
drawn down the central spine,
making us double in a world
where oddness is acceptable only
under the sea, for the lop-sided lobster,
the wonky oyster, the creepily rotated
flatfish with both eyes over one gill;
goodbye to the sweet certitudes of our
mammalian order, where to be
born with one eye or three thumbs
points to not being human. It will come.

In the next world, when this one's gone skew-whiff,
we shall be algae or lichen, things
we've hardly even needed to pronounce.
If the flounder still exists it will be king.

TIME-ZONES

(1991)

Counting

You count the fingers first: it's traditional.
(You assume the doctor counted them too,
when he lifted up the slimy surprise
with its long dark pointed head and its father's nose
at 2.13 a.m. – 'Look at the clock!'
said Sister: 'Remember the time: 2.13.')

Next day the head's turned pink and round;
the nose is a blob. You fumble under the gown
your mother embroidered with a sprig of daisies,
as she embroidered your own Viyella gowns
when you were a baby. You fish out
curly triangular feet. You count the toes.

'There's just one little thing,' says Sister:
'His ears – they don't quite match. One
has an extra whorl in it. No one will notice.'
You notice like mad. You keep on noticing.
Then you hear a rumour: a woman in the next ward
has had a stillbirth. Or was it something worse?

You lie there, bleeding gratefully.
You've won the Nobel Prize, and the VC,
and the State Lottery, and gone to heaven.
Feed-time comes. They bring your bundle –
the right one: it's him all right.
You count his eyelashes: the ideal number.

You take him home. He learns to walk.
From time to time you eye him,
nonchalantly, from each side.
He has an admirable nose.
No one ever notices his ears. No one
ever stands on both sides of him at once.

He grows up. He has beautiful children.

Libya

When the Americans were bombing Libya
(that time when it looked as if this was it at last,
the match in the petrol-tank which will flare sooner or later,
and the whole lot was about to go up)

Gregory turned on the television during dinner
and Elizabeth asked the children to be quiet
because this was important, we needed to watch the news –
'It might be the beginning of the end,' she said.

Oliver, who was seven, said 'But I'm too young to die!'
Lily, who was five, said 'I don't want to die! I don't!'
Oliver said 'I know! Let's get under the table!'
Lily said, 'Yes, let's get under the table!'

So they got under the table, and wriggled around our legs
making the dishes rattle, and we didn't stop them
because we were busy straining to hear the news
and watching the fat bombers filling the screen.

It was a noisy ten minutes, one way and another.
Julia, who was fifteen months, chuckled in her high chair,
banging her spoon for her wonderful brother and sister,
and sang 'Three blind mice, three blind mice'.

What May Happen

The worst thing that can happen –
to let the child go;
but you must not say so
or else it may happen.

The stranger looms in the way
holding an olive-twig.
The child's not very big;
he is beginning to cry.

How can you stand by?
A cloud crushes the hill.
Everything stands still.
Everything moves away.

The stranger is still a stranger
but the child is not your child.
Too soon, before he's old,
he may become a stranger.

He is his own child.
He has a way to go.
Others have lived it through:
watch, and turn cold.

My Father

When I got up that morning I had no father.
I know that now. I didn't suspect it then.
They drove me through the tangle of Manchester
to the station, and I pointed to a sign:

'Hulme' it said – though all I saw was a rubbled
wasteland, a walled-off dereliction. 'Hulme –
that's where they lived,' I said, 'my father's people.
It's nowhere now.' I coughed in the traffic fumes.

Hulme and Medlock. A quarter of a mile
to nowhere, to the names of some nothing streets
beatified in my family history file,
addresses on birth and marriage certificates:

Back Clarence Street, Hulme; King Street (but which one?);
One-in-Four Court, Chorlton-upon-Medlock.
Meanwhile at home on my answering machine
a message from New Zealand: please ring back.

In his day it was factory smoke, not petrol,
that choked the air and wouldn't let him eat
until, the first day out from Liverpool,
sea air and toast unlocked his appetite.

He took up eating then, at the age of ten –
too late to cancel out the malnutrition
of years and generations. A small man,
though a tough one. He'll have needed a small coffin.

I didn't see it; he went to it so suddenly,
too soon, with both his daughters so far away:
a box of ashes in Karori Cemetery,
a waft of smoke in the clean Wellington sky.

Even from here it catches in my throat
as I puzzle over the Manchester street-plan,
checking the index, magnifying the net
of close-meshed streets in M2 and M1.

Not all the city's motorways and high-rise.
There must be roads that I can walk along
and know they walked there, even if their houses
have vanished like the cobble-stones – that throng

of Adcocks, Eggingtons, Joynsons, Lamberts, Listers.
I'll go to look for where they were born and bred.
I'll go next month; we'll both go, I and my sister.
We'll tell him about it, when he stops being dead.

Cattle in Mist

A postcard from my father's childhood –
the one nobody photographed or painted;
the one we never had, my sister and I.
Such feeble daughters – couldn't milk a cow
(watched it now and then, but no one taught us).

How could we hold our heads up, having never
pressed them into the warm flank of a beast
and lured the milk down? Hiss, hiss, in a bucket:
routine, that's all. Not ours. That one missed us.

His later childhood, I should say;
not his second childhood – that he evaded
by dying – and his first was Manchester.
But out there in the bush, from the age of ten,
in charge of milking, rounding up the herd,
combing the misty fringes of the forest
(as he would have had to learn not to call it)
at dawn, and again after school, for stragglers;
cursing them; bailing them up; it was no childhood.

A talent-spotting teacher saved him.
The small neat smiling boy (I'm guessing)
evolved into a small neat professor.
He could have spent his life wreathed in cow-breath,
a slave to endlessly refilling udders,
companion of heifers, midwife at their calvings,
judicious pronouncer on milk-yields and mastitis,
survivor of the bull he bipped on the nose
('Tell us again, Daddy!') as it charged him.

All his cattle: I drive them back
into the mist, into the dawn haze
where they can look romantic; where they must
have wandered now for sixty or seventy years.
Off they go, then, tripping over the tree-roots,
pulling up short to lip at a tasty twig,
bumping into each other, stumbling off again
into the bush. He never much liked them.
He'll never need to rustle them back again.

Toads

Let's be clear about this: I love toads.

So when I found our old one dying,
washed into the drain by flood-water
in the night and then – if I can bring myself
to say it – scalded by soapy lather
I myself had let out of the sink,
we suffered it through together.

It was the summer of my father's death.
I saw his spirit in every visiting creature,
in every small thing at risk of harm:
bird, moth, butterfly, beetle,
the black rabbit lolloping along concrete,
lost in suburbia; and our toad.

If we'd seen it once a year that was often,
but the honour of being chosen by it
puffed us up: a toad of our own
trusting us not to hurt it
when we had to lift it out of its den
to let the plumber get at the water-main.

And now this desperate damage: the squat
compactness unhinged, made powerless.
Dark, straight, its legs extended,
flippers paralysed, it lay lengthwise
flabby-skinned across my palm,
cold and stiff as the Devil's penis.

I laid it on soil; the shoulders managed
a few slow twitches, pulled it an inch forward.
But the blowflies knew: they called it dead
and stippled its back with rays of pearly stitching.
Into the leaves with it then, poor toad,
somewhere cool, where I can't watch it.

234

Perhaps it was very old? Perhaps it was ready?
Small comfort, through ten guilt-ridden days.
And then, one moist midnight, out in the country,
a little shadow shaped like a brown leaf
hopped out of greener leaves and came to me.
Twice I had to lift it from my doorway:

a gently throbbing handful – calm, comely,
its feet tickling my palm like soft bees.

Under the Lawn

It's hard to stay angry with a buttercup
threading through the turf (less and less a lawn
with each jagging rip of the fork or scoop
of the trowel) but a dandelion can

inspire righteous fury: that taproot
drilling down to where it's impossible
ever quite to reach (although if it's cut
through that's merely a minor check) until

clunk: what's this? And it's spade-time. Several hours
later, eleven slabs of paving-stone
(submerged so long ago that the neighbours
who've been on the watch since 1941

'never remember seeing a path there') with,
lying marooned singly on three of them,
an octagonal threepence, a George the Fifth
penny and, vaguely missed from their last home

for fifteen years or so and rusted solid,
Grandpa's scissors, the ones for hairdressing
from his barbering days: plain steel, not plated;
still elegant; the tip of one blade still missing.

Wren Song

How can I prove to you
that we've got wrens in the garden?

A quick flick of a tail
in or out of the ivy hedge
is all you'll ever see of them;

and anyway, I'm asleep.
Not dreaming, though: I can hear him,
the boss-wren, out there in the summer dawn –

his bubbling sequences,
an octave higher than a blackbird's,
trickling silver seeds into my ears.

I'll get the tape-recorder.
But no, it's in another room,
and I've no blank tapes for it;

and anyway, I'm asleep.
Hard to wake up, after a sultry night
of restless dozing, even for the wren.

I've tracked his piccolo solo
in the light evenings, from hedge to apple tree
to elder, sprints of zippy flight in between.

I've looked him up: 'A rapid
succession of penetrating and jubilant
trills, very loud for so small a bird.'

I'll get the tape-recorder.
I'll find an old cassette to record over.
I'm getting up to fetch it now –

but no, I'm still asleep;
it was a dream, the getting up.
But the wren's no dream. It is a wren.

Next Door

You could have called it the year of their persecution:
some villain robbed her window-boxes of half
her petunias and pansies. She wrote a notice:
'To the person who took my plants. I am disabled;
they cost me much labour to raise from seed.'
Next week, the rest went. Then his number-plates.
(Not the car itself. Who'd want the car? It stank.)
A gale blew in a pane of their front window –
crack: just like that. Why theirs? Why not, for example,
mine? Same gale; same row of elderly houses.

And through it all the cats multiplied fatly –
fatly but scruffily (his weak heart, her illness:
'They need grooming, I know, but they're fat as butter') –
and the fleas hopped, and the smell came through the walls.
How many cats? Two dozen? Forty? Fifty?
We could count the ones outside in the cages (twelve),
but inside? Always a different furry face
at a window; and the kittens – think of the kittens
pullulating like maggots over the chairs!
Someone reported them to the authorities.

Who could have done it? Surely not a neighbour!
'No, not a neighbour! Someone in the Fancy' –
she was certain. 'They've always envied my success.
The neighbours wouldn't . . .' A sunny afternoon.
I aimed my camera at them over the fence,
at their garden table, under the striped umbrella:
'Smile!' And they grinned: his gnome-hat, her witch-hair
in the sun – well out of earshot of the door-bell
and of the Environmental Health Inspector.
You could call it a bad year. But the next was worse.

Helianthus Scaberrimus

This is the time of year when people die:
August, and these daisy-faced things
blare like small suns on their swaying hedge
of leaves, yellow as terror. Goodbye,

they shout to the summer, and goodbye
to Jim, whose turn it was this morning:
while in another hospital his wife
lies paralysed, with nothing to do but lie

wondering what's being kept from her, and cry –
she can still do that. August in hospital
sweats and is humid. In the garden
grey airs blow moist, but the mean sky

holds on to its water. The earth's coke-dry;
the yellow daisies goggle, but other plants
less greedily rooted are at risk.
The sky surges and sulks. It will let them die.

House-martins

Mud in their beaks, the house-martins are happy . . .
That's anthropomorphism. Start again:

mud being plentiful because last night
it rained, after a month of drought,
the house-martins are able to build their nests.

They flitter under the eaves, white flashes
on their backs telling what they are:
house-martins. Not necessarily happy.

Below in the mock-Tudor cul-de-sac
two kids on skateboards and a smaller girl
with a tricycle are sketching their own circles –

being themselves, being children:
vaguely aware, perhaps, of the house-martins,
and another bird singing, and a scent of hedge.

Anthropomorphism tiptoes away:
of human children it's permissible
to say they're happy – if indeed they are.

It's no use asking them; they wouldn't know.
They may be bored, or in a sulk,
or worried (it doesn't show; and they look healthy).

Ask them in fifty years or so,
if they're still somewhere. Arrange to present them with
(assuming all these things can still be assembled)

a blackbird's song, the honeyed reek of privet,
and a flock of house-martins, wheeling and scrambling
about a group of fake-half-timbered semis.

Call it a Theme Park, if you like:
'Suburban childhood, late 1980s'
(or 70s, or 50s – it's hardly changed).

Ask them 'Were you happy in Shakespeare Close?'
and watch them gulp, sick with nostalgia for it.

Wildlife

A wall of snuffling snouts in close-up,
ten coloured, two in black and white,
each in its frame; all magnified,
some more than others. Voles, are they?
Shrews? Water-rats? Whiskers waggling,
they peep from under twelve tree-roots
and vanish. Next, a dozen barn-owls,
pale masks, almost filling the dark screens.
Cut; and now two dozen hedgehogs

come trotting forward in headlong pairs:
they'll fall right out on the floor among the
cookers and vacuum-cleaners unless
the camera – just in time – draws back.
Here they come again, in their various
sizes, on their various grass:
olive, emerald, acid, bluish,
dun-tinged, or monochrome. The tones
are best, perhaps, on the 22-inch
ITT Squareline: more natural
than the Philips – unless you find them too
muted, in which case the Sony
might do. Now here are the owls again.

Meanwhile at the Conference Centre
three fire-engines have screamed up. Not,
for once, a student smoking in a bedroom:
this time a cloud of thunderflies
has chosen to swarm on the pearly-pink
just-warm globe of a smoke-detector.

Turnip-heads

Here are the ploughed fields of Middle England;
and here are the scarecrows, flapping polythene arms
over what still, for the moment, looks like England:
bare trees, earth-colours, even a hedge or two.

The scarecrows' coats are fertiliser bags;
their heads (it's hard to see from the swift windows
of the Intercity) are probably 5-litre
containers for some chemical or other.

And what are the scarecrows guarding? Fields of rape?
Plenty of that in Middle England; also
pillage, and certain other medieval
institutions – some things haven't changed,

now that the men of straw are men of plastic.
They wave their rags in fitful semaphore,
in the March wind; our train blurs past them.
Whatever their message was, we seem to have missed it.

The Batterer

What can I have done to earn
the Batterer striding here beside me,
checking up with his blue-china
sidelong eyes that I've not been bad –

not glanced across the street, forgetting
to concentrate on what he's saying;
not looked happy without permission,
or used the wrong form of his name?

How did he get here, out of the past,
with his bulging veins and stringy tendons,
fists clenched, jaw gritted,
about to burst with babble and rage?

Did I elect him? Did I fall
asleep and vote him in again?
Yes, that'll be what he is: a nightmare;
but someone else's now, not mine.

Roles

Emily Brontë's cleaning the car:
water sloshes over her old trainers
as she scrubs frail blood-shapes from the windscreen
and swirls the hose-jet across the roof.
When it's done she'll go to the supermarket;
then, if she has to, face her desk.

I'm striding on the moor in my hard shoes,
a shawl over my worsted bodice,
the hem of my skirt scooping dew from the grass
as I pant up towards the breathless heights.
I'll sit on a rock I know and write a poem.
It may not come out as I intend.

Happiness

Too jellied, viscous, floating a condition
to inspire more action than a sigh –
like being supported on warm porridge

gazing at this: may-blossom, bluebells, robin,
the tennis-players through the trees,
the trotting magpie (not good news, but handsome)

asking the tree-stump next to where I'm sitting
'Were you a rowan last time? No?
That's what the seedling wedged in your roots is planning.'

Coupling

On the wall above the bedside lamp
a large crane-fly is jump-starting
a smaller crane-fly – or vice versa.
They do it tail to tail, like Volkswagens:
their engines must be in their rears.

It looks easy enough. Let's try it.

The Greenhouse Effect

As if the week had begun anew –
and certainly something has:
this fizzing light on the harbour, these

radiant bars and beams and planes
slashed through flaps and swags of sunny vapour.
Aerial water, submarine light:
Wellington's gone Wordsworthian again.
He'd have admired it –
admired but not approved, if he'd heard
about fossil fuels, and aerosols,
and what we've done to the ozone layer,
or read in last night's Evening Post
that 'November ended the warmest spring
since meteorological records began'.
Not that it wasn't wet:
moisture's a part of it.

As for this morning (Friday),
men in shorts raking the beach
have constructed little cairns of evidence:
driftwood, paper, plastic cups.
A seagull's gutting a bin.
The rain was more recent than I thought:
I'm sitting on a wet bench.
Just for now, I can live with it.

The Last Moa

Somewhere in the bush, the last moa
is not still lingering in some hidden valley.
She is not stretching her swanlike neck
(but longer, more massive than any swan's)
for a high cluster of miro berries,
or grubbing up fern roots with her beak.

Alice McKenzie didn't see her
among the sandhills at Martin's Bay
in 1880 – a large blue bird
as tall as herself, which turned and chased her.
Moas were taller than seven-year-old
pioneer children; moas weren't blue.

243

Twenty or thirty distinct species –
all of them, even the small bush moa,
taller than Alice – and none of their bones
carbon-dated to less than five centuries.
The sad, affronted mummified head
in the museum is as old as a Pharoah.

Not the last moa, that; but neither
was Alice's harshly grunting pursuer.
Possibly Alice met a takahe,
the extinct bird that rose from extinction
in 1948, near Te Anau.
No late reprieve, though, for the moa.

Her thigh-bones, longer than a giraffe's,
are lying steeped in a swamp, or smashed
in a midden, with her unstrung vertebrae.
Our predecessors hunted and ate her,
gobbled her up: as we'd have done
in their place; as we're gobbling the world.

Creosote

What is it, what is it? Quick: that whiff,
that black smell – black that's really brown,
sharp that's really oily and yet rough,

a tang of splinters burning the tongue,
almost as drunkening as hot tar
or cowshit, a wonderful ringing pong.

It's fence-posts, timber yards, the woodshed;
it bundles you into the Baby Austin
and rushes you back to early childhood.

It's Uncle's farm; it's the outside dunny;
it's flies and heat; or it's boats and rope
and the salt-cracked slipway down from the jetty.

It's brushes oozing with sloshy stain;
it's a tin at the back of the shed: open it,
snort it ! You can't: the lid's stuck on.

Central Time

'The time is nearly one o'clock,
or half past twelve in Adelaide' –
where the accents aren't quite so . . . Australian
as in the other states, the ones
that were settled (not their fault, of course)
by convicts. We had Systematic
Colonisation, and Colonel Light,
and the City of Adelaide Plan. We have the Park Lands.
It's time for the news at 1.30 –
one o'clock Central Time in Adelaide.

It's early days in Hobart Town,
and Maggie May has been transported
(not such fun as it sounds, poor lass)
to toil upon Van Diemen's cruel shore.
It's 1830 or thereabouts
(1800 in Adelaide?
No, no, this is going too far –
as she might have said herself at the time).

The time is three o'clock, etc.
The time is passing.
You're tuned to ABC Radio.
We'll be bringing you that programme shortly.

It's five o'clock in Adelaide
and Maggie May has found her way
to a massage parlour in Gouger Street.
The Red Light Zone (as we don't call it)
extends from the West Park Lands to Light Square
(named for the Colonel, not the Zone).

The Colonel's in two minds about it;
his fine Eurasian face is troubled.

The Colonel's an anomaly.
There are plenty of those in Adelaide.
Meanwhile, back in Van Diemen's Land,
a butcher bird sings coloratura
in the courtyard of the Richmond Gaol
as tourists file through with their cameras,
wondering how to photograph
a Dark Cell for solitary
from the inside, with the door shut.
Look, they had them for women too!

It's half past eight in Adelaide
and 4 a.m. in Liverpool.
Maggie May wants to ring Lime Street.
You mean they don't have STD?
But I thought this was the New World.

They don't have GMT either;
or BST, as they call it now,
whenever now is.
                          It is now
half past ten in Adelaide,
and in the Park Lands a nasty man
is cutting up a teenage boy
and cramming him into a plastic bag.

In Gouger Street another man,
equally nasty but less wicked,
has taken his wife to a performance
of Wagner at the Opera Theatre
and is strolling with her to their car
past the massage parlour
where something like five hours ago
Maggie May gave him a hand-job.

The Colonel's brooding over his notebooks,
and lying under his stone, and standing
on his plinth on Montefiore Hill.

Maggie May is still on the phone,
arguing with the operator,
trying to get through to Lime Street.
It's the future she wants,
or the past back. Some of it.

You're listening to ABC FM:
12.30 Eastern Standard Time –
twelve midnight in Adelaide.
And now, to take us through the night,
Music to Keep the Days Apart.

The Breakfast Program

May: autumn. In more or less recognisable
weather, more or less recognisable birds
are greeting the dawn. On 5CL the newsreader
has been allotted (after the lead story
on whether the Treasurer might or still might not
cancel the promised tax-cuts) two minutes
to tell us about whatever it is today –
chemical weapons, radioactive rain,
one of those messy bits of northern gloom
from the places where gloom's made (not here, not here!).
He tells us; then the baby-talking presenter
(curious how some Australian women
never get to sound older than fifteen)
contrives a soothing link: 'Grim news indeed,'
she ad-libs cosily. 'Much worse, of course,
if you live in Europe' – writing off a hemisphere.

From the Demolition Zone

Come, literature, and salve our wounds:
bring dressings, antibiotics, morphine;

bring syringes, oxygen, plasma.
(Saline solution we have already.)

We're injured, but we mustn't say so;
it hurts, but we mustn't tell you where.

Clear-eyed literature, diagnostician,
be our nurse and our paramedic.

Hold your stethoscope to our hearts
and tell us what you hear us murmuring.

Scan us; but do it quietly, like
the quiet seep of our secret bleeding.

When we lie awake in the night
cold and shaking, clenching our teeth,

be the steady hand on our pulse,
the skilful presence checking our symptoms.

You know what we're afraid of saying
in case they hear us. Say it for us.

On the Way to the Castle

It would be rude to look out of the car windows
at the colourful peasants authentically pursuing
their traditional activities in the timeless landscape
while the editor is talking to us.
He is telling us about the new initiatives
his magazine has adopted as a result
of the Leader's inspiring speech at the last Party Congress.

He is speaking very slowly (as does the Leader,
whom we have seen on our hotel television),
and my eyes are politely fixed on his little moustache:
as long as it keeps moving they will have to stay there;
but when he pauses for the interpreter's turn
my duty is remitted, and I can look out of the windows.
I am not ignoring the interpreter's translation
but she has become our friend: I do not feel compelled
by courtesy to keep my eyes on her lipstick.
What's more, the editor has been reciting his speech
at so measured a pace and with such clarity
that I can understand it in his own language;
and in any case, I have heard it before.
This on-off pattern of switching concentration
between the editor's moustache and the sights we are passing
gives me a patchy impression of the local agriculture.
Hordes of head-scarved and dark-capped figures
move through fields of this and that, carrying implements,
or bending and stretching, or loading things on to carts.
I missed most of a village, during the bit about the print-run,
but the translation granted me a roadful of quaint sheep.
Now the peasants are bent over what looks like bare earth
with occasional clusters of dry vegetation.
It is a potato field; they are grubbing for potatoes.
There are dozens of them – of peasants, that is:
the potatoes themselves are not actually visible.
As a spectacle, this is not notably picturesque,
but I should like to examine it for a little longer.
The sky has turned black; it is beginning to rain.
The editor has thought of something else he wishes to tell us
about the magazine's history.
Once again, eyes back to his official moustache
(under which his unofficial mouth looks vulnerable).
The editor is a kind man.
He is taking us on an interesting excursion,
in an expensive taxi, during his busy working day.
It has all been carefully planned for our pleasure
Quite possibly he wants to shield us from the fact
that this rain is weeks or months too late;

that the harvest is variously scorched, parched and withered;
that the potatoes for which the peasants are fossicking
have the size and the consistency of bullets

Romania

Suddenly it's gone public; it rushed out
into the light like a train out of a tunnel.
People I've met are faces in the government,
shouting on television, looking older.

The country sizzles with freedom. The air-waves
tingle. The telephone lines are all jammed.
I can't get through to my friends. Are they safe? They're safe,
but I need to hear it from them. Instead

I'll play the secret tape I made in the orchard
two years ago, at Ciorogîla.
We're talking in two languages, mine and theirs,
laughing, interrupting each other;

the geese in the peasants' yard next door
are barking like dogs; the children are squawking,
chasing each other, picking fruit;
the little boy brings me a flower and a carrot.

We're drinking must – blood-pink, frothy –
and a drop of unofficial *ţuica*:
'What do the peasants drink in your country? –
Oh, I forgot, you don't have peasants.'

It's dusk. The crickets have started up:
Zing-zing, zing-zing, like telephones
over the static. Did it really happen?
Is it possible? 'Da, da!' say the geese.

December 1989

Causes

The Farm
(*in memory of Fiona Lodge*)

Fiona's parents need her today –
they're old; one's ill, and slipping away –
but Fiona won't be by the bed:
                 she's dead.
She went for a working holiday
years ago, on a farm that lay
just down the coast from St Bee's Head
in Cumbria, next to – need I say?
                A name to dread.
She was always very fond of the farm
with its rough, authentic rural charm,
and the fields she tramped, and the lambs she fed
                with youthful pride.
Her family saw no cause for alarm –
how could it do her any harm
working there in the countryside?
It would help to build her up, they said.
But it secretly broke her down instead,
                until she died.
There was a leak, if you recall,
at Windscale in the fifties. No?
Well, it was thirty years ago;
                but these things are slow.
And no matter what the authorities said
about there being no risk at all
from the installations at Calder Hall,
buckets of radiation spread,
                and people are dead.
That farm became a hazardous place –
though to look at it you wouldn't know;
but cancers can take years to grow
(or leukaemia, in Fiona's case),
and as often as not they win the race,

                    however slow.
Before long most of us will know
people who've died in a similar way.
We're not aware of it today,
                    and nor are they,
but another twenty years or so
will sort out who are the ones to go.
We'll be able to mark them on a chart,
a retrospective map to show
where the source of their destruction lay.
                    That's the easy part.
But where's the next lot going to start?
At Windscale, Hinkley Point, Dounreay,
Dungeness, Sizewell, Druridge Bay?
                    Who can say?

Aluminium

Ting-ting! 'What's in your pocket, sir?'
Ping! Metal. Not coins or keys:
Sterotabs for the foreign water,
armour against one kind of disease.

'Aluminium: that's what they are –
they set the machine off.' That's it, then:
out of the frying-pan into the fire;
here's awful Alzheimer's looming again.

There wasn't much point in throwing away
your aluminium pots and kettle
if whenever you go on holiday
your drinking water's full of that metal.

Which will you swallow: bacteria soup,
or a clanking cocktail of sinister granules
that'll rust your mental circuitry up
and knot your brain-cells into tangles?

Don't bother to choose. You can't abjure it,
the use of this stuff to "purify".
At home the Water Board's fallen for it:
don't be surprised to see a ring of sky,

grey and canny as a metal detector,
to hear, amidst an aerial hum,
tintinnabulations over the reservoir
warning you of dementia to come.

A Hymn to Friendship

Somehow we manage it: to like our friends,
to tolerate not only their little ways
but their huge neuroses, their monumental oddness:
'Oh well,' we smile, 'it's one of his funny days.'

Families, of course, are traditionally awful:
embarrassing parents, ghastly brothers, mad aunts
provide a useful training-ground to prepare us
for the pseudo-relations we acquire by chance.

Why them, though? Why not the woman in the library
(grey hair, big mouth) who reminds us so of J?
Or the one on Budgen's delicatessen counter
(shy smile, big nose) who strongly resembles K?

– Just as the stout, untidy gent on the train
reading the *Mail on Sunday* through pebble specs
could, with somewhat sparser hair and a change
of reading-matter, be our good friend X.

True, he isn't; they aren't; but why does it matter?
Wouldn't they do as well as the friends we made
in the casual past, by being at school with them,
or living nextdoor, or learning the same trade?

Well, no, they wouldn't. Imagine sharing a tent
with one of these look-alikes, and finding she snored:
no go. Or listening for days on end while she dithered
about her appalling marriage: we'd be bored.

Do we feel at all inclined to lend them money?
Or travel across a continent to stay
for a weekend with them? Or see them through an abortion,
a divorce, a gruelling court-case? No way.

Let one of these impostors desert his wife
for a twenty-year-old, then rave all night about
her sensitivity and her gleaming thighs,
while guzzling all our whisky: we'd boot him out.

And as for us, could we ring them up at midnight
when our man walked out on us, or our roof fell in?
Would they offer to pay our fare across the Atlantic
to visit them? The chances are pretty thin.

Would they forgive our not admiring their novel,
or saying we couldn't really take to their child,
or confessing that years ago we went to bed
with their husband? No, they wouldn't: they'd go wild.

Some things kindly strangers will put up with,
but we need to know exactly what they are:
it's OK to break a glass, if we replace it,
but we mustn't let our kids be sick in their car.

Safer to stick with people who remember
how we ourselves, when we and they were nineteen,
threw up towards the end of a student party
on ethyl alcohol punch and methedrine.

In some ways we've improved since then. In others
(we glance at the heavy jowls and thinning hair,
hoping we're slightly better preserved than they are)
at least it's a deterioration we share.

It can't be true to say that we chose our friends,
or surely we'd have gone for a different lot,
while they, confronted with us, might well have decided
that since it was up to them they'd rather not.

But something keeps us hooked, now we're together,
a link we're not so daft as to disparage –
nearly as strong as blood-relationship
and far more permanent, thank God, than marriage.

Smokers for Celibacy

Some of us are a little tired of hearing that cigarettes kill.
We'd like to warn you about another way of making yourself ill:

we suggest that in view of AIDS, herpes, chlamydia, cystitis and NSU,
not to mention genital warts and cervical cancer and the proven connection
      between the two,

if you want to avoid turning into physical wrecks
what you should give up is not smoking but sex.

We're sorry if you're upset,
but think of the grisly things you might otherwise get.

We can't see much point in avoiding emphysema at sixty-five
if that's an age at which you have conspicuously failed to arrive;

and as for cancer, it is a depressing fact
that at least for women this disease is more likely to occur in the
      reproductive tract.

We could name friends of ours who died that way, if you insist,
but we feel sure you can each provide your own list.

You'll notice we didn't mention syphilis and gonorrhoea;
well, we have now, so don't get the idea

that just because of antibiotics quaint old clap and pox
are not still being generously spread around by men's cocks.

Some of us aren't too keen on the thought of micro-organisms travelling up
    into our brain
and giving us General Paralysis of the Insane.

We're opting out of one-night stands;
we'd rather have a cigarette in our hands.

If it's a choice between two objects of cylindrical shape
we go for the one that is seldom if ever guilty of rape.

Cigarettes just lie there quietly in their packs
waiting until you call on one of them to help you relax.

They aren't moody; they don't go in for sexual harassment and threats,
or worry about their performance as compared with that of other cigarettes,

nor do they keep you awake all night telling you the story of their life,
beginning with their mother and going on until morning about their first
    wife.

Above all, the residues they leave in your system are thoroughly sterilised
    and clean,
which is more than can be said for the products of the human machine.

Altogether, we've come to the conclusion that sex is a drag.
Just give us a fag.

Mrs Fraser's Frenzy

Songs for Music

1

My name is Eliza Fraser.
I belong to some savages.
My job is to feed the baby
they have hung on my shoulder.

Its mother is lying sick
with no milk in her breasts,
and my own baby died:
it was born after the shipwreck.

It was born under water
in the ship's leaky longboat.
Three days I helped to bail,
then gave birth in the scuppers.

My poor James, the captain,
was crippled with thirst and sickness.
The men were all useless,
and no woman to call on.

I believe the First Mate,
Mr Brown, treated me kindly;
he consigned my dead infant
to its watery fate.

But now I have been given
a black child to suckle.
I have been made a wet-nurse,
a slave to savage women.

They taunt me and beat me.
They make me grub for lily-roots
and climb trees for honey.
They poke burning sticks at me.

They have rubbed me all over
with charcoal and lizard-grease
to protect me from sunburn.
It is my only cover.

I am as black as they are
and almost as naked,
with stringy vines for a loincloth
and feathers stuck in my hair.

They are trying to change me
into one of themselves.
My name is Eliza Fraser.
I pray God to save me.

Their men took my husband –
they dragged him into the forest –
but I still have my wedding-ring
concealed in my waistband.

My name is Eliza Fraser.
My home is in Stromness.
I have left my three children
in the care of the minister.

I am a strong woman.
My language is English.
My name is Eliza Fraser
and my age thirty-seven.

2

The ghosts came from the sea, the white ghosts.
One of them was a she-ghost, a white woman.
We took her to the camp, the white she-ghost.
She was white all over, white like the ancestors,
white like the bodies of dead people
when you scorch them in the fire and strip off the skin.
She was a ghost, but we don't know whose.
We asked her 'Whose ghost are you?
Which ancestor has come back to us?'
She wouldn't say. She had forgotten our language.
She talked in a babble like the babble of birds,
that ghost from the sea, that white she-ghost.
She was covered with woven skins, but we stripped her;
she had hairs on her body, but we plucked them out;
we tried to make her look like a person.
She was stupid, though. She wouldn't learn.
We talked to her and she didn't listen.
We told her to go out and collect food, to dig for roots.
We told her to climb trees, to look for honey.
She couldn't, not even when we beat her.
She seems to have forgotten everything,
that ghost from the sea, that white woman.
We send her out for food every day
and she brings back a few bits, not enough for a child.
We have to throw her scraps, or she would starve.
All she is fit for is to suckle a baby,
that ancestor woman, that white ghost.
We have put her among the children until she learns.

3

I am a poor widow.
I do not own a farthing –
bereft in a shipwreck
of all but my wedding-ring.

    You are a liar, Mrs Fraser.
    You own two trunks of finery

and £400 subscribed
by the citizens of Sydney.

I am a poor widow.
My fatherless children
are alone up in Orkney
while I beg for money.

The Lord Mayor of Liverpool,
the Lord Mayor of London,
the Colonial Secretary:
they will none of them help me.

> You are a liar, Mrs Fraser.
> You are not even Mrs Fraser.
> You have another husband now –
> you married Captain Greene in Sydney.

I am a poor widow,
the victim of cannibals.
They killed my dear husband
on the shores of New Holland.

They skinned him and baked him;
they cut up his body
and gorged on his flesh
in their villainous gluttony.

Their hair is bright blue,
those abominable monsters;
it grows in blue tufts
on the tips of their shoulders . . .

> You are a liar, Mrs Fraser.
> Your sad ordeals have quite unhinged you.
> You were a decent woman once,
> prickly with virtue. What has changed you?
> Tell us the truth, the truth, the truth!
> What really happened that deranged you?

4

Not easy to love Mrs Fraser.
Captain Fraser managed it, in his time –
hobbling on her arm, clutching his ulcer,
falling back to relieve his griping bowels;
and hauling timber, a slave to black masters:
'Eliza, wilt thou help me with this tree? –
Because thou art now stronger than me.'
But they speared him, and she fainted, just that once.

Her children had to love her from a distance –
from Orkney to the far Antipodes,
or wherever she'd sailed off to with their father,
cosseting him with jellies for his gut:
'I have received a letter from dear Mamma.
I am looking for her daily at Stromness.'
Daily they had no sight of Mrs Fraser –
who had secretly turned into Mrs Greene.

And Captain Greene? Did he contrive to love her?
He never saw her as her rescuers did:
'Perfectly black, and crippled from her sufferings,
a mere skeleton, legs a mass of sores.'
He saw a widow, famous, with some money.
He saw the chance of more. He saw, perhaps,
a strangeness in her, gone beyond the strangeness
of anything he'd met on the seven seas.

5

I am not mad. I sit in my booth
on show for sixpence: 'Only survivor'
(which is a lie) 'of the *Stirling Castle*
wrecked off New Holland' (which is the truth),

embroidering facts. There is no need
to exaggerate (but I do), to sit
showing my scars to gawping London.
I do it for money. This is not greed:

261

I am not greedy. I am not mad.
I have a husband. I am cared for.
But I wake in the nights howling, naked,
alone, and starving. All that I had

I lost once – all the silken stuff
of civilisation: clothes, possessions,
decency, liberty, my name;
and now I can never get enough

to replace it. There can never be
enough of anything in the world,
money or goods, to keep me warm
and fed and clothed and safe and free.

Meeting the Comet

1

She'll never be able to play the piano –
well, not properly. She'll never be able
to play the recorder, even, at school,
when she goes: it has so many little holes . . .

We'll have her taught the violin.
Lucky her left hand's the one with four
fingers, one for each string. A thumb
and a fleshy fork are enough to hold a bow.

2

Before the calculator – the electronic one –
there were beads to count on; there was the abacus
to tell a tally or compute a score;
or there were your fingers, if you had enough.

The base was decimal: there had to be
a total of ten digits, in two sets –
a bunch of five, another bunch of five.
If they didn't match, your computations went haywire.

3

On the left hand, four	and a thumb.
On the right, a thumb	and just two.
Proper fingers, true,	fitted out
in the standard way;	but not four.

Baby-plump, the wrist	on the left.
On the right, the arm	narrows down
to a slender stem	and a palm
like a little tube	of soft bones.

263

4

Leafy lanes and rus in urbe were the thing
for a sheltered childhood (not that it was for long,
but parents try): the elm trees lingering
behind the coach factory; the tense monotonous song

of collared doves; the acres of bare floor
for learning to gallop on in the first size
of Start-Rite shoes; the peacock glass in the front door;
and the swift refocusing lurch of the new baby-sitter's eyes.

5

The Duke of Edinburgh stance: how cute
in a five-year-old! She doesn't do it much
when you're behind her; then it's hands in armpits
or pockets. School, of course, would like to teach

that well-adjusted children don't need pockets
except for their normal purposes, to hold
hankies or bus-tickets. She'll not quite learn
what she's not quite specifically taught.

6

Perhaps I don't exist. Perhaps
I didn't exist till I thought that;
then God invented me and made me
the age I am now (nearly eight);

perhaps I was someone else before,
and he suddenly swapped us round, and said
'You can be the girl with two fingers
and she can be you for a change, instead.'

7

'Give us your hand – it's a bit muddy here,
you'll slip.' But he's on her wrong side: her right's
wrong. She tries to circumnavigate him
('Watch it!' he says), to offer him her left –

and slips. It comes out. 'There!' she says. 'You see!'
'Is that all? Fucking hell,' he says, 'that's nothing;
don't worry about it, love. My Auntie May
lost a whole arm in a crash. Is it hereditary?'

8

'Some tiny bud that should have split into four
didn't, we don't know why' was all they could offer.
Research, as usual, lags. But suddenly, this:
'A long-term study has found a positive link

between birth defects and exposure to pesticides
in the first twelve weeks of pregnancy . . . the baby's
neural crest . . . mothers who had been present when
aerosol insecticides . . .' Now they tell us.

TRAVELLING

9 *So Far*
She has not got multiple sclerosis.
She has not got motorneuron disease,
or muscular dystrophy, or Down's Syndrome,
or a cleft palate, or a hole in the heart.

Her sight and hearing seem to be sound.
She has not been damaged by malnutrition,
or tuberculosis, or diabetes.
She has not got (probably not got) cancer.

10 Passport

Date of birth and all that stuff: straightforward;
likewise, now that she's stopped growing, height.
But ah, 'Distinguishing marks': how can she smuggle
so glaring a distinction out of sight?

The Passport Office proves, in one of its human
incarnations, capable of tact:
a form of words emerges that fades down
her rare statistic to a lustreless fact.

11 Stars

She's seeing stars – Orion steady on her left
like a lit-up kite (she has a window-seat),
and her whole small frame of sky strung out
with Christmas-tree lights. But what's all that

behind them? Spilt sugar? Spangled faults
in the plane's window? A dust of glittering points
like the sparkle-stuff her mother wouldn't let her
wear on her eyes to the third-form party.

12 Halfway

Does less mean more? She's felt more nearly naked
in duffel-coat and boots and scarf
with nothing showing but a face and her bare
fingers (except, of course, for the times

in fur gloves – mittens – look, no hands!)
than here on a beach in a bikini:
flesh all over. Look at my legs, my
back, my front. Shall I take off my top?

13 *At the Airport*

Shoulders like horses' bums; an upper arm
dressed in a wobbling watermelon of flesh
and a frilly muu-muu sleeve; red puckered necks
above the bougainvillaea and sunsets

and straining buttons of Hawaiian shirts;
bellies, bald heads, a wilting grey moustache
beneath a hat proclaiming 'One Old Poop'.
The tour guide rounds them up: his travelling freak-show.

14 *Comet*

'There will be twenty telescopes in the crater
of Mount Albert.' White-coated figures man them,
marshalling queues in darkness: not the Klan
but the Lions raising funds for charity.

$2 a look. No lights – not even torches;
no smoking (bad for the optics); no moon
above the tree-fringed walls of this grassy dip.
Nothing up there but stars. And it, of course.

15 *Halley Party*

A glow-worm in a Marmite jar
like the one her mother brought her once:
'I dreamt you woke me in the night and showed me
a glow-worm in a Marmite jar.'

So these wee kids in dressing-gowns
will remember being woken up
for honey sandwiches and cocoa
and a little light in a ring of glass.

16 Orbit

'It's not like anything else, with its stumpy tail:
just a fuzz, really, until you get up close –
but of course you can't. With binoculars, I meant,
or a telescope. Actually the tail's fading.'

Higher than Scorpius now, higher than the Pointers,
high as the mid-heaven, she's tracked it nightly,
changing. 'I'm not the only one, but I'm once
in a lifetime.' As for close, that's something else.

AFTER

17

Landing at Gatwick on a grey Sunday when
the baggage handlers seem to be on strike as
they were at the airport before last (but no,
it's merely Britain being its old self) she's

her old self – a self consisting also of
more hand-luggage than she'd thought she was allowed
plus her at last reclaimed suitcase: all of which,
however she may dispose them, hurt her hand.

18

Rise above it! Swallow a chemical:
chuck down whisky, Valium, speed,
Mogadon, caffeine; bomb it or drown it.
But wait! If chemicals did the deed

pandering to their ways compounds
the offence. Resist: you know they lead
to trouble. Find another obsession.
Face a healthier form of need.

19

Saving the world is the only valid cause.
Now that she knows it's round it seems smaller,
more vulnerable (as well as bigger, looser,
a baggy bundle of dangerous contradictions).

There's room for such concerns in student life,
if you stretch it. So: Link hands around the world
for peace! Thumbs down to Star Wars! Hands off
the environment! Two fingers to the Bomb!

20

'Of course you'd have a natural sympathy . . .
I always thought it was quite sweet, your little hand,
when we were kids; but we don't want other kids
walking around the world with worse things . . .

I'm not upsetting you, am I?' No, she's not,
this warm voice from the past, this candid face.
'Right. See you tomorrow. The coach leaves at 8.
Oh, and we've got a wonderful furious banner.'

21

The fountain in her heart informs her
she needn't try to sleep tonight –
rush, gush: the sleep-extinguisher
frothing in her chest like a dishwasher.

She sits at the window with a blanket
to track the turning stars. A comet
might add some point. The moon ignores her;
but dawn may come. She'd settle for that.

22

There was a young woman who fell
for someone she knew rather well –
a friend from her school: confirming the rule
that with these things you never can tell.

The person she'd thought a fixed star –
stuck on rails like a tram, not a car –
shot off into orbit and seemed a new planet,
and a dazzler, the finest by far.

23

She wants to see what it looks like on
a breast. She puts it on a breast –
not the one she has in mind
but her own: at least it's a rehearsal.

Three weeks later, the first night:
a nipple, darker than hers, framed
in a silky, jointed bifurcation.
There is also dialogue. And applause.

24

And she never did learn to play the violin.
So it will have to be *Musica Mundana*,
'the harmony of the spheres' (coming across a map
of the southern skies cut out of some Auckland paper)

or the other kind: what was it? *Instrumentalis*
and – ah, yes – *Humana*. (Listen: Canopus, Crux,
Carina, Libra, Vela choiring together. She
has glided right off the edge of the star-chart.)

LOOKING BACK

(1997)

I

Where They Lived

That's where they lived in the 1890s.
They don't know that we know,
or that we're standing here, in possession
of some really quite intimate information
about the causes of their deaths,
photographing each other in a brisk wind
outside their terrace house, both smiling
(not callously, we could assure them),
our hair streaming across our faces
and the green plastic Marks and Spencer's bag
in which I wrapped my camera against showers
ballooning out like a wind-sock
from my wrist, showing the direction
of something that's blowing down our century.

Framed

(*Sam Adcock, 1876-1956, & Eva Eggington, 1875-1970*)

What shall we do with Grandpa, in his silver
frame? And why is he in it, may we ask?
Why not Grandma, still shyly veiled in her
tissue paper and photographer's cardboard?

Of course, there's his moustache: we can't miss that;
nor would he wish us to. It must have taken
hours and all his barbering skills to wax
and twirl the ends into these solemn curlicues.

We can't keep that in a drawer – or he couldn't.
But Grandma, now, in her black, nervously smiling,
one hand barely poised on the same ridiculous
Empire chairback: what a stunner she was!

Why did he not frame her? After all, her looks
are what he married her for. He fell in love
with her portrait (not this one) in a photographer's
window, and hunted down the woman herself.

She was a dressmaker's cutter (cool hands);
he was an extrovert – a talker, mixer
(the Lodge, the Church, the Mechanics' Institute,
the Temperance Movement). And it all came true:

seven years of engagement, fifty more
together. You can almost map their marriage,
decade by decade, through the evolution,
flourishing and decline of his moustache.

At twenty, not a whisker; at thirty or so,
this elaborate facial construct. In Manchester
it throve; then what did he do but export it
to droop and sag in the bush at Te Raua Moa,

on his dairy farm (how those cattle depressed him –
was New Zealand not such a bright idea after all?).
But it perked up for his passport in the 30s,
with a devilish Vandyke beard, for their last trip Home.

Not a handsome man, he must have decided
to take a bit of trouble and pass for one;
while Grandma, with the eyes and the bone structure
and that tilt of the head, decided to be plain.

She took to bobbed hair and wire-framed glasses,
and went grey early. He never did (unless
there was some preparation he knew about?)
Here they are in a 50s Polyfoto –

she with her shy smile, he with a muted version
of the moustache, wearing his cameo tie-pin
and a jubilant grin, as if he'd just slammed down
the winning trick in his favourite game of 'Sorry!'

The Russian War

Great-great-great-uncle Francis Eggington
came back from the Russian War
(it was the kind of war you came back from,
if you were lucky: bad, but over).
He didn't come to the front door –
the lice and filth were falling off him –
he slipped along the alley to the yard.
'Who's that out at the pump?' they said
'– a tall tramp stripping his rags off !'
The soap was where it usually was.
He scrubbed and splashed and scrubbed,
and combed his beard over the hole in his throat.
'Give me some clothes,' he said. 'I'm back.'
'God save us, Frank, it's you!' they said.
'What happened? Were you at Scutari?
And what's that hole inside your beard?'
'Tea first,' he said. 'I'll tell you later.
And Willie's children will tell their grandchildren;
I'll be a thing called oral history.'

227 Peel Green Road

Failing their flesh and bones we have the gatepost.
Failing the bride in her ostrich-feathered hat,
the groom bracing his shoulders for the camera,
we have the garden wall, the path, and the gatepost:

not the original gatepost, but positioned
in exactly the same relation to the house –
just as the windows have been modernised
but we can see their dimensions are the same

as the ones behind the handsome brothers' heads
under their wedding bowlers. The gatepost
stands to the left, where nine-year-old Nellie
ought to be standing, in her home-made dress,

her boots and stockings and white hair-ribbon,
leaning her wistful head against Marion –
her next-best sister, who will have to do
now that Eva's married and going away.

Father and Mother, corpulent on chairs,
young Harry wincing in his Fauntleroy collar,
James in his first hard hat, a size too large,
have faded away from bricks and wood and metal.

Failing the sight of Mary, flowered and frilled,
the married sister, simpering on the arm
of Abraham with his curled moustache (the swine:
he'll leave her, of course) we may inspect the drainpipe:

not the authentic late-Victorian drainpipe
but just where that one was, convincing proof
(together with the gatepost and the windows)
that this is it, all right: the very house –

unless it's not; unless that was a stand-in,
one the photographer preferred that day
and lined them up in front of, because the sun
was shining on it; as it isn't now.

Nellie
(i.m. Nellie Eggington, 1894-1913)

Just because it was so long ago
doesn't mean it ceases to be sad.
Nellie on the sea-front at Torquay
watching the fishing-boats ('Dear Sis and Bro,
I am feeling very much better') had
six months left to die of her TB.

She and Marion caught it at the mill
from a girl who coughed and coughed across her loom.
Their father caught it; he and Marion died;
the others quaked and murmured; James fell ill.
So here was Nellie, with her rented room,
carefully walking down to watch the tide.

When she'd first been diagnosed, she'd said
'Please, could Eva nurse me, later on,
when it's time, that is . . . if I get worse?'
Eva swallowed hard and shook her head
(and grieved for fifty years): she had her son
to consider. So their mother went as nurse.

Nellie took her parrot to Torquay –
her pet (as she herself had been a pet,
Eva's and her father's); she could teach
words to it in the evenings after tea,
talk to it when the weather was too wet
or she too frail for sitting on the beach.

Back in Manchester they had to wait,
looking out for letters every day,
or postcards for 'Dear Sis'. The winter passed.
Eva and Sam made plans to emigrate.
(Not yet, though. Later.) April came, and May –
bringing something from Torquay at last:

news. It was Tom's Alice who glanced out,
and called to Eva; Eva called to Sam:
'Look! Here's Mother walking up the road
with Nellie's parrot in its cage.' No doubt
now of what had happened. On she came,
steadily carrying her sharp-clawed load.

Mary Derry

The first spring of the new century
and there I was, fallen pregnant!

Scarcely out of winter, even –
scarcely 1800 at all –

with not a bud on the trees yet
when the new thing budded in me.

They said I ought to have known better:
after all, I was over thirty.

William was younger; and men, of course . . .
but he came round fair in the end.

We couldn't sit the banns through,
giggled at for three Sundays –

not in Lichfield. He got a licence
and wedded me the next morning

in Armitage. July, it was
by then, and my loose gown bulging.

The babe was christened in Lichfield, though.
You knew he died? The wages of sin.

*

So this is where we began again:
Liverpool. Can you hear the seagulls?

A screeching city: seagulls and wagons,
drawbridges, floodgates, lifting-gear,

and warehouses huge as cathedrals.
We lived down by the Duke's Dock,

one lodging after another.
The family grew as the city grew.

William sat on his high stool
inscribing figures in a ledger.

My care was the children, bless them.
I ferried most of them safely through

the perilous waters of infancy,
and saw them married. Then I died.

                    *

Well, of course you know that.
And you know what of : consumption,

a word you don't use; an unwilled
legacy to go haunting down

one line of my long posterity
to Frank's son, and his son's son,

and fan out in a shuddering shadow
over the fourth generation.

And what I have to ask is:
was it the city's fault, or mine?

You can't answer me. All you hear
is a faint mewing among the seagulls.

Moses Lambert: The Facts

The young cordwainer (yes, that's right)
got married at the Old Church –
it's Manchester Cathedral now.
That was the cheapest place to go.

They married you in batches there –
a list of names, a buzz of responses,
and 'You're all married,' said the clerk.
'Pair up outside.' (Like shoes, thought Moses.)

After the ceremony, though,
he and Maria waited on.
They had an extra thing to do:
their daughter needed christening.

The baby's age is not recorded.
The bride was over twenty-one –
full age. The bridegroom (never mind
what he might have said) was seventeen.

The young Queen was on the throne;
they'd have to be Victorians now.
Meanwhile, two more facts: they were
from Leeds. One of them had red hair.

Samuel Joynson

He looked for it in the streets first,
and the sooty back alleys. It wasn't there.

He looked for it in the beer-house;
it dodged away as soon as he glimpsed it.

It certainly wasn't there at work,
raining down with the sawdust on to
his broad-brimmed hat as he stood sweating

in the pit under the snorting blade.

He looked all over the house for it –
the kitchen the scullery the parlour
the bedroom he shared with two of his brothers –
and shrugged. Of course it wasn't there.

So he tied a noose around where it should have been,
and slipped his head into it, for one last look.

Amelia

It went like this: I married at 22,
in 1870. My daughter was born
the following year – Laura, we called her.
(No reason for the name – we just liked it.)
In '72 my brother hanged himself.
Laura died exactly a year later,
when I was pregnant with her brother Thomas
(named for my dead father). In '74
three things happened: my baby Thomas died,
then my sister; then I gave birth to John,
my first child to survive. He was a hunchback.
(I don't suppose you care for that expression;
well, call it what you like.) He lived to 20,
making the best of things, my poor brave lad.

After him, I got the knack of producing
healthy children. Or perhaps it was the gin.
Yes, I took to the bottle. Wouldn't you?
By the time it killed me I'd five living –
a little Band of Hope, a bright household
of teetotallers, my husband at their head.
I died of a stroke, officially; 'of drink'
wasn't spoken aloud for forty years.
These youngsters have my portrait proudly framed –
an old thing in a shawl, with a huge nose.
They also have a photograph – a maiden

with frightened eyes and a nose as trim as theirs.
Both are labelled 'Amelia'. Which one
was I? I couldn't have been both, they're sure.

Barber

They set the boy to hairdressing –
you didn't need to be strong, or have
a straight back like other people.

It was the scissors he liked – their glitter
and snicker-snack; the arts, too,
of elegant shaping. Oh, and the razors.

He served his time, and qualified young;
it's on his death certificate:
'Hairdresser (Master). Age 20.'

In the next column, 'Spinal disease,
15 months. Abscess, 12 months.'
That sounds like cancer. It felt like blades

burning, slicing – a whole year
to play the Little Mermaid, walking
on knife-edges, with hand-glass and comb.

Flames

Which redhead did I get my temper from?
I've made a short ancestral list
by hair-colour and moods. But, more to the point,
what are the odds on Alzheimer's?

Which ones went funny in their seventies?
Mary Ellen, perhaps, found in the coal-shed
hunting for her Ship Canal shares
after her fiery hair turned grey.

My hair's not red. I like flames, though.
When I get old and mad I'll play with them –
run the flimsy veils through my fingers
like orange plastic film, like parachute-silk.

My hands will scorch and wither, if I do.
I shall be safe and dead. It won't matter.
It's something to look forward to,
playing with fire. That, or deep water.

Water

I met an ancestor in the lane.
She couldn't stop: she was carrying water.
It slopped and bounced from the stoup against her;
the side of her skirt was dark with the stain,
oozing chillingly down to her shoe.
I stepped aside as she trudged past me,
frowning with effort, shivering slightly
(an icy drop splashed my foot too).
The dress that brushed against me was rough.
She didn't smell the way I smell:
I tasted the grease and smoke in her hair.
Water that's carried is never enough.
She'd a long haul back from the well.

No, I didn't see her. But she was there.

A Haunting

'Hoy!' A hand hooks me into a doorway:
'Here!' (No, that's not it: too many aitches;
they'd have been short of those, if I recall . . .)
'Oy, there!' (Never mind the aitches, it's his
breath now, gin and vinegar – I'm choking –

and fire on my neck; the hand grinding my shoulder.
I'm a head taller, nearly, but he's strong.)
'Look at me! I'm your ancestor.'

Eyes in a smudged face. Dark clothes. A hat . . .
'Look at me!' A stunted stump of a man.
Boots. No coat, although it's cold. A jacket
crumpled at the elbows. (I'm shivering.)
What kind of hair? If I can get
my hands to move, I'll push his hat off. There:
black, above a gleam of white skin (oh you poor
factory rat, you bastard you, my forebear!).

'Which one are you? Which ancestor?' Won't say.
Won't talk now. Stands there, shaking me now and then,
staring. Dark-haired – but then so were they all
in the photographs: brown hair, red hair, grey,
all dark for the cameras; and unsmiling.
This one's before photography,
still on the verge of things: a pre-Victorian,
pre-Temperance, pre-gentility; and angry.

He shows a snaggle of teeth (pre-dentistry);
means another thing now: 'Give us a kiss!'
No. No, I can't. 'Why not? You're family.'
That's not a family expression on his face.
'You're a woman, aren't you? One of ours?
A great-great-great-granddaughter?' He looks
younger than me, thirtyish. How do you talk
to a young man who's been dead a hundred years?

'Not unless you tell me who you are.'
'A part of you,' he cackles. 'Never mind
which part.' (Is it compulsory, I wonder,
to like one's ancestors? I couldn't stand
that laugh of his for long.) 'You were so set
on digging us up. You thought it was romantic,
like all that poetry they talk about
(not me – I can't read). Well, I'm what you dug.

So: what'll you give me for the favour, lass?
You wouldn't be on this earth if it weren't for me.'
That scorching gin-breath. 'Let me find my purse.'
We stagger together, a step or two, and I'm free.
His hat's on the cobbles. I rattle it full of money.
Not sovereigns, no: pound coins, worth less than a kiss –
base metal to him, proleptic wealth, no use
for more than a century to come. I'm sorry.

The Wars

When they were having the Gulf War
I went to the 18th century.
I could see no glory in this life.

Awake half the night with the World Service,
then off on an early train for news –
secrets, discoveries, public knowledge

lurking on microfilm or parchment:
'I bequeath to my said daughter Mary Adcock
my Bedd and Bedding my oak Clothes Chest and Drawers

my Dressing Table and Looking Glass my Arm chair
my Clock standing in my said Dwelling house,
And one half part or share of all my Pewter.'

When it was over and not over,
and they offered us the Recession instead,
I went back further, pursuing the St Johns,

the Hampdens, the Wentworths to their deathbeds:
'Item I give to my wives sonne . . .'
(Ah, so she had been married before!)

'. . . Mr Edward Russell fiftie pounds,
and to John his brother ten pounds by the yeare
to be paid him soe long as he followes the warrs . . .'

Sub Sepibus

'Many of this parish in the years ensuing were marryed clandestinely,
i.e. sub sepibus, and were excommunicated for their labour.'
Note after entries for 1667 in Parish Register for Syston, Leicestershire

Under a hedge was good enough for us,
my Tommy Toon and me –
under the blackthorn, under the may,
under the stars at the end of the day,
under his cloak I lay,
under the shining changes of the moon;
under Tom Toon.

No banns or prayer-book for the likes of us,
my Tommy Toon and me.
Tom worked hard at his frame all day
but summer nights he'd come out to play,
in the hedge or the hay,
and ply his shuttle to a different tune –
my merry Tom Toon.

The vicar excommunicated us,
my Tommy Toon and me.
We weren't the only ones to stray –
there are plenty who lay down where we lay
and have babes on the way.
I'll see my tickling bellyful quite soon:
another Tom Toon.

Anne Welby

(died 9 May 1770, Beeby, Leicestershire)

For her gravestone to have been moved is OK.
I know she isn't here, under the nettles;
but what did I want to do, after all –
burrow into the earth and stroke her skull?

Would that help me to see her? Would she rise
from the weeds ('Dormuit non mortua est')
and stand clutching at elder branches to prop
her dizzy bones after centuries of sleep?

The nettles, in fact, have also been removed:
a kind man with a spade has just slain them
so that I could kneel on the earth and scan
the truths, half-truths and guesses on her stone.

'Here lie the earthy remains' (I like 'earthy')
'of Ann the wife of Henry King'; then (huge
letters) 'Gentleman'. Not quite, I think:
it was his children who cried out their rank.

Henry was a grazier in his will;
but Anne, his lady, brought him eighty acres
and a fading touch of class; then lived so long
they buried a legend here – her age is wrong.

Homage (or weariness) called her 95,
adding perhaps five years. Her birth's gone under
the rubble of time, just as her grave was lost
when the church expanded a few yards to the east.

But I know who she was. I've traced her lineage
through wills and marriage bonds until I know it
better than she herself may have done, poor dear,
having outlived her age. And yes, she's here:

I've brought her with me. As I stroke the stone
with hands related to hers, I can feel
the charge transmitted through eight steps
of generations. She's at my fingertips.

Beanfield

Somehow you've driven fifty miles to stand
in a beanfield, on the bumpy ridges
at the edge of it, not among the blossom
but under the larks – you can hear but not see them;
and it's not even where the house was –
the house, you think, was under the airfield
(beanfield, airfield, ploughed field) –
they ploughed the house but left the twitter of larks,
a pins-and-needles aerial tingling;
yet somehow this, you're sure, is Frances St John.
How do you know? It just is.
She's here; she's not here; she was once.
The larks are other larks' descendants.
Four hundred years. It feels like a kind of love.

Ancestor to Devotee

What are you loving me with? I'm dead.
What gland of tenderness throbs in you,
yearning back through the silt of ages
to a face and a voice you never knew?

When you find my name in a document
or my signature on a will,
what is it that makes you hold your breath –
what reverent, half-perverted thrill?

'Flesh of my flesh,' we could call each other;
but not uniquely: I've hundreds more
in my posterity, and for you
unreckoned thousands have gone before.

What's left of me, if you gathered it up,
is a faggot of bones, some ink-scrawled paper,
flown-away cells of skin and hair . . .
you could set the lot on fire with a taper.

You breathe your scorching filial love
on a web of related facts and a name.
But I'm combustible now. Watch out:
you'll burn me up with that blow-torch flame.

Frances

Her very hand. Her signature –
upright, spiky, jagged with effort –
or his hand on hers, was it,
her son's grasp locked on her knuckles?

'F. Weale'. Third of her surnames.
I Frances Weale of Arlesey,
widowe, being weake in body
but of perfecte memory,

doe make this my last will
in the yeare 1638 . . .
Item I give to my sonne Samuell Browne
my halfe dozen of silver spoones . . .

*

They've had quite a history, those spoons.
My first husband bequeathed them to my second –
or at least to his mother, Goodwife Weale:
'one haulfe dozen of silver spoones
which are alone and seldom occupied' –
little guessing they'd come back to me.

I was supposed to go away quietly
and live at Ashby Mill in Lincolnshire,
there to 'rest myself contented' and not
(repeat *not* – he did go on about it)
sue for my thirds, my widow's right in law.
Nicholas wasn't one for women's rights.

I was to have the bringing up of Samuel,
our older son; but John, our younger boy,
was to stay behind with the man Nicholas called
his 'trustie frende', Thomas Weale of Polebrook,
his joint executor. I was to be the other –
as long as I didn't claim my thirds, of course.

I was to keep the buildings in repair;
I wasn't to fell any of the trees . . .
he was going to rule us all from beyond the grave,
my iron rod of a husband, Nicholas Browne,
BA, BD, Rector of Polebrook, Prebendary
of Peterborough Cathedral; puritan.

Well, I wouldn't be ruled. I was done with that.
I'd had eleven years of being meek.
So when he tried to shunt me off up north
to the dull retreat he'd set aside for me
(such a fiddly, scholar's will), I didn't go.
I stayed at home and married Thomas Weale.

Yes, I know I was taking another master,
but this time I was doing it by choice;
and believe me if I tell you he was different –
a yeoman, not a cleric; less cold;
and, above all, my little John's guardian.
By marrying Thomas I kept both my children.

We made an execution of the will
to our joint satisfaction, I and Thomas
(I was still young, remember). We did our duties –
to Nicholas's estate, and to the boys
(we had no other children), and to each other.
Thomas Weale was a 'trustie frende' to us all.

No nagging about thirds when his time came:
he left me both his houses, and some land
(for my life-time only – but even a man, I think,

290

needs little land when he's dead), and his goods and plate.
Of which to my son John my silver bowl,
to his wife my silver cup; and the spoons to Samuel.

In witnes whereof I have set to
my hande the day & yeare above written . . .

*

F. Weale. Her final signature.
Her own fingers twitching across
this very page. Not John's hand –
he wasn't there. Not clever Samuel's –

his legal glibness would have made
a brisker job of it. The wobbling
jabs of the quill are hers, an image
of weakness spelling out her strength.

At Great Hampden

That can't be it –
not with cherubs.
After all, they were Puritans.

All the ones on the walls are too late –
too curlicued, ornate, rococo –
17th century at least.

Well, then, says the vicar,
it will be under the carpets:
a brass.

He strips off his surplice,
then his cassock,
hardly ruffling his white hair.

He rolls the strip of red carpet;
I roll the underfelt.
It sheds fluff.

A brass with figures appears. Not them.
Another. Not them.
We've begun at the wrong end.

Room for one more? Yes.
There, just in front of the altar,
a chaste plaque and a chaste coat of arms.

It says what the book says:
'Here lieth the body of Griffith Hampden . . .
and of Ann . . .' No need to write it down.

Now we begin again, the vicar and I,
rolling the carpet back,
our heads bent to the ritual;

tweaking and tidying the heavy edges
we move our arms in reciprocal gestures
like women folding sheets in a launderette.

A button flips off someone's jacket.
Yours? I offer it to the vicar.
No, yours. He hands it back with a bow.

At Baddesley Clinton

A splodge of blood on the oak floor
in the upstairs parlour, near the hearth.

Nicholas Brome splashed it here
five centuries ago, the villain.

Not his blood; he kept his,
apart from what he handed down

292

(drops of it circulating still
in my own more law-abiding veins).

It was a priest's blood he squirted:
out with his sword and stuck it into

the local parson, whom he caught
'chockinge his wife under ye chinne'.

Not the same class of murder
as when he ambushed his father's killer.

That was cold blood at the crossroads;
hot blood in the parlour's different.

But he got the King's and the Pope's pardons,
and built the church a new west tower.

There it stands among the bluebells:
'NICHOLAS BROME ESQVIRE LORD OF

BADDESLEY DID NEW BVILD THIS STEEPLE
IN THE RAIGNE OF KING HENRY THE SEAVENTH.'

His other memorial was more furtive;
it trickled down under the rushes

and stayed there. Easy to cover it up,
but more fun now for the tourists

to see it crying out his crime.
It is blood: they've analysed it.

On some surfaces, in some textures,
blood's indelible, they say.

Traitors

'. . . For that preposterous sinne wherein he did offend,
In his posteriour parts had his preposterous end.'
      MICHAEL DRAYTON: Poly-Olbion
        (on Edward II, murdered by Roger de Mortimer, 1327)

Naughty ancestors, I tell them,
baby-talking my cosy family –
the history ones, the long-ago
cut-out figures I've found in books.

Cut up, too, a few of them: quartered –
you, for instance, regicide
who cuddled a king's wife, and then
had her husband done away with.

You never touched him yourself, of course;
but wasn't it your own vision,
to roger him to death like that,
a red-hot poker up his rear?

Well, he had it coming to him,
you might have sneered (I see you sneering:
a straight man, in that you preferred
women to Eddy-Teddy-bears).

It's never only about sex.
Power, as usual, was the hormone;
and two of those who had the power
were my other naughties, the Despensers.

It wasn't Hugh the king's playmate
but Hugh his father who begat us,
through a less blatant son. Both Hughs
lost their balls before the scaffold.

That was how the sequence went,
for treason: chop, then hang, then quarter.
So fell all three. Only the king
died without a mark on his body –

or so they say. It's all hearsay.
Perhaps the king and Hugh the younger
were just good friends; perhaps the murder
wasn't a murder; perhaps the blood

of traitors isn't in my veins,
but just the blood of ambitious crooks
with winning Anglo-Norman accents
and risky tastes in sex. Perhaps.

Blood must be in it somewhere, though;
I see them bundled into a box,
dismembered toys, still faintly squeaking,
one with royal blood on his paws.

Swings and Roundabouts

My ancestors are creeping down from the north –
from Lancashire and the West Riding,
from sites all over Leicestershire,

down through the Midlands; from their solid outpost
in Lincolnshire, and their halts in Rutland,
down through Northants and Beds and Bucks.

They're doing it backwards, through the centuries:
from the Industrial Revolution
they're heading south, past the Enclosures

and the Civil War, through Elizabethan times
to the dissolution of the monasteries,
the Wars of the Roses, and beyond.

From back-to-backs in Manchester they glide
in reverse to stocking-frames in Syston,
from there back to their little farms,

then further back to grander premises,
acquiring coats of arms and schooling
in their regression to higher things.

They're using the motorways; they're driving south
in their armour or their ruffs and doublets
along the M1 and the A1.

They've got as far as the South Mimms roundabout.
A little group in merchants' robes
is filtering through London, aiming

for a manor-house and lands in Chislehurst
across the road from a school I went to;
and somewhere round about Footscray

they'll meet me riding my bike with Lizzie Wood
when I was twelve; they'll rush right through me
and blow the lot of us back to Domesday.

Peter Wentworth in Heaven

The trees have all gone from the grounds of my manor –
the plums, quinces, close-leaved pears –
where I walked in the orchard, planning my great speech;
and the house gone too. No matter.

My *Pithie Exhortation* still exists –
go and read it in your British Library.
I have discussed it here with your father;
he was always a supporter of free speech.

The trouble it brought me it is not in my nature
to regret. Only for my wife I grieved:
she followed me faithfully into the Tower;
her bones lie there, in St Peter ad Vincula.

I would not have gone home to Lillingstone Lovell,
if my friends had gained my release, without her,
'my chiefest comfort in this life, even
the best wife that ever poor gentleman enjoyed'.

She was a Walsingham; her subtle brother
was the Queen's man; he guarded his own back.
Any fellow-feeling he may once have cherished
for our cause he strangled in his bosom.

I was too fiery a Puritan for him.
His wife remembered mine in her will:
'to my sister Wentworthe a payre of sables'.
Not so Francis: he was no brother to us.

Well, we are translated to a different life,
my loyal Elizabeth and I.
We walk together in the orchards of Heaven –
a place I think you might find surprising.

But then you found me surprising too
when you got some notion of me, out of books.
Read my Exhortation, and my Discourse;
so you may understand me when we come to meet.

Notes

276: **Mary Derry** married William Eggington in 1800 and was the great-great-grandmother of Samuel Adcock's wife Eva Eggington.

278: **Moses Lambert**: the facts: Moses Lambert, 1821–1868, was the father of Mary Ellen Lambert (not the premarital baby in this poem but a later child), who married William Henry Eggington and was the mother of Eva.

278: **Samuel Joynson** was Amelia Joynson's brother.

279: **Amelia**: Amelia Joynson, 1847–1899, married John Adcock, 1842-1911, and was Samuel Adcock's mother.

280: **Barber**: John Adcock, 1874–1895, was the son of John and Amelia, and brother of Sam Adcock.

284: **Anne Welby** married Henry King, 1680–1756. Their granddaughter Elizabeth King married William Adcock, 1737–1814, Samuel Adcock's great-great-grandfather.

285–7: **Beanfield and Frances**: Frances St John married Nicholas Browne, rector of Polebrook, Northants, in 1597, and was Anne Welby's great-great-grandmother.

285–90: **At Great Hampden**: Griffith Hampden, 1543-1591, and his wife Anne Cave were the parents of Mary Hampden who married Walter Wentworth, son of Peter. Their daughter Mary Wentworth married John Browne; these were the great-grandparents of Anne Welby.

290–2: **At Baddesley Clinton and Traitors**: These assorted villains figure in the family tree of Elizabeth Ferrers, mother of Griffith Hampden. Baddesley Clinton is in Warwickshire; the house belongs to the National Trust.

294: **Peter Wentworth in Heaven**: Peter Wentworth, MP, 1524–1597, was imprisoned in the Tower of London several times by Elizabeth I for demanding that Parliament should be free to discuss the succession and other matters without interference. His wife Elizabeth Walsingham died in 1596 in the Tower. Her sister-in-law who mentioned Elizabeth in her will was Sir Francis Walsingham's first wife, Anne.

Tongue Sandwiches

Tongue sandwiches on market-day
in the King's Head Hottle (I could read;
my sister couldn't.) Always the same
for lunch on market-day in Melton.

No sign of a bottle in the hottle –
or not upstairs in the dining-room;
the bottles were in the room below,
with the jolly farmers around the door.

I didn't know we were in a pub,
or quite what pubs were: Uncle managed
to be a not unjolly farmer
with only tea to loosen his tongue.

And what did I think 'tongue' was?
These rose-pink slices wrapped in bread?
Or the slithery-flappy tube behind
my milk-teeth, lapping at novelties

(yes, of course I'd heard of 'ho-*tells*')
and syphoning up Midlands vowels
to smother my colonial whine?
(Something new for Mummy and Daddy,

coming to visit us at Christmas,
these local 'oohs' and 'ahs', as in
'Moommy, there's blood in the lavatory!
Soombody moost have killed a rabbit.')

On the way back to Uncle's cart
(how neat that his name was George Carter!)
we passed the beasts in the cattle-stalls –
their drooling lips, their slathering tongues.

The horse was a safer kind of monster,
elephant-calm between the shafts
as Auntie and Uncle loaded up
and we all piled on. Then bumpety-bump

along the lanes. I was impatient
for *Jerry of St Winifred's* –
my Sunday School prize, my first real book
that wasn't babyish with pictures –

to curl up with it in the armchair
beside the range, for my evening ration:
'Only a chapter a day,' said Auntie.
'Too much reading's bad for your eyes.'

I stuck my tongue out (not at her –
in a trance of concentration), tasting
the thrilling syllables: 'veterinary
surgeon', 'papyrus', 'manuscript'.

Jerry was going to be a vet;
so when she found the injured puppy
and bandaged its paw with her handkerchief,
and the Squire thanked her – well, you could see!

As for me, when I sat for hours
writing a story for Mummy and Daddy,
and folded the pages down the middle
to make a book, I had no ambition.

The Pilgrim Fathers

I got a Gold Star for the Pilgrim Fathers,
my first public poem, when I was nine.
I think I had to read it out to the class;
but no one grilled me about it, line by line;

no one asked me to expatiate on
my reasons for employing a refrain;
no one probed into my influences,
or said 'Miss Adcock, perhaps you could explain

your position as regards colonialism.
Here you are, a New Zealander in Surrey,
describing the exportation of new values
to America. Does this cause you any worry?

And what about the title, 'Pilgrim Fathers' –
a patriarchal expression, you'll agree –
how does it relate to the crucial sentence
in stanza one: 'Nine children sailed with we'?

Were you identifying with your age-group?
Some of us have wondered if we detect
a growing tendency to childism
in your recent poems. Might this be correct?'

No one even commented on the grammar –
it didn't seem important at the time.
I liked the sound of it, is all I'd have said
if they'd questioned me. I did it for the rhyme.

Paremata

Light the Tilley lamp:
I want to write a message,
while the tide laps the slipway
and someone else cooks sausages.

Make the Primus hiss:
twizzley music. Dusk time.
Bring back the greeds of childhood;
forget young love and all that slime.

Camping

When you're fifteen, no one understands you.
And why had I been invited, anyway? –
On a camping holiday with my Latin teacher
and her young friends, two men in their twenties.
I didn't understand them, either.

The one I fancied was the tall one
with soft brown eyes. He was a hairdresser.
One day the Primus toppled over
and a pan of water scalded his foot.
The skin turned into soggy pink crêpe paper –
grisly; but it gave him a romantic limp
and a lot of sympathy.
Once he condescended to lean on my shoulder
for a few steps along a wooded path.
Next time I offered, he just laughed.

Funnily enough, two days later
I scalded my own foot: not badly,
but as badly as I dared.
                    It didn't work.
Everyone understood me perfectly.

Bed and Breakfast

They thought he looked like Gregory Peck, of course;
and they thought I looked like Anne somebody –
a name I vaguely recognised: no one special,
not Greer Garson or Vivien Leigh.
What they really must have thought I looked like
was young. But they were being kind;
and anyway, we'd asked for separate rooms.

When it was late enough, Gregory Peck
came into mine – or did I go into his?
Which of us tiptoed along the passage
in our pyjamas? And to do what?
                              Not sex,
but what you did when you weren't quite doing sex.
It made you a bit sticky and sweaty,
but it didn't make you pregnant,
and you didn't actually have to know anything.
You didn't even take off your pyjamas.

Unfortunately since it never got anywhere
it went on most of the night. No sleep.
At breakfast, though, I can't have looked too haggard:
Gregory Peck was not put off.
For that I could thank the resilience of youth –
one of the very few advantages,
as far as I could see, of that hateful condition.
Anne Whatsit might have looked worse;
but then I suppose she'd have had makeup.

Rats

That was the year the rats got in:
always somebody at the back door
clutching a half-dozen of beer,
asking if we felt like a game of darts.

Then eyes flickering away from the dartboard
to needle it out. What were we up to?
Were we really all living together –
three of us? Four of us? Who was whose?

And what about the children? What indeed.
We found a real rat once, dead
on the wash-house floor. Not poison:
old age, perhaps, or our old cat.

We buried the corpse. Our own victims
were only our reputations, we thought –
bright-eyed with panic and bravado.
It can take thirty years to find out.

Stockings

The first transvestite I ever went to bed with
was the last, as far as I know.
It was in the 60s, just before tights.
He asked if he could put my stockings on –
on me, I thought; on him, it turned out.
His legs weren't much of a shape,
and my suspender-belt was never the same
after he'd strained it round his middle.
But apart from that, things could have been worse.
The whisky helped.

I never went out with him again;
and I never, ever, told his secret –
who'd want to? (He must have counted on
the inhibiting power of embarrassment.)
But I still went to his parties.
At one of them I met Yoko Ono.

A Political Kiss

In the dream I was kissing John Prescott –
or about to kiss him; our eyes had locked
and we were leaning avidly forward,
lips out-thrust, certain protuberances
under our clothing brushing each other's fronts,
when my mother saw us, and I woke up.

In fact I've never kissed an MP.
The nearest I got was a Labour peer
in a telephone box at Euston station
(one of the old red kiosks –
which seemed appropriate at the time).
But I don't suppose that counts, does it?

An Apology

Can it be that I was unfair
to Tony Blair?
His teeth, after all, are beyond compare;
but does he take too much care
over his hair?

If he were to ask me out for a meal,
how would I feel?
Would I grovel and kneel,
aflame with atavistic socialist zeal?
No, I'm sorry, he doesn't appeal:
he's not quite real.

In the House he sounds sincere,
but over a candlelit table, I fear,
his accents wouldn't ring sweetly in my ear.
Oh dear.

I'd love to see him in No. 10,
but he doesn't match my taste in men.

Festschrift

Dear So-and-so, you're seventy. Well done!
Or is it sixty? It's a bit confusing
remembering which, of all my ageing friends,
is the one about whose talents I'm enthusing.

I'm getting on myself, a fact which makes one
occasionally vague – as you may know,
having achieved such venerable status;
although in you, of course, the years don't show.

Anyway, I'm delighted to contribute
to the memorial volume which your wife –
or publisher – is secretly arranging
to mark this splendid milestone in your life.

As one of your most passionate admirers
I'm glad to tell the world of my conviction
that you've transformed the course of literature
by your poetry – or do I mean your fiction?

Oh dear. Well, never mind. Congratulations,
from a near contemporary, on your weighty
achievements; and you'll hear this all again
in ten years' time, at seventy – sorry! eighty.

Offerings

A garland for Dame Propinquity, goddess
of work-places, closed circles and small towns,
who let our paths cross and our eyes meet
so many times in the course of duty
that we became each other's pleasure, and every
humdrum encounter a thundering in the veins.
We place at the hem of her fluted marble robe
this swag of meadow flowers, picked nearby,
as much a bribe as a thank-offering,

asking her to smile on our extensions
and elaborations of what she began.
And now, to be on the safe side, a recherché
confection of orchids and newly hybridised lilies
for her sister, Lady Novelty: not to leave us.

Danger: Swimming and Boating Prohibited

This tender 'V' of thighs below my window
is one end of Kuba's mother,
sprawled for the May sun in her bikini.
I hardly know her face. 'Ku-baah!' she calls,
and scolds him drowsily in Polish.

Kuba's off with his bikie friends,
the big boys, old enough for school.
'Ku-baah!' they shout. Their accent's perfect.
They bump their tyres in circles over the grass,
towards and then away from the glinting water.

In winter, I'm told, the swans come up
and tap their beaks on the windows, begging.
Today a lone brown female mallard
waddles quacking forlorn parodies
of a person doing duck imitations.

Kuba tries to run her down.
She flaps off, squawking, back to the Broad.
It's a rough male world down there;
the drakes are playing football hooligans,
dunking each other, shamming rape –

well, what else is there to do
while their sober mates are hatching eggs?
Only one brood's appeared so far.
I count the ducklings every day:
eight, five, four, still four (good!), three . . .

I'll go and check again in a minute.
'Grow up!' I'll tell them. 'Hang on in there!'
Downstairs the front end of Kuba's mother,
a streaked blonde top-knot, pokes out of a window.
'Kuba!' she calls again. 'Ku-baah!'

Risks

When we heard the results of our tests
we felt rather smug (if worried);
we said to each other loudly in public
'Well, that's it for space-travel;
we mustn't go up there again.
We can't afford to be bombarded
with any more radiation, dammit!'

No more risks: that was the policy.
In which case what are we doing here
scrambling along this rocky gorge
with hardly a finger-hold to bless us,
and the bridge down, and a train coming,
and the river full of crocodiles?
(I think I invented the crocodiles.)

Blue Footprints in the Snow

But there's no snow yet: the footprints
are made by a rubber stamp, a toy
I daren't give to a child. (Warning:
'Ink not guaranteed to wash out.')

First the gale, and now the rain,
and soon the sleet, and then the footprints.

The TV weather map is stamped
with rows of identical cloud-shapes,
each dangling two white crystals
and striding briskly south from Scotland.

But the feet are close together, jumping
kangaroo-hops on a white page.

We thought we were stuck on Crusoe's island,
marooned in summer, dry and stranded
under clouds that would come to nothing –
or nothing anyone could want.

Earth-based, earth-bound, paper-bound,
we had to play with toy footprints.

Now, though, prophetic silhouettes
emerge from a computer to bless us.
The clouds leap up; the crystals fall
and multiply on roofs and gardens.

The feet are lifting off the page
to bite blue shadows into the snow.

Summer in Bucharest

We bought raspberries in the market;
but raspberries are discredited:

they sag in their bag, fermenting
into a froth of suspect juice.

And strawberries are seriously compromised:
a taint – you must have heard the stories.

As for redcurrants, well, they say
the only real redcurrants are dead.

(Don't you believe it: the fields are full of them,
swelling hopefully on their twigs,

and the dead ones weren't red anyway
but some mutation of black or white.)

We thought of choosing gooseberries,
until we heard they'd been infiltrated

by raspberries in gooseberry jackets.
You can't tell what to trust these days.

There are dates, they say, but they're imported;
and it's still too early for the grape harvest.

All we can do is wait and hope.
It's been a sour season for fruit.

1990

Moneymore

Looked better last time, somehow, on a wet weekday
from under an umbrella – rain
blurring my lens and rinsing the handsome faces
of the Drapers' Company buildings, lights on early,
golden glimmers in puddles, cars growling
at each other over parking spaces –

than on this mild and spacious Sunday afternoon,
no car but ours parked in the High Street
by the painted kerbstones – white, blue, red, white, blue,
with lads loafing in front of the Orange Hall
and an old woman, daft in the sunshine,
greeting strangers: 'How are you? How are *you?*'

Oh, yes, and that parked van outside the Market House . . .
but time's up; I've a plane to catch.
If we take the Ballyronan road
we shan't see Magherafelt, a town I've always
wanted to visit; where ten hours from now
another van will discharge its sudden load.

The Voices

The voices change on the answering-machines:
not the friend but the friend's widow;
not the friend but the other friend.

'I'm not here' the machine tells you.
'This is the job I never did –
this fluent interface with the world.

He/she did it; but I'm learning.
Now all the jobs are mine or no one's.
There's no one here. Leave a message.'

Willow Creek

The janitor came out of his eely cave
and said 'Your mother was a good swimmer.
Go back and tell her it's not yet time.'

Were there no other animals in Eden?
When she dives under the roots, I thought,
an eel is the last shape she'll want to meet.

Her brother was the one for eels: farm-wise,
ruthless about food. You roll the skin back
and pull it off inside out like a stocking.

He grew up with dogs, horses and cattle.
She was more at home with water and music;
there were several lives for her after the creek.

In one of them she taught my younger son
to swim in the Greek sea; and walked through Athens
under a parasol, to buy us melon.

Fruit for the grandchildren; nectarines and pears
for the great-grandchildren; feijoa-parties . . .
'There's more of that to come,' said the janitor.

'But no more swimming. Remember how she plunged
into a hotel pool in bra and knickers,
rather than miss the chance? She must have been sixty.'

I had some questions for the janitor,
but he submerged himself under the willows
in his cavern where I couldn't follow –

you have to be invited; I wasn't, yet,
and neither was she. Meanwhile, she's been allowed
a rounded segment of something warm and golden:

not pomegranate, paw-paw. She used to advise
eating the seeds: a few of them, with the fruit,
were good for you in some way – I forget.

Long life, perhaps. She knows about these things.
And she won't let a few eels bother her.
She's tougher than you might think, my mother.

Giggling

I mustn't mention the hamster's nose –
it sets you off. You giggle like Auntie Lizzie
forty-odd years ago, when she was your age:
heading for ninety. Great gigglers,
you and your mother and your aunt.
They were white-haired and well-padded;
you were too skinny for a mother,
we thought, with our teenage angst,
afraid of turning into you.

'It just struck me funny,' said Auntie Lizzie,
' – that old drunk in his coffin
with all those flowers. I got the giggles.'
Her comfortable shoulders heaved
as yours do, now that you're her shape.
She lived to a hundred and three,
blind and deaf at the end, but not to be fooled:
when her daughter died, she knew.
I hope you'll be spared that extremity.

Of course it wasn't the hamster's nose:
that's just shorthand. It was the fireman's;
he'd given it the kiss of life,
and the hamster . . . oh, well, never mind –
you know the story. You're off again.
I never guessed old age was so much fun.

Trio

Julia has chocolate on her chin,
and isn't getting far with the cut-out stick
they've given her as a bow. It doesn't matter;
the music's there, behind her serious eyes.

Lily's in her knickers and a sweater
passed down from Oliver, who hated it,
her shiny hair glinting above her shiny
half-sized (or is it quarter-sized?) violin.

Oliver's playing his cello: he knows how;
and that's not all he knows about: he made
the cardboard fiddle – bridge and strings and struts
and curves, a three-dimensional miracle

of Sellotaping – for Julia to play at
playing like Lily, and for family harmony.
Soon, after her birthday, when she's four,
she'll have Suzuki lessons and the real thing.

The Video

When Laura was born, Ceri watched.
They all gathered around Mum's bed –
Dad and the midwife and Mum's sister
and Ceri. 'Move over a bit,' Dad said –
he was trying to focus the camcorder
on Mum's legs and the baby's head.

After she had a little sister,
and Mum had gone back to being thin,
and was twice as busy, Ceri played
the video again and again.
She watched Laura come out, and then,
in reverse, she made her go back in.

NEW POEMS

(2000)

Easter

On the curved staircase he embraced me.
'You've got a ladybird in your hair.
Without hurting it, come closer,'
one of us said, in a daze of dream.

But I thought we were in Jerusalem?
– That is indeed the name of this city.
It would be difficult to wind down further
below the ground than to this cave of birth.

All the best dreams have a baby in them.
Year after year I give birth to my son.
Clutch him in his blanket, close in your arms;
the chill from the walls burns colder than marble.

30 March 1997

High Society

Here, children, are the pastel 50s for you:
everything, even to Bing Crosby's trousers,
is powder-blue – if it isn't petal-pink,
like Grace Kelly's cashmere sweater.

The name of the song is 'True Love'.
We may have crooned it over your cradles.
The name of the age was 'Innocence Incorporated'.
We bought it, along with the first LPs.

Why do you think we turned out as we did? –
We, your parents, that is. You turned out OK:
you didn't have to rebel against it;
you were only just being conceived.

We dressed you in pink or blue,
popped nipples into your mouths (we were big on breast-feeding),
and cigarettes into our own (same thing),
then went to the next party. The jazz was good.

Now you're rebelling against our rebellions.
You haven't been married as often as us.
Your kids have shrugged and taken to computers.
We worry about them; it's what we do these days.

Our parents worried about our divorces
(so Hollywood!) and then embarked on their own.
But we've had enough of Technicolor;
after all, we were conceived in black and white.

For Meg
(*i.m. Meg Sheffield, 1940–1997*)

Half the things you did were too scary for me.
Skiing? No thanks. Riding? I've never learnt.
Canoeing? I'd be sure to tip myself out
and stagger home, ignominiously wet.
It was my son, that time in Kathmandu,
who galloped off with you to the temple at Bodnath
in a monsoon downpour, both of you on horses
from the King of Nepal's stables. Not me.

And as for the elephants – my God, the elephants!
How did you get me up on to one of those?
First they lay down; the way to climb aboard
was to walk up a gross leg, then straddle a sack
(that's all there was to sit on), while the creature
wobbled and swayed through the jungle for slow hours.
It felt like riding on the dome of St Paul's
in an earthquake. This was supposed to be a treat.

You and Alex and Maya, in her best sari,
sat beaming at the wildlife, you with your camera
proficiently clicking. You were pregnant at the time.
I clung with both hot hands to the bit of rope
that was all there was to cling to. The jungle steamed.
As soon as we were back in sight of the camp
I got off and walked through a river to reach it.
You laughed, but kindly. We couldn't all be like you.

Now you've done the scariest thing there is;
and all the king's horses, dear Meg, won't bring you back.

A Visiting Angel

My angel's wearing dressing-up clothes –
her sister's ballet-skirt, her mother's top,
some spangles, a radiant smile.

She looks as if she might take off
and float in the air – whee! But of course
you've guessed: she's not an angel really.

Her screeches when you try to dress her
make the neighbours think of child abuse.
She has to be in the mood for clothes.

Once, for the sake of peace, when she wouldn't even
part with her soggy night-time nappy,
I took her to the shops in her pyjamas.

And what about the shoe she left on the train?
But then she sat like Cinderella,
serene and gracious, trying on the new ones.

Has she been spoilt? Her big sister,
no less pretty, gave up the cuteness contest
and settled for being the sensible one.

It's tough being sister to an angel
(a burden I bore for years myself),
but being an angel's grandmother is bliss.

I want to buy her French designer outfits.
Madness. It would be cheaper and more fun
to go to Paris. So we all do that.

A special deal on Eurostar.
Halfway there, she comes to sit beside me
on Daddy's knee, and stares into my face.

'Fleur,' she says thoughtfully, 'I love you.'
Wow! That's angel-talk, no doubt of it.
Where can I buy her a halo and some wings?

It's Done This!

(*for Mia, Kristen and Marilyn*)

Help! It's hidden my document,
and when I try to get it back,
tells me it's already in use.
It keeps changing the names of my files.
Why won't the Edit Menu appear?
It takes no notice of me. Help!

'You have made changes which alter
the global template, Normal. Do you
want to save them?' Oh, please, no –
what have I altered? The ozone layer?
Help! But Help refuses to help;
the message goes on glaring at me.

There are some things you can't cancel –
or, if you have, you wish you hadn't.
'This may damage your computer.'
What may? 'Windows is closing down.'

But Windows isn't. Who can I ring
to rescue me, at nearly midnight?

Somehow, between us, we survive,
even though I've lost page 4
and all the margins have gone crazy.
What if I've bought the wrong scanner?
What if my printer's rather slow?
I'm getting rather slow myself.

It's nearly midnight once again,
and Windows isn't closing down –
nor do I want it to, just yet.
We're in it together. So be it.
I'll sit here, at the end of an age,
and wait for the great roll-over.

Kensington Gardens

Droppings

Poetry for the summer. It comes out blinking
from hibernation, sniffs at pollen and scents,
and agrees to trundle around with me, for as long
as the long days last, digesting what we discover
and now and then extruding a little package of words.

Poetry Placement

They suggest I hold court in the Queen's Temple
(hoping it doesn't smell of urine).
Too exposed, I say; no doors or windows.
We settle for a room by the Powder Store (1805):
where else should poets meet but in a magazine?

Peter Pan

What was the creepiest thing about him?
The callousness? The flitting with fairies?
The detachable shadow? No,
that feature that was most supposed to entrance you:
the 'little pearls' of his never-shed milk-teeth.

The Fairies' Winter Palace

Queen Caroline, I think, planted these chestnuts
with their spiralling ridged bark. In another world
Peter and his freaky friends claimed this hollow one,
capacious enough for several children, if they dare,
to stand inside, holding their breath. Don't try it!

Heron

A seagull on every post but one;
on the nearest post a heron.
Is he asleep? Stuffed, nailed to his perch?
He hunches a scornful shoulder, droops
an eyelid. Find out, fish!

Handful

Now that there are no sparrows
what I feel landing on my outstretched hand
with a light skitter of claws
to snatch up a peanut and whirl off
are the coloured substitutes: great tits, blue tits.

Jay

A crow in fancy dress
tricked out in pink and russet
with blue and black and white accessories
lurks in a tree, managing not to squawk
his confession: 'I am not a nice bird.'

*

Sandy

A cold day, for July, by the Serpentine.
She brings us up to date on her melanoma:
some capillary involvement, this time.
Just here is where her grandparents first met.
She still hopes to finish her family history.

*

Aegithalos Caudatus

Don't think I didn't see you in the apple tree,
three of you, hanging out with the gang, your long tails
making the other tits look docked; and in the roses –
all that dangling upside-down work – feeding, I hope,
on aphids. Come any time. My garden's all yours.

*

Birthday Card

This Winifred Nicholson card for my mother's birthday,
because she loves Winifred Nicholson's work –
or did, when she had her wits. Now, if all that's forgotten,
she may at least perhaps like it, each new time
it strikes her: 'That's nice . . . That's nice . . . That's nice.'

*

Polypectomy

'You need a bolster,' said the nurse, strapping a roll
of gauze under my nose, when my dressings threatened
to bleed into my soup. I sat up in bed
insinuating the spoon under my bloody moustache
and crowing internally: after all that, real life.

Butterfly Food

The Monarch caterpillars were crawling away,
having stripped bare the only plant they could fancy.
We raced to the Garden Centre for two more,
and decked them with stripy dazzlers – lucky to have hatched
in NZ and not in the GM USA.

Checking Out

In my love affair with the natural world
I plan to call quits before it all turns sour:
before the last thrush or the last skylark,
departing, leaves us at each other's throats,
I intend to be bone-meal, scattered.

Goodbye

Goodbye, summer. Poetry goes to bed.
The scruffy blue tits by the Long Water are fed
for the last time from my palm – with cheese, not bread
(more sustaining). The chestnut blossoms are dead.
The gates close early. What wanted to be said is said.

DRAGON TALK

(2010)

To the memory of my mother
Irene Adcock, née Robinson
(1908-2001)

Dragon Talk

How many years ago now
did we first walk hand in hand –
or hand in claw –
through Alice's Wonderland,

your favourite training ground,
peopled with a crew
of phantasms – Mock Turtle, Gryphon –
as verbal as you?

Your microphone, kissing my lips,
inhaled my words; the machine
displayed them, printed out
in sentences on a screen.

*

My codependant,
my precious parasite,
my echo, my parrot,
my tolerant slave:

I do the talking;
you do the typing.
Just try a bit harder
to hear what I say!

I wait for you to lash your tail
each time I swear at you.
But no: you listen meekly,
and print 'fucking moron'.

*

All the come-ons
you transcribed as commas –
how can we conduct a flirtation
in punctuation? –

Particularly when,
money-mad creature,
you spell doom to romance
by writing 'flotation'.

*

I can't blame you for homonyms,
but surely after a decade
you could manage the last word
of Cherry Tree 'Would'?

Context, after all,
is supposed to be your engine.
Or are you being driven
by Humpty Dumpty?

*

I take it amiss
when you mis-hear the names
of my nearest and dearest;
in particular, Beth.

Safer, perhaps, if I say Bethany.
Keep your scary talons
off my great-granddaughter:
don't call her 'death'.

*

You know all the diseases
and the pharmaceuticals:
bronchopneumonia,
chloramphenicol

are no trouble to you,
compulsive speller,
hypochondriac,
virtual dealer.

*

You're hopeless at birds:
can't get wren into your head –
too tiny, you try to tell me:
it comes out as rain or ring.

Let's try again: blackbird, osprey,
hen, (much better), kingfisher, hawk,
duckling. But I have to give up
and type Jemima Puddleduck.

*

What am I thinking of,
dragon bird?
How could I forget
that you too have wings?

Fly to me;
let me nuzzle your snout,
whisper orders, trust you
to carry them out.

*

Do I think of you as 'he'? –
Beyond male or female;
utterly alien,
yet as close as my breath –

invisible, intangible,
you hover at my lips –
am I going too far?
Are we into theology?

*

Animal, vegetable or mineral?
Who's playing these games? –
Abstract, with mineral connections
and a snazzy coat of scales.

Gentle dragon, stupid beast,
why do I tease you?
Laughter's not in your vocabulary:
all you understand are words.

*

Today I saw you cresting the gable
of someone's roof: a curly monster
smaller than me, but far too large
to hide yourself inside a computer.

They'd painted you red – was that your choice?
But this was only your graven image.
Your private self was at home, waiting
for reincarnation through my voice.

My First Twenty Years

Kuaotunu

This is the schoolhouse at Kuaotunu,
on the hill, with Daddy's school next door,

and this is my little red watering-can;
I've just been splashing some dirt with it.

In the kitchen is Jammy Jean,
washing the dishes; Mummy's sitting

on the verandah, feeding the baby.
I'm the big sister now; I'm two.

The fireguard is made of blackboard
for me to chalk on. I'm drawing a face.

Inside my head I can see it clearly,
but my fingers won't do what I tell them.

It turns out to be a round patch
of scribble. It looks more like the world.

Linseed

The knees I'm embracing through her skirt
are Grandma Robinson's; above them
is a dark blue jumper, a bit scratchy.

I can just reach it. I must be three.
She's trying to sweep the kitchen floor,
and I'm tripping her up. She's not cross yet.

There's some linseed boiling on the stove –
tiny brown jellies, with seeds in them.
I can't be expected to know what for.

The milk she squeezes out of the cow
turns into butter when she churns it.
Life's mysterious, but I'm used to that.

Illiterate

That gaping boredom before I learned to read –
sitting on the sheepskin rug, wailing
'Mummy, I don't know what to do!'

(The baby asleep, no one to play with,
no kindergarten until the morning,
and no idea when the afternoon would end.)

'Why don't you do some colouring in?' she'd say.
'Here are the crayons' – except I thought she called them
'crowns', like what the King wore on his head.

It was sometimes hard to get a grip on words.
That snail bread, for example: I watched her slice it,
waiting for the knife to expose a shell.

There was always something new to puzzle out,
and old stuff to unlearn (the singular
of matches, it turned out, was match, not 'matcher').

Thank God Chicken Licken came along,
a year or two later, to rescue me.
Life makes a lot more sense when you can spell.

Food

Spanish cream, cloudy with beaten egg-white,
standing in a cold bath until it jells;
stewed prunes in a bowl in the pantry;

butter in the safe, except for some
left on the table; I climb on a chair
and am caught raiding it. (I like salt.)

My favourite meal is mashed potatoes,
with gravy or with a buried treasure
of butter to find. I don't mind cabbage.

Once, as an experiment, I bite off
a chip of apple and ram it up my nose.
What pain, until it shrivels and falls out!

And yet how superior I feel
coming in from the sandpit to report
'Mummy, Baby's eating sand again.'

Lollies

The only chocolate I still like
is crisp and dark as the shards of Easter egg
my father shared with me when I was four

outside in the caravan: a treat
to keep me quiet, and avoid disturbing
the household so early in the morning.

We were not brought up to eat sweets.
'If someone offers you lollies,' they told us,
'say no, thank you, they're bad for my teeth.'

Little prigs, we obeyed at first.
Only later, in England, did they relent –

if something's rationed, you must be allowed it.

But back there in pre-war New Zealand
sweets were medicinal: barley sugar
if you felt sick in the Baby Austin,

or for me, after the surgeon
had scraped the flesh off my poisoned finger,
bribes to let my mother change the dressing:

a choice of pastel-coloured cachous –
mauve, pink, pale-green or lemon – powdery
and perfumed like a handkerchief sachet.

Rangiwahia

When the kitten got its head stuck
in a cream-jug Mummy ran across
to a plumber laying drains next door
at the school. He slid his tin-clippers

beween the enamel neck of the jug
and the soft, furry neck inside.
Out shot the kitten, up a drainpipe
and into our memories for life.

The other scene presented to me
for my retention was the earthquake.
It made the playground ripple, they said,
pointing out into the dark.

But I was too sleepy, snatched from bed
and clutched under a safe doorframe;
my focus wouldn't open out
further than their wondering faces.

My own chief marker for the place
was nothing visual; it was the wind

moaning in the telegraph wires
as I hung swinging on the gate –

bored, waiting for Daddy to come
from the school for tea; hearing the sky:
the loneliest music in all the world.
How could air make you feel so sad?

Drury Goodbyes

What with getting in the way of the packing
and not being allowed to go to
the big event, Great-granny's funeral,

we found something silly to do, and did it:
we sat the new dolls on the potty
after we'd done wees in it ourselves.

Next day we were going away in a boat
so big that you could stand up in it,
they said, and it wouldn't tip over.

There was no time to dry the soggy dolls;
they were left behind – all but my Margaret,
who wouldn't bend enough to dunk her bottom.

3 September 1939

Hindsight says we were in the Red Sea,
heading for Suez. Late afternoon;

sultry, I guess. I woke up half dazed
to a flurry in the darkish cabin:

that being-late feeling, Mummy in a rush.
She trotted us to the empty dining-room.

'We fell asleep and missed the children's dinner,'
she said. They rustled up a meal for us –

turkey minced in some kind of sauce –
as they told her 'That's not all you missed.'

A fricassee, I think, is what you'd call it.

Sidcup, 1940

I was writing my doll's name on the back of her neck
when Mummy caught fire — a noisy distraction.

She was wearing a loose blue flowered smock
(an old maternity smock, I now deduce,

from her pregnancy with my sister four years earlier,
being used as an overall, not to waste it);

the hem flapped over the hearth she was sweeping,
and caught on a live coal from last night's fire.

I tore myself away from writing 'Margaret'
to save her life. 'Lie down, Mummy!' I said,

and helped to smother her flames in the hearthrug.
So much is memory. The rest was praise:

What a good girl, how sensible, how calm!
But 'how well-taught' is what they should have said.

She saved her own life, really. She'd made sure
we knew fire travels upwards, and needs air.

After all, this was the 'phoney war' –
she was waiting for all of England to catch fire.

My First Letter

Dear Mammy [Auntie's spelling, I suspect:
a Leicestershire phonetic transcription
from my still slightly New Zealand accent,

soon to be lost]. *We sat on the platform*
three times last Sunday. We did like it.
We go to school. We like to go to school.

That's all, apart from half a page of kisses
and a rather fine drawing on the other side.

What was it we liked, then, exactly?
Sunday School? Did sitting on the platform
make us important? We certainly liked school –

or I did; Marilyn was not so keen,
but she was only four. And we liked the farm,
and our new Auntie and Uncle, and Betty and Jean.

We liked Mummy, too – and Daddy, of course –
but they weren't there. You can't have everything.

Ambulance Attendant

What happened to that snapshot of my mother
in her grey Ambulance Service overcoat

and a tin hat, her gas-mask hanging
from a diagonal strap across her chest?

It wasn't flattering. She may have burnt it,
out of vanity. Too late: I can still see it.

All she ever told us about that year
was the tale of how they parked over a time-bomb –

unscathed, of course; a big joke, afterwards.
But the picture grows clearer by the minute:

the double row of buttons; the pockets;
the collar; her determined chin.

Off Duty at the Depot

There stands my father in ARP overalls
with his arm around a plump blonde lady.
They are both holding tennis racquets;
their heads are tilted towards each other.

Who took the photo? Some colleague of theirs,
no doubt – you can see the depot behind them.
Not my mother. But 'Auntie Joan'
ripened into a friend of the family.

Later, when I was eleven or so,
she came with presents for Christmas. Mine
was *The Rubaiyat of Omar Khayyam*.
I found it totally seductive.

Just in Case

'If anything happens to us,' they said,
sitting down with us at the farmhouse table
on one of their rare visits from the Blitz –

'it won't, of course – don't worry – but if it did
you'd go back to live in New Zealand
with Auntie Alma'.
                    Why Auntie Alma?

Couldn't we go to Grandma and Uncle Len
and Auntie Cynthia and Rose and Don?
Couldn't we just stay here?
                              Apparently not;

it was Auntie Alma with her rimless glasses
and Uncle Leslie and his stamp collection.
What a good thing nothing happened!

Fake Fur

Instead of a teddy there was Bobby, my dog.
I hugged him bald, and his legs went wobbly:
you could see the folded straw inside the cloth.

Later, when I could sew, I covered him
in white satin, trimly stitched to fit,
with black velvet for the perky terrier tail:

perfect, up to the shoulders – at which point
my creativity failed. But the eyes, I thought,
serene in the threadbare face, forgave me.

A Rose Tree

When we went to live at Top Lodge
my mother gave me a rose tree.

She didn't have to pay for it –
it was growing there already,

tall and old, by the gravel drive
where we used to ride our scooters.

No one else was allowed to pick
the huge pale blooms that smelt like jam.

It was mine all through that summer.
In October we moved again.

But even never seeing it
couldn't stop it from being mine:

one of those eternal presents.
At the new house I had a duck.

Glass

On the bus, you added up the numbers
on your ticket: if they came to 21
that meant you were going to get a sweetheart.

But if you walked to school, you might be able
to add to your collection of coloured glass:
rubies and sapphires; bits of saints and martyrs.

Casein

The knife handles were made out of milk,
my mother said: like cheese. I thought of the skin
on cocoa, and had to believe her;
the handles looked creamy, after all.

But when it came to buttons, that was harder;
and knitting-needles – so many colours,
and that smooth, clicky feel against your teeth
when you tapped them: all made out of milk.

Teeth were quite interesting, too.

Glitterwax

That winter's craze, in 1943:
slabs of the greenest green, the frostiest white,
all colours the most intense and shiny.

You warmed them in your hands, and genius flowered.
I fashioned a perfect snowdrop, on a stiff wire –
bell cup, green dots. You could mould anything.

It was the apotheosis of modelling clay:
silky as poison, the plasticine of the gods.
Yet the world has decided to live without it.

Bananas

The first banana I'd seen for years
was at school assembly, tenderly swaddled
in cotton wool. Someone's father

had brought it home on leave with him.
The raffle tickets were 6d each,
for the Red Cross. I forget who won it.

The next was sliced and drowning in custard –
'Auntie' Lena's way of stretching it.
Sacrilege. But then this was a woman

whose husband left his clothes by a river
to get away. (A dozen years later
he popped up alive, and she took him back.)

Not that I knew all this at the time;
but even before the banana, you could
tell by her corsets she had no taste.

Clay

Just before we left the farm by the brickworks
Peter Jackson smashed my clay tea-set,
thus ensuring that I'd remember him for ever.

Each lumpy cup, saucer, jug, plate or bowl
I'd fashioned out of the beige-blue squelchiness
had taken days to bake hard in the sun.

No time to make more; our holiday was over.
My mother, coming to collect us, said:
'It will all be the same in a hundred years'.

I quoted it back at her after the first fifty –
still unconsoled. But now, too late to tell her,
I give in. So it will, Mother. Clay crumbles.

The Mill Stream

And what was the happiest day I remember?
It was when we went to the Mill Stream –

my sister and I and the Morris kids.
We wore our bathing-suits under our dresses

(subterfuge), crossed the live railway lines
(forbidden), and tramped through bluebell woods.

There was a bridge with green and brown shadows
to lurk among in the long afternoon.

Chest high in the stream, with pointy water-snails
as escorts, I could hardly believe my luck.

Happiness is chemical. Sunshine and water
trigger it. (And I couldn't even swim.)

Morrison Shelter

Marilyn was frightened of snakes, mostly –
quite convinced a boa-constrictor lurked

under the eiderdown, or perhaps just
a nest of adders. I was full of scorn:

even real snakes didn't bother me –
and how could they have got into her bed?

My own nightmares (fewer – I was older)
were about ghosts: doors couldn't keep those out.

Oddly enough, being in bed with Mummy –
that outgrown childhood remedy – did the trick.

It also worked for pythons in the blankets.
So when we all slept in the table shelter

nobody woke up screaming. After all,
being scared of bombs was just for grown-ups.

Direct Hit

I
The way they told it to us at the time,
if he hadn't swapped his day off with a friend
to come home for his birthday, he'd have been killed.

But the friend, unlike our father, was not a driver,
and therefore hadn't run to where the cars were
when he heard the siren, and was thus not killed.

So that was all right, or not so bad – until
you thought about it, which they hoped we wouldn't:
somebody had to run and start the cars.

II
The way he told his parents, two weeks later:
'Times have been quite exciting. Fortunately
I still have my lucky star and am safe and sound.

Our depot, however, was completely demolished,
which explains why this letter is not typed . . .
I have lost both my cars but they will be covered

by war damage insurance . . .' Typewriter? Cars?
No word of people? – Not while it's still going on.
But on the day after his next birthday,

June 1945, one sentence:
'Just a year ago today I was helping
to dig my friends from the debris of the depot'.

III
So who was killed? They're in the *Kentish Times*
('FLYING BOMBS HIT SOUTHERN ENGLAND.
First-Aid and Rescue Service Depot Destroyed'):

Mrs W. Symes; Miss L. Hancock;
Mr B. Hopwell; Mr E. Ingram;
Mr Norman White; and a messenger named Smith.

Mr Dolman

My mother, dusting Mr Dolman's parlour
in the winter of 1944,

misplaced one of his Staffordshire dogs
by an inch or two. 'Oi keeps ee thur !'

the old man snarled, as he moved it back.
Thirty years later, 'Oi keeps ee thur',

I'd say to my son as he searched for something.
Thirty more years, and the Wiltshire burr

resounds again in Andrew's own house,
away in a different hemisphere –

washing the dishes, I hold up a jug:
'Where does this go?' 'Oi keeps ee *thur*'.

Do his daughters think of it as merely
something Dad says, or will they confer

another generation of currency
on a soundbite uttered they don't know where

by someone their grandmother's family lodged with
for a month or two in the Second World War?

Tunbridge Wells Girls' Grammar

Even snow not being what it was,
the crumbly stuff they grant us nowadays
can't match the shapely stars that hypnotised me

as they posed on my navy woollen coat-sleeves
for long enough to distract me from caring
whether or not they made me late for school.

Frant

Bliss cottage, in retrospect:
woods just across the road, a duckpond
in the field behind, cowslips . . .

even at the time we loved it.
Living in Sussex, going to school in Kent:
how travelled we sounded!

I had my eleventh birthday there:
books, and cake for tea in the back parlour
we rented from Mrs Gain.

We all used the big kitchen
with the range whose lid she lifted one day
when Stanley Gain (about my age,

but a boy, unfortunately)
came in dangling from a long stick something
murkily white with loops at each end:

'What's this, Mum?' 'I don't know; give it here' –
into the sizzling coals. He smirked and left.
She clanked the lid, and honoured me

with a complicit glance, as if
I were old enough to use things like that
or know what name she'd call them by.

Biro

Always one for a new invention, my father
was much taken with the clever device
he brought home to show us, early that spring:

a ballpoint pen. Where did he get it?
It was 1945. You couldn't buy one.
But the RAF were issued with them

for use at high altitudes – or so I read now.
He used to lecture to forces personnel
in the south of England. Case solved – I think.

Woodside Way

'When are we going back to Woodside Way?'
No answer; or 'Not just yet; we'll have to see.'

We couldn't make them grasp how much it mattered:
a quarter or so of our lives in one place –

and one with actual woods at the end of the road
to make free with, and friends living nearby.

It was as if a few Doodlebug raids
had jolted them into forgetting the word 'home'.

We'd moved to Scalford, Corsham, Chippenham, Frant,
and finally (a name from the past) Sidcup –

five changes of school in less than a year –
before they confessed: we had a new home now.

Woodside Way went on without us. Our friends
had other friends. New people lived in our house.

Surely they could at least have taken us back –
one little outing by train – to say goodbye

to the Morrises, and Edna and Diana
and the others, and the house itself, and the woods,

and the field beside them, ploughed for victory
each year, and Middle Bush, where the owl roosted?

Sidcup Again

Had we become suddenly posh, then, living
in this enormous house in Hatherley Road
with three storeys, rambling cellars, outbuildings,
and a garden that was an orchard as well?

Not quite. There were also Mr and Mrs Ash,
and Miss Miller, and Mr and Mrs Curtiss
and Mr Ferris – all at the same time –
and others now and then to be squeezed in.

We never knew where we'd be sleeping next:
upstairs at the back, downstairs at the front,
or al fresco in the coach house or stables
(roofed, it's true, but each of them short of a wall).

One winter our parents took to the cellar.
It was the kind of thing New Zealanders did –
unlike the Burtonshaws across the road;
nobody else lived in their house but them.

My sister and I were fond of Miss Miller
(a teacher), and the Curtisses were friendly.
They invited us to tea; we had shrimps
for the first time, and played with the baby.

Mr Ferris, who was a friend of theirs,
had a thin moustache, and looked like a spiv.
One evening he and Mr Curtiss fell out
and tumbled down the stairs in a violent clinch.

I didn't see the gun they were grappling over –
my mother screamed at me to stay in my room –
but I heard the police arrive. (Poor Marilyn
was asleep, and missed it all). No one was shot.

Mr Curtiss's thumb was broken. Mr Ferris
crawled on the floor to search for his gold tooth.
A bit of an anti-climax. Still, it was all
quite fun. I hope the Burtonshaws were jealous.

August 1945

After queueing sixteen hours for tickets
he brought us to the land beyond the war.

In Donegal he came in with a newspaper.
'They've split the atom!' And then he explained.

When VJ Day happened we were in Dublin.
Our landlady gave us some kindly advice:

'Best not to wear red, white and blue rosettes –
they might get torn off, and your lapels with them.'

Even so, when we went to the pictures –
'The Commandos Strike at Dawn' – and the camp guards

hoisted the swastika, we still couldn't quite
believe our ears when the audience cheered.

Signature

It was not sensible to write my name
by dragging my feet through the ankle-deep snow
on the playing-field – it clotted in my shoes
and short white socks. Think of the chilblains!

But I was thirteen, and sensible only
intermittently; and this famous winter –
arctic, rattling with icicles – was my last
in England; and I didn't want to leave.

On the SS *Arawa*

Torn away from England at thirteen,
like Juliet from Romeo, I dreamed
a plane swooped on the deck to whisk me back.
No chance. I had to look for distractions.

I read the entire Bible at a gallop
in five weeks (skipping the minor prophets).
I learned to swim. I wrote a comic play,
and we put it on (tickets a penny).

I found an actual Romeo, a steward,
to moon over. One night the other kids
persuaded him to kiss me, while they giggled:
not ideal, but something for my diary.

That was the kind of stuff it flourished on,
together with our exotic ports of call –
Curaçao, with bananas galore
and Dutch currency; polyglot Panama.

The doll I made for Marilyn from a pair
of pink knickers featured; and our quarrels.
I didn't mention (though I still remember)
what songs the crew's accordion used to play

on the afterdeck, those tropical evenings;
or the green-black sea and the tempting rail;
or how, in spite of Louis's Italian eyes,
my dreams were still of Surrey, Wiltshire, Sidcup.

Unrationed

I
My diary of our holiday in Ireland
is full of references to being sick.

It also describes a series of breakfasts:
eggs, bacon, fried bread, brown bread with real butter –

more grease in one meal than our weekly ration.
You'd think I might have made the connection.

II
'Legs like pea-sticks,' the aunties complained,
welcoming us home from austerity
with bulging tea-trolleys of cream sponges.

'We'll fatten you up.' Cream, butter, cheese:
New Zealand's dairy industry set to –
and failed. Fat legs were not my destiny.

The Table

What they should have taken back to New Zealand
was the oval walnut dining-table

picked up for almost nothing during the Blitz
when antiques were no one's priority:

the smoothest, most colourfully-grained,
prettiest slab of wood we ever ate off.

Once or twice, when the Doodlebugs came,
we even slept with our heads under it,

before our Morrison shelter was delivered.
But no; they took the piano instead.

It was her choice (although the table had been
hers too: her lucky find, her gleeful purchase;

he was far too busy to go shopping,
and only home on leave one night a week).

Was she trying to say she was the person
who, for a couple of years during a lull,

had a plate beside her door with letters on it
(LTCL, LRSM, etc),

and not just a furnisher of tables?
But New Zealand was full of pianos.

Back from the War

A bit over the top, I thought, the lectern
my grandfather presented to the church

(St John's, Drury – proud of its bullet-holes
from what we could still then call the Maori Wars):

'A thank-offering from Mr and Mrs S. Adcock
for the safe return of their son . . . and family . . .'

After all, we hadn't been to the front.
A few air raids, and none that struck home, were all.

Bad enough when Grandpa, standing beside me
in the pew, decided to sing falsetto.

Now here I was, implicitly included
('and family') in his embarrassing monument.

Well, I grew up. And it's gone now, the lectern –
replaced by a brass eagle, though the plaque survives.

A pity; I'd have liked another look at it.
I rather suspect the dear man made it himself.

Temporary

Adelaide Road was not a good address –
we didn't mention it at our new schools –
but it appealed to our taste for squalor.

Poverty was romantic. Was this it?
The cabin trunk we ate off, seated on boxes,
would suggest so, and the bare floorboards.

Sausage curry with potatoes and carrots,
our staple dish (though our mother afterwards
always denied it) seemed appropriate too.

My sister even relished the hot whiffs
of toffee or peppermint oozing up
from the sweet factory downstairs.

Our parents had a bed. We had inflatable
army surplus lilos, joined-up tubes
of smelly rubber with lives of their own.

It was easy to slip off on to the floor
where Marilyn's dolls were ranged for their schooling,
ready to lose their English accents.

Strangers on a Tram

I was on a tram going home from school
when who should get on it but my mother,
wearing the brown tweed costume Mrs Dowle
passed on to her before we left England.

This wouldn't have been so bad except that
she'd let the hem down because Mrs D.
had said skirts were going to be longer.
Well, if so New Zealand had not yet heard.

Mothers were supposed to be stout, with grey hair,
and not go around predicting the New Look.
There were some girls on the tram I sort of knew.
I pretended this woman was a stranger.

Amazingly, she pretended the same
(apart from giving me a furtive wink).
How dare she have the cheek to understand me!
It was hard to work out what to resent.

Her First Ball

For the school dance I wore a circular skirt –
full length, and a full-circle swirl of apple green;
I bought the pattern; my mother made the frock.

But what to do with my hair: so little-girlish,
too long? Auntie Phil came up with a green snood
and an Alice-band on which (her brainwave)

she pinned sprigs of daphne – most waxen-petalled,
extravagantly-scented of real flowers,
from the bush by our door – to intoxicate,

as it turned out, my classmate Dell's very tall
brother Ken, who danced with me all evening,
his nose hovering above the honeyed wafts.

After my friends' lunchtime coaching in the gym
I managed the quicksteps and foxtrots all right,
even in gold sandals (we all wore gold sandals).

As for underneath, I'd been given no option:
Phil and my mother had tracked down in some shop
a pair of kneelength, scratchy woollen drawers

to protect my kidneys from chills, they insisted.
I was too naive to see at the time
what it was they really wanted to guard.

Precautions

I sat on the stairs and fiddled with something
as my mother braved the pre-wedding chat:

it seemed you wrote to a doctor in Christchurch
who would send supplies under plain cover,

and – well, that was it. Struck dumb by the notion
of parental sex, I asked no questions.

We never wrote to the dubious doctor,
nor did Alistair slink into chemists' shops.

In fact we did nothing much at all;
and only after my first baby,

when my GP decided to fit me
with a diaphragm, and explained what it was,

did I get the point of my friend's grim saga
about her trek from doctor to doctor

before her wedding, being turned away
as immoral, until she found the one

who slashed her hymen with surgical scissors –
she haemorrhaged all over the couch.

At least we hadn't had that problem.

Miramar

Miramar? No, surely not – it can't be:
the cream, clinker-built walls, the pepper tree,
the swan-plants under my bedroom window . . .
But if it is, I'll open the back door
to the sun porch, with its tang of baked wood.

You'll be lying propped on the shabby couch,
writing; you won't be pleased to see me,
home from school already, with my panama
and my teenage grumps, though you'll pretend
you're a gracious mother, and I a loving daughter.

After the chiropractor's fixed your back
and growing up improved my temper,
we'll learn to be good friends for forty years,
most of them spent apart, vocal with letters:
glad of each other, over all the distances –

until this one, that telescopes your past,
compacting the whole time from postwar England
to your present house into a flattened slice
of Lethe; tidily deleting my teens
from your tangled brain; obliterating Miramar.

Summer Pudding

Dare I assume I'll remember the summer pudding
I made last week with a heap of mixed berries
and shiny red currants? It was the first for years.

My mother used to make them during the war
from hedgerow blackberries and the sugar ration,
saved for the purpose, with top-of-the-milk for cream.

And then she forgot. Not just the occasions,
but the method – the bread-lined basin, the small plate
for a lid, with a weight on it; the lot.

She came across the recipe, when she was old,
and announced 'I've made my first summer pudding'.
It was to be for Christmas, the following week.

But she'd made it too early. It sat in the fridge
getting soggier and more slimy. When the day came
we ate it, to please her. It was disgusting.

Lost

She is prowling around the flat
all night, looking for the children.

Her granddaughter comes and tells her
they are safely tucked up in bed.

'No, not your children,' she says, 'mine.
Where can they be? I can't find them.'

By daylight she finds us often:
two grown women, in our sixties.

Only in her dreams are we lost,
as sometimes she was lost in ours.

But what if we had found her then,
when we were still her little girls –

woken up in the night and found
a 90-year-old great-granny

crying out in our mother's voice,
and no mother to comfort us?

That Butterfly

(i.m. Irene Adcock, 1908-2001)

It's true about the butterfly –
a peacock, no common tortoiseshell –
that surged in through my open window.

You were in your coffin in New Zealand.
I was here, in my hot London study,
trying to get my voice to work

as Marilyn held the telephone
over your dead face. You couldn't wait:
you fluttered in at once to comfort me.

You were no showy beauty, dear mother,
but your personality was bright rainbow,
and your kindness had velvety wings.

An Observation

Walking about from room to room
to find the source of all this moonlight
I notice I can still remember
the rules for the declension of adjectives
after the article in German:
'der volle Mond; ein voller Mond' –

and there it is, in front of the house,
not even halfway around it yet
but shining full and flat into my eyes;
which means it can't be as late as I thought
(not much past 3 a.m., it turns out);
and I am still a day off 70.

Outside the Crematorium

Flirting with death, after my third funeral
in a month, I chat with the undertaker,
a dashing figure in his designer beard
and frock-coat. He was at school with my son.

They used to play in his father's workshop.
'One day I'll come here in my coffin,'
I tell him. 'I'd like you to see me off.
Andrew will arrange it. How's the family?'

The last stragglers have viewed the flowers
and are drifting towards their cars. The vicar
has apologised to me for the 'poem'
he read with such professional gravity.

Some of my neighbours are walking home –
Peggy was local (the pet-shop lady).
The sun is shining calmly. I could almost
get used to this death business – except

that our last funeral was for a baby,
whose grandmother has just been telling us
how she helped to wash and dress her for it,
and how hard it was to get her vest on.

A Petition

Lord, let me learn to love
the pumping station at the edge of the wood
where the wild arum lilies grew.

Help me to welcome loft extensions,
and in particular the one replacing
the roof where the housemartins always nested.

Teach me the charms of the neighbours' cat
who slaughtered our thrushes, widowed the robin,
and wiped out all the dunnocks, one by one.

Convince me that a hedge of Leylandii
and some grass are better for the frogs
than the pond that seethed with tadpoles every spring.

Make me a devotee of Health and Safety,
hostile to trees (you never know,
their branches might fall off on someone).

Let concrete be my favourite colour,
and petrol fumes my drug of choice,
that I may live happy in my skin.

To the Robins

Innocent receptacles of my love
which I convey in the form of mealworms
when I can get them, or at other times
disguised as tiny morsels of cheese,

I gaze into your eyes, one at a time,
and you gaze back, trying to predict me,
lurking hopefully on the windowsill
but ready to fly if I turn nasty.

Your love is only for each other.
It is embodied mostly in food;
what you really like is 'courtship feeding' –
beak to beak, as if posing for 'Springwatch'.

When he jumped on you (at this point the pronoun
bifurcates from dual to singular),
my fellow female, he was off in a second.
You quivered with astonishment for minutes.

You definitely preferred the foreplay –
the chocolates and champagne, as it were;
in view of which, accept my platonic
offering: a bowl of little wrigglers.

A Garland for Rosa

Skype

More technology, and it brings me Rosa,
captured in mid-scamper by a parent
to wave hello to her London grandma.

'Baby,' she says, in an almost French accent –
the pure vowels of the novice talker,
although she's a New Zealand child: 'Bébé!'

What she sees is her miniaturised self
in the lower left hand corner of the screen;
and in the centre, wistfully beaming, me:

to whom she's half blowing a kiss – it's planted
on her hand, but she forgets to throw it;
and I can't quite reach to it through the glass.

Rosa Mundi

Dear Rosa, twenty years before I knew
that one day there might be someone like you
I planted this: a rose with which you share
part of your name – as also with 'the Fair
Rosamund'; the rose of the world, it means.
The colours are pinks, whites, reds and in-betweens,
all mingled. Roses come in many types,
but how could I resist one that has stripes? –
a bit like Milly-Molly-Mandy's dress

and a bit like a long-ago princess.
You'll see it one day. But although I'm fond
of the rose, you might prefer what's in the pond
beside it, flicking its slender tail: a newt,
a miniature dragon. What could be more cute?

Fenlanders

These are the fens.
And suddenly I half expect

the ghosts of your local ancestors
to flap up, hooting,

out of the black soil
some of them helped to drain.

How will they be disguised?
Geese, will they be? Snipe, mallards?

Two centuries ago
when all this was water

they were hatched around here.
Their very names have wings:

Samuel Spinks and his grandmothers
Anne Bird and Elizabeth Sparrow.

(I am not making this up,
and you are too young to think it odd.)

Perhaps they'll waddle in
kitted out in bills and feathers

with fluffy, strokeable breasts.
Would you like that, my little ducky?

Fast Forward

Holding the photograph of Mary Ellen,
my great-grandmother the midwife,
to gaze more closely at her face,
I see on my desk behind the frame
another picture, in another frame:
my blonde granddaughter holding her baby.
They are standing in a doorway,
just off to a lecture on *Beowulf.*

Suddenly a rushing of wings
as the generations between accelerate
like a fan of pages riffling over
or like the frames that rattled past
as I swooped into the anaesthetic
for my tonsillectomy, when I was nine.
Face after face, all with our imprint,
humming forwards. We can do anything.

GLASS WINGS

(2013)

For Gregory and Andrew

At the Crossing

The tall guy in a green T-shirt,
vanishing past me as I cross
in the opposite direction,
has fairy wings on his shoulders:
toy ones, children's fancy-dress wings,
cartoonish butterfly cut-outs.

Do they say gay? No time for that.
He flickers past the traffic lights –
whoosh! gone! – outside categories.
Do they say foreign? They say young.
They say London. Grab it, they say.
Kiss the winged joy as it flies.

Traffic swings around the corner;
gusts of drizzle sweep us along
the Strand in the glittering dark,
threading to and fro among skeins
of never-quite-colliding blurs.
All this whirling's why we came out.

Those fragile flaps could lift no one.
Perhaps they were ironic wings,
tongue-in-cheek look-at-me tokens
to make it clear he had no need
of hydraulics, being himself
Hermes.
           Wings, though; definite wings.

For Michael at 70
Michael Longley, 2009

I wish I had a gift for you to match
those packets of ghosts I used to send you
when I was teasing out your ancestry:

the Kentish farmers in their Wealden hamlets;
your great-grandfather, the 'Wood Reeve' –
or 'Peasant' (no apparent irony)

on a certificate; his son Charles Longley,
born in chocolate-box Chiddingstone, married
in Lambeth, propelled there by history.

It urged them all to London, in the end –
these, and your tobacco pipe makers
from Bucks – to change their lives, and link up with

your other lines: the Dorset brickmakers
(who must have talked, we think, like William Barnes),
and from Somerset the horsehair weaver

Henrietta (whose farm servant mother
her master took advantage of, she hints);
and that arch-Londoner and shape-shifter

William Braham: son of an engraver
born who knows where, and himself an artist,
jeweller, commission agent in the City,

pawnbroker – (conman, I suspect) – fit forbear
for your artist daughter, or for anyone
in the risky trickster trade of poetry.

They flit among their demolished streets, dodge
into unlit doorways, or slither behind
a hedge or haystack. They are shy of us.

All I can do is call them up again
to marvel at the poet they've produced.
Here are your ancestors. They don't explain you.

An 80th Birthday Card for Roy

Roy Fisher, 2010

Happy birthday! I'm sorry this is not
that clutch of long-tailed tits you always wanted
or a melodious charm of goldfinches.
They would certainly fly more gracefully
than my stumbling public-private poem
(you know how tricky such commissions are –
although you'd bring to them your customary
elegance, intelligence and wit).

In any case, you're doing all right for birds:
swallows dashing out from under your eaves,
thrushes and a blackbird both nesting
outside your kitchen window.
                                        Here, I see,
I should slip in a flattering metaphor
about your lyric voice. It wouldn't be apt:
your poems are not songs; they are to think with.
Thank you for them; and not for them only.

I could start reminiscing – Arvon courses,
Bucharest, Burton Dassett, the Marsden hat –
but you know all that; and it's your birthday.
Happiness, we've agreed, tends more and more
these days to be bird-shaped. For a present,
if I can manage teleportation,
I'll zoom a pair of kingfishers your way;
or a golden oriole; a Phoenix.

Finding Elizabeth Rainbow

i.m.

Elizabeth Rainbow was lurking under the earth
a few yards from the west door. Someone
had scratched a window into the shallow turf
over her fallen gravestone. I called to Joyce –

Joyce was alive then – and she went to fetch you,
halfway to the car (you could still walk then).
You plodded back, this time with a gait
that almost demanded the word 'sprightly'.

That woman with the posse of children called them –
the little gigglers, the skinny black girl,
the teenager with cornflowers on his straw hat –
and they scrabbled at the soil like a pack of terriers.

Elizabeth was nestled into the ground
like the church itself, with its organically
sloping floor. We'd given up too soon.
You leaned on your stick just feet from your ancestor.

The clods flew, I knelt to copy down
the rest of the inscription as it emerged,
Joyce clicked her camera; the sunlight was on us all.
These were the glories of Burton Dassett.

Spuggies

The spuggies are back –
a word I lifted from Basil Bunting
and was never entirely sure how to pronounce,
having only seen it in print, in *Briggflatts*,
and at the time had little cause to adopt
with the London sparrow in extinction;
but now three are cheeping in my lilacs.

The other word I learned from Basil Bunting
he spoke aloud, the last time I met him:
'bleb', meaning condom – as used, he said
(to his severe disapprobation)
by 12-year-old girls on the Tyne & Wear
housing estate where we were calling on him.
I think they asked him if he had any.

Fox

Our old fox creaks into the garden,
a rusty shadow. He finds a patch of sun,
curls up for ten minutes; dozes.

Then suddenly he's bounding into the air,
leaping on imaginary frogs in the periwinkle
and snatching intently at the lawn.

What can he be chewing in his long, long jaws?
I peer from the bedroom through binoculars.
Grass. I shall never understand him.

The Saucer

Round here I saw a flying saucer once
on a sultry night like this: July, still light.
I was walking with my gaze fixed on the moon
over the rooftops when it loomed: the classic

flattened dome, almost a cartoon version.
I tracked it all along Fortis Green,
to the High Road. No one else seemed to see it;
normal people don't look up at the sky.

I marched after it among dawdling couples.
A man came out of the chip shop, munching;
I was tempted to clutch him as a witness –
but you don't, do you? And it moved so fast,

scooting low to the south over Highgate,
then out of sight. An advertising gimmick,
I told myself: a motorised balloon,
some kind of airship; not worth mentioning.

But now I think of the disappointed creatures,
wistful in their skyborne chapter house,

as they chugged back to the mother planet
taking whatever they had brought for us.

The Belly Dancer

Across the road the decorators have finished;
your flat has net curtains again
after all these weeks, and a 'To Let' sign.

I can only think of it as a tomb,
excavated, in the end, by
explorers in facemasks and protective spacesuits.

No papers, no bank account, no next of kin;
only a barricade against the landlord,
and the police at our doors, early, with questions.

What did we know? Not much: a Lebanese name,
a soft English voice; chats in the street
in your confiding phase; the dancing.

You sat behind me once at midnight Mass.
You were Orthodox, really; church
made you think of your mother, and cry.

From belly dancer to recluse, the years
and the stealthy ballooning of your outline,
kilo by kilo, abducted you.

Poor girl, I keep saying; poor girl –
no girl, but young enough to be my daughter.
I called at your building once, canvassing;

your face loomed in the hallway and, forgetting
whether or not we were social kissers,
I bounced my lips on it. It seemed we were not.

They've even replaced your window frames. I still
imagine a midden of flesh, and that smell
you read about in reports of earthquakes.

They say there was a heart beside your doorbell
upstairs. They say all sorts. They would –
who's to argue? I don't regret the kiss.

Ingeburg

Putting it in a poem is no use,
but she won't see it on the Internet
(she's blind) or hear it on the radio,
drawn to her attention by some friend –
last time we spoke she had none; even
her late husband's boring niece had died.

An old, blind, bad-tempered, scholarly
Jewish widow with a German accent,
half-paralysed, stuck in a born-again
Christian care home in small-town Canada.

Except that now she's gone. No, not dead, and
no, they couldn't tell me any more.

No doubt they thought I was after her money.

                          *

Exactly how was she so irritating?
Being bossy (well, she was a teacher);
befriending and pestering my parents;
interfering; forcing me (thank God)
to study Greek.
                          But mostly it was that
I didn't care for being doted on.

Not just 'the best student she'd ever had'
but my 'funny little nose pressed against
the windowpane' that day we spilt the ink,
Diane and I, on her front room carpet
while she was out. The flat stank for weeks
of the milk we sloshed on so it wouldn't stain.

Fancy forgiving me for that!

Of course she scored points with us for her 'secret'
affair with a married professor; we found
the hypocrisy most entertaining.
(My father knew him; he spoke at my wedding).
And after a while we all moved on,
she and I to live in different countries.

                              *

I've not spoken to her for eighteen months.
What would I want, if I could track her down?
To know she's all right – or whatever
constitutes being 'all right' for someone
of ninety-four, other than being dead,
which in her state of health would be my choice.

I'd like to hear her voice. I'd like to know
if there's anything I can send her.
I'd like to apologise.

I'd quite like to be forgiven again.

Alfred

i.m. Alfred Robinson, 1861-1934

Suddenly I've outlived my grandfather:
the one for whom I was unique, his only
grandchild, although eleven more were to come.

An infant bundle on his bedside rug,

I must have heard the not yet fathomable
murmurs of his farewell to my mother.

'Tell her about me when she's older,' he said.
She did better than that: she gave me
his complete Shakespeare, 1928,

bought the year after, on Shakespeare's birthday –
just the kind of thing I might have done.
The print is tiny, to my ageing eyes.

Thirty-seven plays, in eight-point type.
I read them in my teens, lying on the carpet
in my bedroom, and ticking them off as I went:

Hamlet (tick), Macbeth (tick), Henry the Fifth (tick) –
goodbye, Grandpa   The Tempest (tick) – thank you –
and the sonnets, of course; and Romeo . . .

Match Girl

She grew up, the little match girl;
leapfrogged a century, survived,
became my little sister: small-boned
and slender still, but breakable.

When she had measles I was there;
I remember her chickenpox,
her whooping cough, her grumbling appendix,
and when she ran into the barbed wire.

But how can someone younger than me
have osteoporosis, and sit
googling up a substance that might
help it, or give her phossy jaw?

Phosphorus. It can strengthen brittle
bones – or turn them into rubble.

Alumnae Notes

Beautiful Ataneta Swainson is dead.
I had a crush on her when she was a prefect
(hers is the face that swims into my head

when Katherine Mansfield's Maata is mentioned);
and Barbara Murray, my fellow cyclist
and fan of Rupert Brooke, has dementia.

The class photos fade. But Marie and I,
face to face on Skype in full colour
and still far too animated to die,

can see we've not yet turned to sepia.

Nominal Aphasia

On the bus, 'mirage' was waiting for me.
I had left it there on my way out, dodging
under the seats, refusing to be collared,

lurking among 'deception' and 'illusion'
and 'fantasy' and 'phantom' and, I confess,
'oasis' (you can see the logic there).

It was in a dim, swimming, sandy turmoil
of desert vistas. I couldn't even get
that it might begin with 'm', or be French.

But the minute I stepped aboard, going home,
the word skipped briskly into my head,
impatient at having been kept waiting.

Walking Stick

Parading on the pharmacy carpet
as I try out the height, I'm taken back
to the time I bought my first high heels
(brown suede, with little bows, if you must know);
walking with something new is a knack.

I can still see Grandma Adcock's pursed lips.
'Never mind,' whispered Mother; 'once in a while
it's nice to buy something your grandmother
disapproves of.' Well, this respectable
piece of apparatus is just her style.

'It's only temporary,' I say – 'a sprain –
you know these rough pavements – I had a fall.'
Yes, temporary this time.   But who's fooled?
The stick's a folding one, in a plastic case.
I'll keep it hanging ready in the hall.

Macular Degeneration

For a start, I'm fairly sure they're not swans:
too many (this is not Coole Park),
although flapping such wide white underwings.
Also too squat.   Are they geese, perhaps?
If I could work out the scale; if they were
closer . . . Or what about seagulls?

All this restless taking off and landing
doesn't help; it's a very broad pond –
more a lake – and they're on the other side.
I need something to measure them against:
that moorhen, for example, bumbling around
(these glasses are useless) – unless it's a coot?

Now they're off again, wheeling and swooping,
waterskiing. If only they would

kindly stop all this buggering about
and proceed calmly in my direction.
The light's not too good for judging colours.
Settle down, damn you! I think they're ducks.

Mrs Baldwin

And then there's the one about the old woman
who very apologetically asks the way
to Church Lane, adding 'I ought to know:
I've lived there since the war.' So you go with her.

This comes with variations, usually leading
(via a list of demented ancestors)
to calculations of how much time you've got
before you're asking the way to your own house.

But it's not so often that you find the one
about how, whenever you hear of someone
diagnosed with cancer, you have to hide
that muffled pang that clutched you, at fifteen,
when you saw Pauline Edwards holding hands
with the boy from the Social Club you'd always fancied.

Charon

Where is Dr Shipman when we need him
to ferry us across the fatal stream
and land us gently in Elysium?

Shipman, boatman, ferryman – whatever
the craft he plies to help us cross the river –
we seem to have been waiting here for ever.

How did we get the timetable so wrong?
Things are becoming vague, and we're not strong.
Life was OK, but it went on too long.

When we've forgotten how to keep afloat,
scoop us up, Doctor, in your kindly boat,
and carry us across the final moat.

Having Sex with the Dead

How can it be reprehensible?
The looks on their dead faces, as they plunge
into you, your hand circling a column

of one-time flesh and pulsing blood that now
has long been ash and dispersed chemicals.
The half-glimpsed mirror over their shoulders.

This one on the floor of his sitting-room
unexpectedly, one far afternoon;
that one whose house you broke into, climbing

through his bathroom window after a row.
The one who called you a mermaid; the one
who was gay, really, but you both forgot.

They have all forgotten now: forgotten
you and their wives and the other mermaids
who slithered in their beds and took their breath.

Disentangle your fingers from their hair.
Let them float away, like Hylas after
the nymphs dragged him gurgling into the pool.

Robert Harington, 1558

Get you, with your almain rivetts (latest
fad from Germany), and your corselet,
and your two coats of plate! How much harness

does a man need? None, when he's in his grave.
Your sons may have it, together with your
damask and satin gowns to show off in;

while you go to lie down in Witham church,
and the most armour I've seen in a will
rusts or turns ridiculous in this world.

Anthony Cave, 1558

One monument to her dear Antony
was not enough. Even his will allowed for
two: 'no sumptuous pomp,' he said, but
a stone 'of no great value' in the north aisle

and 'a picture of death upon the wall.'
It hovers above him, engraved in brass,
a skeleton trussed in a transparent shroud
like a polythene bag: '*So shall you be.*'

Elizabeth, who would have cradled his bones,
saw all done; and then, as she must,
married twice more – Chicheley was a prize.
Eighteen years later, widowed a third time,

her four daughters dowried and settled,
and the future of the house secure,
she was Anthony's again; and yielded
to a degree of sumptuous pomp.

This is the third monument: of marble –
with caryatids, I'm afraid, and columns.
In front lies a naked corpse, hands clasped
modestly over its parts; above this

a row of kneeling figures – short-lived son
behind him, train of daughters behind her –
and they two, face to face across a desk,
gazing and gazing at each other.

Alice Adcock, 1673

Sitting by the widow's bed, the vicar
made notes: to her sons and her daughter
£2 apiece; to every grandchild
five shillings; her bed and bedding; a chest . . .

Then it began to be all petticoats:
to her daughter, 'my jersey petticoat';
'my petticoat and my hat' (to a friend);
'my green petticoat and the body of

my jersey gown' (to her son Robert's wife);
'my tawny coat' (to her son William);
and (to his wife) 'my ordinary wearing
petticoat and the coat I wear under it.'

Even allowing for the fact
that a petticoat was merely a skirt
and not underwear, this is confusing:
what, in the context, was a coat?

The vicar dutifully wrote it up.
But her brother-in-law, named executor,
flinched from allocating such tricky
female garments and renounced the task.

Instead her son Robert shouldered it –
as he did that of generating,
in their eventual multitudes,
all the subsequent Adcocks in Syston.

Luke Sharpe, 1704

'I, Luke Sharpe of Langham, desiring
that all my children may live together
in peace and love . . . do make
this my last will and testament.

To my daughters one hundred pounds apiece . . .
my son Luke Sharpe my executor . . .'
and then a growl from the beyond: 'My will
notwithstanding the above is that

if my daughter Elizabeth Sharpe
be married to Mr Kempe of Oakham
or any other man without consent
and liking of my executor

she shall have but one shilling for her portion.'
The same goes for Mary, vis-à-vis
Thomas Bodell (not even '*Mr*' Bodell).
I'd like to think she ran away with him.

As for Elizabeth, she knuckled under,
let her brother talk her into a match
with Mr William Lacer of Syston
(she was past thirty); became an ancestor.

William Clayton, 1725

'I give and bequeath to my beloved son
John Clayton all my tools
proper for the trade of a carpenter' –
this among careful provisions
for his two daughters and their families:
a cottage that he's lately rebuilt,
a rood of land each in the common field.

Twenty-three years later, the will
of John Clayton of Syston, carpenter –
half the length, and more perfunctory,
with all that he owns left to his wife, and
after her death to a list of daughters:
Mary, wife of William Adcock,
Elizabeth, wife of John Taylor,
Ann, Katherine, Hannah, Sarah and Jane
Clayton – the seven survivors
of nine female births in a row
uninterrupted by anything male.

No carpentry tools are mentioned.

James Heyes, 1726

To be a prizer is a solemn task –
to value all his Goods, Cattells and Chattells
for a *True and perfect Inventory,*
the stock first: *Two old Cows and two Calves,*
£6 5s, one old Horse, one Colt . . .
assessing his crops – *Wheat and Barley*
upon the ground £8; Oats 5 shillings;
Pottatoes £1.10s (good soil
for root crops now they've drained part of the Mere
around Burscough); *A few garden pulse –*

then his cart and husbandry implements;
and in the house the *Grate & Crow & Tongues*,
the *Rakins and other Iron Geere*,
his *Two Small old brass pans*, his *One brass pott*,
All the Pewter (no need to count it);
his diverse tubs and vessels: *One Eshin*,
One Piggin (let the clerk spell them), *One*
Salting Turnall, One Washing Turnall,
One Stoond (for beer); *One Tresl; Four old Chears;*
One fall board; One Table & the Forme . . .

We recognise these things; we have their like
in our own houses; his *Old Fether bed*
with its Furnature might be one of ours.
We have apprized his every item,
even to the *old Grindle Stone* (sixpence),
but the total, just over £30,
is £4 short of the poor fellow's debts –
and his eldest lad barely come of age,
with three young sisters . . . Well, here is our list,
duly signed. *William Foreshaw. William Prescot.*

Henry Eggington, 1912

'I want no funeral service
in any shape whatsoever . . .'

It may not have been what Eva
expected of her father's will:

'I instruct my executors
(Eva and her brother Thomas)

to have my body cremated
as soon as possible. No flowers

nor black to be worn but simply
taken to the Withington Road

crematorium, and the ashes
scattered to the four winds of the earth.'

*

'And that no person follow my
remains but the executors.'

Eva may have disobeyed him –
she and Nellie were photographed

in black dresses about this time
(unless that was for Marion,

recently dead at twenty-four).
But to follow her father's coffin

I hope she had a winter coat
in dutiful grey, brown or blue,

for a January morning
in Manchester; or a warm shawl.

*

'No one to attend the reading
of my will but those interested'—

that is to say, mentioned in it:
his wife, of course; Thomas, Eva,

James, Nellie, Harry. Not Mary
(who was married to a scoundrel

and far too fond of money herself)
or Willie (what had Willie done?)

The rest set out, obediently
disguised as non-mourners, hoping

their nervous mufti would provoke
no reaction from the neighbours.

*

To have TB at sixty, caught
from nursing a daughter till she died,

and to hear another daughter
(the pet, the youngest) and a son

already coughing the same cough
can sicken a man of playing,

as he once did, Moody and Sankey's
jolly hymns on the harmonium.

Nellie and James would both be dead
within three years (and Willie, too –

of something quite unsuspected).
Meanwhile those who had to do it

incinerated Henry's beard,
his rotten lungs, his broken heart,

his anger, and cast them to the four winds.

William Dick Mackley

For 'general dealer' read 'fence': he served
a year in Warwick jail for receiving
'12 tame fowls, feloniously stolen'.
Arrogant enough to plead not guilty,
he went down for twice as long as the thief.

But yes, he was a general dealer too,
with his scrapyard in Catherine Street
full of everything, or pieces of it –
an embarrassment, no doubt, to Rosetta's
more genteel cousins if they should pass by.

No doubt? But the whole thing rattles with doubts:
was he really, for example, a Gypsy,
or just a besotted hanger-on who
travelled with fairground people, dodged the census
as often as not; lived in a caravan?

Ah, that Diccon-the-Gypsy glamour! Of course
Rosetta fell: married him in Leicester,
seven months pregnant; hawked fish in Swindon
under a false name; buried dead infants
along the way to wherever might be next.

For twenty years the shadows engulf them –
drifting, disguised. Then in 1901
they trundle into town with the funfair –
Ada Ann, their only surviving child,
is a 'travelling shooting gallery'.

Ten years later William is breaking stones,
with Rosetta left in charge of the business,
an entry in the Leicester directory –
The Van, Catherine Street – and her will made
(decades too early). I seem to see her

in shawl and braids on the steps of the van,
smoking a pipe on a summer evening.
(I try to obliterate the pipe; no,
it won't go). But she died in a 'rest home',
smashed up falling from a bedroom window.

William inherited £2,000
(solid money from her solid father?)
and left nearly twice that to his new wife.
Not exactly a Gypsy thing, a will.
And how did Rosetta fall out of the window?

The Translator

(*In memory of my ancestor Robert Tighe, d.1616*)

I
Anne Browne's grandfather, he turned out to be.
No wonder she bequeathed books in her will:
'*Charnocks sermons upon the attributes
and Doctor Burnetts church history*' – these
to a son-in-law; then '*Item I give
to my daughter Hurst my Cambridge Bible.*'

That Bible might have been a clue; first, though,
where was she from: Kirby? Careby? Some small
Danelaw village near the Rutland border
in Lincolnshire. They all sounded the same
to the vicar of St Mary Woolnoth
in London when he married her parents.

But two years later, 1631,
in the register at Carlby, '*Anne Tigh
daughter to John Tigh baptised June vij*'.
John was swallowed up in the Civil War;
during which same commotion Anne married
Samuel Browne of Stockinghall, Rutland.

Carlby, then. But the register patchy,
no earlier Tighe entries, John's mother
buried as her second husband's widow
'Marie Bawtrie' (to be unmasked later).
So who was her first? The Lay Subsidy
returns, for the land tax, surrendered him:

in the 8th regnal year of James I,
'[. . .] Tyghe doctor in Divinity' – first name
obliterated. It doesn't matter;
there was only going to be one match.
The Oxford and Cambridge alumni lists
rolled out his multiple identities:

*'Tighe, Robert, of Deeping, Lincs. BA from
Trinity College, Cambridge. BD and
DD, Magdalen College, Oxford. Vicar
of All Hallows'* (from whose tower Pepys would
view the fire). *'Archdeacon of Middlesex.
One of the translators of the Bible.'*

II
Being him:
sifting through flakes and flecks
of Hebrew; winnowing out
seeds of meaning; choking
on obscurities, the chaff
of mistranscriptions, howlers,
ambiguities, the never-before-seen.

Dreaming it:
the braids of upside-down-looking
words trailing through his sleep,
tripping him up or winding themselves
into suddenly obvious patterns:
truth leaping out;
no room for argument.

But arguing anyway:
someone, Tyndale or whoever,
may have got it wrong –
just this one term,
perhaps, for a beast or a tree;
an odd verb; a tribal name;
a turn of phrase that needed to be recast.

III
After all, they had chosen him for it:
celeberrimus textuarius –
the lad from a dull yeoman family
in Deeping St James, who went to Cambridge
and grew into a 'profound linguist'
(as Fuller has it) – rose to his moment.

After his doctorate, after he left
scholastic seclusion to get an heir,
found a wife and a parish, began to
baptise his own children (most of whom died),
and stuffed the graveyard with plague burials
while the new Scottish King quaked and delayed,

came the call: to join the First Westminster
Company under Lancelot Andrewes
and re-examine an allotted chunk
of the Old Testament. Andrewes himself
took the Pentateuch, with a few yes-men;
Tighe and his fellows broached the histories.

Elsewhere, companies of learned divines
combed their way through the Hebrew and Greek texts
of the remaining Scriptures (without pay –
their other duties had to support them)
for some five years: conferring, reviewing,
meeting again, squabbling for perfection.

Selden relates how they went about it:
one reading, the others interrupting
to correct any fault. It was all done
by voice, testing it on the ear for sense
and euphony. Almost no one took notes.
The great process lies buried in hearsay.

IV
And Robert? No sooner excavated
from the silt of documentary darkness
than he slithers away again: a black gown
among other such around a table,
offering suggestions when the urge impels him
but not, it seems, writing anything down.

We have his signature as vicar
on page after page of the register
at All Hallows; but otherwise
no identifiable word of his:
no letters, no books or sermons,
even his will declared invalid and lost.

He has merged into a composite –
we can make contact with that mind
only in his assent, grudged or willing,
quite often tacit, no doubt,
as the procedural rules enjoined,
to Joshua, Judges, Ruth, Samuel, the books of Kings.

Intestate

What was she supposed to use for ink –
blood? Breast milk? Amniotic fluid?

Too late for those. Too late altogether.
Some things are impossible to write.

Campbells

Elegy for Alistair

(i.m. Alistair Te Ariki Campbell, 1925–2009)

Now he is dead, who wrote
'Now he is dead, who talked
of wild places and skies
inhabited by the hawk' –

thereby captivating
readers and composers,
envious fellow-poets,
multiple admirers

of his romantic looks,
and silly girls like me,
foolish enough to marry
what I wanted to be

before I knew who I was
but wise enough to have chosen
a kind and dedicated
father for our children

who happened as well to have
an exquisite ear and eye
for a rhythm or a phrase.
Beautiful poet, goodbye.

Port Charles

It must have been August. I was nineteen.
My husband and I and our friend John Thomson

hitchhiked for hours, pole-axed by Marzine,
on sick-making bends to that far bay.

The bach was a rustic hut in the bush:
bellbirds by day, and by night moreporks

and an atmospheric trek with a torch
through ferny rustles to the outside dunny.

Alistair pretended to be joking
when he quailed and shuddered; but no: it seemed

we couldn't tease him back into reason.
I had married a man who suffered from ghosts.

He had been a child in the haunted islands
where his parents were buried. Too much darkness.

For me, though, the prevailing spirit
was of something beginning to dawn.

I was prospectively possessed by
the phantom of the yet-to-be-born:

an inconceivable, newly conceived
co-presence, visible so far only

as a coded smudge under my eyes.
Who says you can't be 'slightly pregnant'?

What the 1950s Were Like

As if you'd scarcely even noticed
the lavatory was across the yard
in the wash-house, and you all had to go
outside, day or night, raining or not,
pregnant or not, for every pee;

and since your mother had never told you
tipping in Harpic was not enough,
the lodger had to speak out, fed up
with her teenage landlady, who'd never
learnt to use a lavatory brush.

Student life was one state (Miss Gillon
ruling over her warren of arty youths
at 191 The Terrace), living at home
another. This was a third condition:
student marriage, it could have been called.

Clues: the Festival of Britain curtains,
the record-player, the new LPs,
the no TV (this was New Zealand);
and, with luck, Bohemian role models
calling in on the way home from the pub.

The Royal Visit

I took my baby to see the Queen.
He was not yet born, but she wouldn't wait.
She was wearing an evening gown
of silver brocade, although it was lunchtime;
but then she was opening Parliament.

I had on a maternity smock –
it wasn't the thing to parade your bulge,
even for a respectable woman
like me, married more than a year.
Pregnancy was a little bit rude.

It took five minutes from my house,
facing the bulk of Tinakori Hill,
to Parliament and the sunshiny crowds.
I didn't wave, but the baby inside me
waggled his limbs in a loyal kick.

S.S. Gothic was chugging south
around the coastline to scoop up the Queen
from Bluff on a date long preordained.
Meanwhile biology and hormones
were organising my own rendezvous.

Two months later, when I'd turned twenty
and given birth, I'd find myself chanting
'I've got a B.A. and a B.A.B.Y.'
I could almost believe my life would glide on
with the smoothly oiled timing of a royal tour.

The Professor of Music

Standing behind me at the counter
of that old general store in Molesworth Street
where the National Library now looms,

Freddie Page remarked of my purchases –
a tin of black pepper and a mousetrap –
'What a surrealistic pair of objects!'

Later, on a rare visit to our house,
he teased us for having acquired a fridge.
Could we be getting above ourselves?

But ever since the time when a small maggot
had trekked across the plate of a guest
at our table, from a slice of cold lamb,

I couldn't quite trust our meat-safe;
and we had a young child now; and also
my sister had an opulent Frigidaire.

Coconut Matting

Trying to save our marriage, my parents
laid linoleum over the matting
I'd stitched seam by seam with a curved needle,

and glued fake Formica on my deal table
for a surprise when we came back.
Sterile beige smothered our living-room.

How could they get it so wrong? And how could we
tell them? We muttered some nothings,
and slunk away in different directions.

Let's rush up to heaven right now and cling together,
all of us, in a huddle of sobs,
apologising and forgiving each other.

Epithalamium
(*For Gregory's wedding to Angela, Wellington, 8 December 2007*)

Jetlagged again, I greet my precious firstborn
through the usual haze of 'Am I still awake?'

Our ups and downs, through half a century,
could be described as aeronautical:

though you're the qualified pilot, I'm the one
who, far too often, flew away from you.

Well, here I am again, for yet another
rediscovery of my grown-up son.

Remember when we tootled off as tourists
to the South Island (early '76)?

First the flight to Dunedin (still a treat
for a struggling student – 'All you need is money',

396

you said in wonderment); then the hire car
(I paid, you drove), and off to Central Otago

through landscapes where I'd hitchhiked with your father
a quarter of a century before.

Tracking memories, we constructed more –
I'm thinking of that pub in Alexandra

where the pianist, who turned out to be psychic,
struck up 'Careless Love' before we could ask.

Now you and Angela take off together
in love that's neither flyaway nor careless.

All the best for the future, then, my darlings.
Bon voyage, and many happy landings.

A Novelty

(*For my great-grandson Seth Lucas Campbell,*
born 19 November 2011)

What was the bun they had in the oven?
Another girl for my charm bracelet
of granddaughters and great-granddaughters?
Or a male of the species, crested not cloven:
a son, a lad, a fellow, a fella,
heir to the family name, a princelet,
a chap, a bloke, a joker, a geezer,
a guy, a man-child, a mister, a master,
a chip off the old block for his father,
a grandson for Gregory, a joy
for his grandmothers in their several degrees
to cherish, a new kind of cuddly toy
for his aunts and little cousins to squeeze?
Yes! Ollie and Kirsty have had a boy.

My Life With Arthropods

Wet Feet

I was up to my knees in the slit trench
alongside the common, after tadpoles,
when a miniature crocodile bit my leg.

I exaggerate, of course; it nibbled.
I snatched it off, saw what was in my hand,
and flung it back in the water: a monster.

Much later I learned its romantic name:
damsel-fly nymph – a fit inhabitant,
by the sound of it, for my fairy poems.

Meanwhile my sister and I, fossicking
in the ditch at the end of our garden,
found what some kids told us were caddis-flies:

tiny cylindrical clumps of debris –
leaf litter, chopped stalks, diminutive stones –
that would creep nervously across your hand.

They were grubs, really, naked inside their
cunningly decorated sleeping-bags.
You wouldn't have wanted to undress one.

That the wet and squidgy was a kingdom
of shape-shifters, where anything you found
might have plans to turn into something else,

came as a part of the portfolio
handed from child to child, together with
where best to go scrumping, and the local

version of Eeny-meeny-macka-racka.

Dung Beetle

Not easy to forget, the 'sacred beetle' –
excavator, scavenger, hoarder
of what we all want to be rid of –
a creature, I have to confess,
I've never set eyes on, but read about
indelibly in *The Insect Man*:

it burrowed into my nine-year-old mind,
head down, walking backwards, hind legs
rolling a great ball of shit and instinct
and science wrapped up holus-bolus
for me to store in my own underground
larder and feed on, like a beetle's child.

Caterpillars

In the last August of the war, my
caterpillars died of starvation:
all of them, large or small, green or striped,
the hawk moth one with his spiky tail,
the long floppy ones off the poplar,
the black woolly bear, my favourite
(I kidded myself that he'd escaped).

We'd gone on holiday to Ireland.
I had asked Derek, the boy upstairs,
to feed them. He had full instructions.
He was twelve, a year older than me;
he had seemed all right.
                          But how could I
have entrusted my helpless infants –
sealed in their shoe boxes and jam jars,
each with the right leaves, and totally
reliant on me for fresh supplies –
to a boy, even if he promised?
A boy, no matter which one? A boy.

Stag Beetle

'Dead Baby Stag Beetle' reads the caption
in my illustrated nature diary.
Other pages have 'Bee on Hollyhock
(from life)', 'Fungus (from life)'. The beetle sketch
is pedantically subtitled not

'from death' (too histrionic, did I think?)
but 'from the real one'. More reality
or more biology would have told me
that this was just any dead black beetle;
a juvenile stag beetle is a grub.

If I'd been introduced to one, and known
its future (a small black Spitfire, whirring
through the dusk to clash in armoured battle
over its mate), the scientist in me
would no doubt still have contrived to be charmed.

Praying Mantis

Green as a leek, this unlikely insect
is squatting on Grandma's flowering hedge
in dragon pose, but with long arms folded
under its triangular head, to pounce.

We had to ask its name; no one told us
about mantises – mantids? Mantidae? –
how can you relate to a creature that
doesn't even have a proper plural?

Are they new here, like us? I remember
the house and garden from when I was five,
but not these coloured paper cutouts, poised
silently on unusual foliage.

Grandma and our parents have things to do.
We drift around the orchard, gossiping
about life on the boat – our favourite
stewards; those lavatories in Panama.

Then back to nature study. Why am I
reminded of the Wizard of Oz, when
Jiminy Cricket is more to the point?
We seem to be living in a cartoon.

Flea

One excellent quality of the flea
is its capacity to embarrass,
for example, the wealthy art dealer
who kindly drove you and two of your friends
from Dorset to London, but who wouldn't
acknowledge what you'd caught in his back seat;
his discomfiture will be repeated
until he stops being in denial
and takes the car to be fumigated.

Another pleasure is the fatal crunch
when you compress one between two thumbnails.

Then there's the fun of seeing how they hop
shamelessly from one host to another –
as on the train when a flea you've acquired
by visiting a cat-owning household
jumps from your sleeve to the one beside you.
It seems too late for an apology;
better to pretend you haven't noticed.

The first I ever met were chicken fleas
caught from playing in an empty henhouse;
peering down the front of my vest, I could

watch them scurry off under my armpits.
Auntie's reaction was gratifying.

My own reaction was allergic.

Hoppy

Found on the hillside above Urbino:
a grasshopper missing one long leg,
instantly named by eight-year-old Andrew
and almost as swiftly immortalised
by my camera, once I was back from
running down to our Pensione for it;
during which time he had sat raptly guarding
the small shadow you can still see on his hand:

the tenderness of the future vet, perhaps –
who dropped out, having mistaken his calling;
the future anthropologist, musician,
publisher and family man; the kind child
who was to reveal, as perhaps even then
I should have been able to prophesy,
that of all the gifts blossoming in him
his supreme talent is for fatherhood.

Stick Insects

Sweeping the kitchen floor I scooped up
in the dustpan an angular wiry tangle –
part of my grandchildren's construction kit?
(This was their house). A clutter of dead twigs?
Some kind of three-dimensional puzzle?
That, certainly: a pair of stick insects
locked in complicated sexual congress.

Phasmids. Phasmatidae. Lives devoted to
being something else; relying on dignity,

for want of speed – standing around looking
vegetal, ligneous or metallic.
Once I saw one stalking across a road
by the Botanical Gardens, caught out
behaving for a change like flesh and blood.

These two had risked invading a house
(she the explorer, he clinging piggyback)
until my broom scuttled them. They seemed unhurt
and not at all inclined to disengage.
That part of Karori is green with bush.
I carried them respectfully on the dustpan,
still in their embrace, to a matching tree.

To the Mosquitoes of Auckland
(*On discovering that I am not allergic to them*).

Come, then, mosquitoes of my youth:
feel free to munch me with impunity.
Your forebears, nibbling at my infant flesh,
blessed me with permanent immunity.

Crayfish

Of course with all those legs they're arthropods –
crayfish, lobsters and their armoured ilk.
At school one day a bunch of us nipped out
in our lunch-break and bought a prickly hulk
to have our way with, rip apart and crunch.

It was like eating a pterodactyl –
morally, I mean, in retrospect –
but the sea-drenched jelly when I snapped
a leg from the carapace, cracked it and sucked in
ecstasy . . . no, that's no way to talk.

Think of the blood-orange-pink smashed shards,

the pimpled plates of the exoskeleton,
reduced to midden-debris, wrapped
in newspaper in the prefects' room bin;
think of the handsome creature; feel the guilt.

Archaic, slow to mature, not adult
for ten years, it lurks deep among rocks:
the spiny or rock lobster – the one that lacks
claws. To shock predators when attacked
it screeches with its quavering antennae:

friction, not vocalisation. Moult by moult,
given time, it can grow to the bulk
of a dog. Cilla McQueen said it can walk
all the way across the bed of the Tasman
to Australia, feeler to feeler with its kin.

Slaters

The English woodlouse doesn't curl up
into a neat ball when you touch it
like the slater of my childhood
(your pill bug or roly-poly, perhaps).

It seems a missed opportunity
to introduce more entertainment
into the garden; so thank God
for that other multi-nominal

dome-shaped creature, the ladybird
(ladybug, lady cow, if you wish) –
gloss-coloured, with counting-lesson spots
and its own personal nursery rhyme –

commemorated in my house
by the fridge-magnet Cait left behind
(but has since told me I may keep),
lost under the sofa when she was three.

Ella's Crane-Flies

Dear Ella, this is a gentle plea
for the daddy-longlegs population
that haunts your room. Don't hoover them up:
let me convert you to conservation.

A dozen years ago I might
have told you they were fairies in disguise,
but now that you're of age I'll say
try seeing them as skinny butterflies.

No? It was never going to work;
phobias aren't susceptible to words.
You'll never love the leggy wisps.
But think of the planet; think of the birds.

Insects are edible, even these
fragile flitters in their gossamer dance.
Let them be hunted; shoo them out
through the open windows to take their chance.

Orb Web

My tiger flashing stripy legs
up and down the geometry
suspended in my pantry window,
scurrying over cleats and crossings

or twinkletoes across a guy-rope
to sniff with diagnostic feet
at whatever she may have trapped
in her tensile architecture,

can't comprehend the role of 'pet'
which I try to impose on her
by fending off arachnophobes
and hurling greenfly into her net –

all very sweet if the present tense
were not in this case historic,
referring ('wistfully') to an autumn
back in the decade before last

when half the garden was out of bounds,
zigzagged with no-go filaments,
the omphalos of every web
studded with a hirsute acorn

squatting plumply in the ether;
I had to deflect the window-cleaner
from the front of the house, to save
luscious danglers draped on the panes.

These days the only ones we harbour
are floor-scuttlers with no charisma
or miniatures, indulged in corners,
trawling for midges with formless wisps.

Come back, defectors: find your way
from brambles in secluded thickets;
come, furry-trousered velvet raisins,
come and bedizen my house again!

My Grubby Little Secret

Under armchairs, inside the carpet:
rows of miniature white papooses

in which, when I tugged an occupant,
it stretched into a prehensile thread.

All the chemicals that work are banned;
there was only the vacuum-cleaner,

with its cruel attachments, to mince,
grind and suck up the little victims

together with their woolly foodstuff
into a sickening fluffy mash.

But no one looks under furniture;
I had only to stay in control,

slaughtering on the quiet – until
I found two new nurseries, thriving.

That was it. I'd have the lot stripped out;
enough of this maggoty lifestyle.

I ordered an invented fibre
no moth would touch. There was just the shame . . .

but the carpet fitters were as cool
as a proctology clinic nurse

viewing yet another shy bottom;
they knew half the houses in my street.

In Provence

You know you're not in England when
at siesta time you open
what seemed a sealed pack of biscuits,
take an unguarded bite, and find
you're being bitten in return.

A rush to the bathroom mirror
reveals a sketchy black moustache
inscribed along your upper lip:
the smallest ants you've ever seen,
hotly exacting their revenge.

Well, what did you expect? Vineyards
and lavender-fields accoutred
with nothing more aggressive than
a limelight-hogging swallowtail?
Ants are the maquis. Blame the sun.

Unmentionable

'Crab lice, author's experience of'
is an index entry you won't find
in my not-to-be-written memoirs,

although I could tell a tale or two
about the man who gave them to me
(he left them out of his own such books),

and the far too curious GP
who saw my predicament as a
personal invitation to him;

not to mention my naive young friend,
wearing a woolly hat in summer,
who told us he'd caught some from his wife,

who told him she'd caught them (oh, really?)
from her social work with the homeless.
But in fact I think those were head lice.

Phobia

My little sister fell off a dry-stone wall
when a wasp flew down the back of her dress.

That same summer in Wiltshire, our mother
turned over some pears in a greengrocer's

and suddenly lay down on the floor.
An allergic family; so what of me,

whose face a mere Venetian mosquito
could turn into the Elephant Man's?

For decades I quailed, but was never stung.
I read about anaphylactic shock –

how Susan Hill, barefoot in her bedroom,
stepped on a tiny corpse and nearly died;

how a wasp on his ice cream killed a child.
Would my own death zing in yellow stripes?

It seemed I was destined not to find out,
until one August in a leafy alley

something explosive shot under my hat
and stabbed my forehead just at the hairline.

Nothing happened. I didn't faint, or choke,
or feel ill; what I felt was exultant.

I soared above the pavements all the way
to a pharmacy (for antihistamine,

just in case), barely resisting the urge
to babble like an earthquake survivor.

Blow Flies

If you liked them, how your heart might have lifted
to see their neat trapezium shapes studding
the wall like a newly landed flight of jet
ornaments, the intensity of their black
gloss, with secret blues and greens half-glinting through,
and the glass wings, not so unlike those of bees –

if you could bring yourself; if they occupied
a niche in creation nudged fractionally
sideways –
                because it's not their present forms, it's
their larval incarnations that you can't stop
heaving into view, white nests moistly seething
in a dead pigeon or a newspaper-wrapped
package leaking beside a path (but enough –
the others will kindly absent themselves, please!)

And wondering what, where – under the floorboards
or behind the freezer – suddenly hatched these.

Bat Soup

But it's diluted with sky, not water,
the aerial plankton on which they sup.
Our solitary pipistrelle flickers
over her chosen suburban quarter,
echo-locating, to siphon it up.
It nourishes birds as well as bats –
high-flyers that feed on the wing,
swifts, house-martins – this floating gruel
of hymenoptera, midges and gnats,
thunderbugs, beetles, aphids, flies,
moths, mosquitoes, and flying dots
almost too small to be worth naming.

Some of it swirls at a lower level –
a broth of midges over a pool
at dusk or a simultaneous hatch
of mayflies boiling up from Lough Neagh:
swallow-fodder, and also a splotch
to plaster on any passing windscreen,
though even at speed there's never so much
as of yore; bad news for the food-chain,
but somehow '*ou sont les neiges d'antan*'
sounds too noble a note of dole
for a sullying mash of blood and chitin.
(And we can't hear what the bats are screaming).

Lepidoptera

Before there were butterflies, there was a moth
cupped in my mother's palm for me to stroke
and not be frightened. I remember no fear:
only soft brown fur under my finger.

*

Such light walkers, with such delicate legs
to support the ornate curtains of their wings.
But that's why they need the air to waft in –
and ours they find less wholesome year by year.

Long past summers were frilly with butterflies.
I could stare down from my bathroom window
at peacocks, red admirals, painted ladies:
extra blossoms adorning the buddleia.

Occasional refugees came for shelter,
like the overwintering tortoiseshell
clamped on top of the lavatory cistern
(I had to protect it from the plumber),

and another under the tread of a stair,
camouflaging its closed brown underwings
against the carpet, as if safe on bark.
Sometimes our house was just an extra tree.

The years deleted them. They've left only
one frayed wing in a bowl of foreign coins;
and the great dark moths have gone, that thudded
into the lamps in sulphurous heatwaves.

                          *

Instead I've been given this handsome corpse
from the butterfly house at Lancaster:
Papilio memnon agenor, male form –
the Great Mormon, with its five-inch wingspan,

black as a collage from a rook's feathers,
framed in a three-dimensional surround
from Paperchase, and sent to me by post.
I'd say it has a baleful look about it.

Bees' Nest

Bumble-, not honey-; and not a hive.
Ignore those trim little boxes, fitted
with a glass inner lid for viewing
and an entry tunnel of the right gauge,
in friends-of-the-planet catalogues.

Such things may do the trick for blue tits,
with their predictable minds. This bee
won't be invited into your parlour.
She'll build in your compost heap; she'll squat
in a disused mouse-hole; or she's

a cross noise buzzing inside the lawn
so that you desist from using clippers,
and an ever-larger moss-thatched skull
rises from the earth like the Green Man,
his head crowning, being slowly born.

With luck it will be in a summer
rich with visitors, so that a child
may find herself transfixed by a procession
of bees, all in the house uniform,
popping out of the grass, just like that,

to go browsing in the buddleia
or shove their snouts into yellow toadflax,
until they or their clone-kin zoom back
unerringly to the secret trapdoor
that gives access to their waxen dome.

But you worry that you haven't enough
flowers in your garden to feed them,
and that being more rare now they'll never
come back after this year's nest has sagged
into ruin. And they don't come back.

Dragonfly

In the next life I should like to be
for one perpetual day
a dragonfly: a series of blue-green
flashes over Lily Tarn,
a contraption of steel and cellophane
whose only verbs are dart, skim, hover.
One day is enough to remember.

THE LAND BALLOT

(2014)

i.m. Cyril John Adcock, 1904–1987
and
Samuel Adcock, 1876–1956
Evangeline Adelaide Mary Adcock,
née Eggington (Eva), 1875–1970

Life is real! Life is earnest!
And the grave is not its goal;
Dust thou art, to dust returnest,
Was not spoken of the soul.
HENRY WADSWORTH LONGFELLOW

Life is butter.
Life is but a
melon cauliflower,
melancholy flower.
Life is butter melon,
life is butter melon
cauliflower,
cauliflower.
CAMPFIRE SONG

We had some very happy times at Te Rau-a-moa and
were very fond of our 'Squirrel'.
CONDOLENCE CARD FROM DOSSIE
(DOROTHEA) McMONAGLE, NÉE DASSLER

Where the Farm Was

He is not there/I am not there,
but we are haunting it somewhat,
gliding a few feet above the ground
in perhaps detectably thin air.

I am half-occupying the eyes
of my young father, still in his teens –
much of which he spent, like his schoolmates,
in bare feet on the back of a horse.

Therefore as we scan the horizon
two equine ears (which he doesn't notice,
being used to them) swing up and down
at the lower frame of our field of vision.

Probably he's keeping a lookout
even now for those confounded cattle,
five of them, that strayed into the bush
as in a nursery rhyme. Our conjoined sight

is in his keeping. When I gained access
by wriggling into his optic nerves
it was as a hitchhiker, merely;
he controls direction and focus.

In return I get the benefit
of his 20/20. Distant green froth
resolves into identifiable
trees, with specific leaves. Any minute

beyond the newly brought-in land
(fields, would he still say, or paddocks?)
flickers of movement will solidify
into the birds he never mentioned.

The Sower

In the beginning was the axe, then fire.
The first instalment happened before they came:
his father had arranged for Mr Daysh
to fell fourteen acres of standing timber,
lop off and burn the smaller branches,
and leave an area ready to be sown.

Sam was working dawn to dusk on the house,
but sowing was a job a boy could do.

Into the velvety ash, once it had cooled,
he walked like an image from the New Testament
broadcasting seed from a sack at his waist
in swathes and arcs and parabolas
to bring forth a fresh green beard:
the potash would turn it into a meadow.

That was the second power he harnessed.
The first was his first horse: ha ha!

(You've seen the photograph: a lad of eleven
in knickerbockers, reins in his hand,
posing aloft for the glass negative;
although this was earlier, at Te Rahu –
some special occasion, else why would his father
be standing beside him in a three-piece suit?)

But what do I know? Only what he told us,
and what Sam wrote in that pocket diary.

The Pioneer

The way the land ballot worked was like this:
if your name came up you might be offered
the block you'd applied for or another,
which you had to take, or you got nothing.
Meanwhile you looked for something else to do.

Sam was a master packing-case maker,
but New Zealand made no packing-cases.
His other mastery was hairdressing;
he found a job in Te Awamutu
with a barber called Dwen, and they waited,

renting the teacher's house at Te Rahu
three miles away, befriending the farmer
next door, learning to milk, and waiting, while
ballot after ballot came up null, and
waiting, and buying a horse, and waiting.

When they heard, he rushed hot-foot to see it:
his hundred and fifty acres of bush
at Te Rauamoa, halfway along
the road (if road it deserved to be called)
from Otorohanga to Kawhia.

As if to meet a new mail-order bride
he strode off, perhaps quaking a little
(things turn folkloric if you wait too long).
He went by train to Otorohanga
and then walked – it may have been twenty miles.

At one point he had to cross a river;
unable to swim, he waded through it.
One mile road frontage of native forest,
to be transformed somehow into pasture,
waiting on that mountainside. Up he trudged.

Sam's Diary

I

For 1914, but with an afterlife:
blue cloth binding, falling apart,
the *Order of the Sons of Temperance
Friendly Society* badge on the cover,

the back pages overflowing with
a 40-year palimpsest of addresses,
and those at the front with payments, notes, accounts,
and cryptic visitations from the future.

In the centre months a sprinkle of entries
for 1914 itself, chatty at first:
*June 20: Set sail 2.15,
passed the Welsh coast and Isle of Anglesey*

*where Pilot left us at 7 o'clock;
found two stowaways. Retired 9.30.
June 21: felt bad all day*
[and so on through the Bay of Biscay];

*children very costive, gave castor oil.
June 23: got up feeling better.*
After which life rolled on unrecorded:
Cyril pushing his baby cousin's pram

up and down the deck (not that Sam tells us),
Eva doing whatever she quietly did,
ports flitting by – Las Palmas, Durban –
names only. No mention of the storm

in the Indian Ocean, against which
hatches were battened down and oil poured
literally on the waves – one metaphor
after another brought to life – in vain.

Then on August 8, four days after
the official declaration was made,
News of the war,
followed by silence.

II

Scantling
Rough lining
Clean weather board
Dressed timber flooring

Scantling
Weather bd
Dressed timber
Sills
F boards –

pencil notes ghosting the pages
intended for January 1914.
Then a flutter of dates blown in from elsewhere,
with just enough details to anchor them:

Came to Te Rau Moa Wed May 17
Mr Daysh helped Thurs May 18 – 6 hrs
Frid May 19 – 6 hrs
[and so on to Wed May 24].

These fit the calendar for 1916 –
where suddenly, it seems, we've arrived –
all hands helping to clear the site,
burn off debris and build the house:

the Daysh boys and their father employed
by the hour for such time as they could spare;
the hired carpenter, Bebbington,
for seventeen days running into June;

421

Sam, himself no mean joiner, sawing up
scantling for joists and keeping accounts:

Oilcloth 10 yds 2s 3d	*£1.2.6*
5 yds 2/-	*10.6*
3 ft stretcher & mattress	*17.3*
Enamel	*2.6*
Oats & bag	*7.3*
Bicycle	*£3*

And a bucolic note: *Cow served*
November 21st 1915;
due August 1916. Not long
to wait; she was pregnant when they bought her.

District News: Te Rau-a-moa
(*Own Correspondent*)

A number of new houses have lately been erected here, all the bricks for
the chimneys being burned at the local kiln. Mr Bebbington is erecting a
commodious residence for Mr Murrell. All the timber has been cut and the
joinery made locally.

The timber is already on the ground for Mr Adcock's new house on Pirongia
West junction, the owner intending to reside on his farm at an early date. It
will be remembered that Mr Adcock's land was acquired only a few months
ago from the Crown, it being a locked reserve for nearly twenty years.

The district has other locked lands – about 5,000 acres – partly bush and
partly fern. Blackberries have lately been spreading over these lands at a rapid
rate, and it is hoped the Crown Lands Department will take steps to clear
these weeds or else throw the block open for selection.

The Okoko Valley, where the blackberries grow most abundantly, has for
several years been a favourite blackberrying spot for the settlers for miles
around. This valley, which is richly carpeted with native grass and partly
grown over with native bush, is an ideal picnic ground, and has been used

as such for the last fifteen years. It is a pity a few acres were not cut out as a picnic ground for all time.

WAIPA POST, 31 March 1916

Bedtime Story

But there are no tigers in this forest
to run round and round a tree until they

turn into butter; this is not jungle
but unbroached New Zealand bush, and it is

the trees themselves – rimu, hinau, tawa,
totara – that because they cannot run

will be turned step by step first into ash
then grass, then milk, then, yes, into butter.

I trust no one has any objections?
(Hang around as the century scrolls by.)

The Fencer   (*Cyril speaks*)

'Fencing to begin with was a pragmatic
zigzaggy affair, taking advantage
of the logs lying pell-mell everywhere –

you couldn't walk a dozen steps for logs –
and rolling or stacking smaller stuff to bridge
the gaps between one huge felled trunk and the next.

Once the first grass was up, and we'd made
enough makeshift barriers like this
we could turn the horse out, and buy a cow.

When the time came for proper fencing
you'd saw a log into fencepost lengths
and split them with a maul and wedges.

Not every type of wood was suitable –
put rimu in the ground, for example,
and after five years you could knock it over.

Totara was best, but not a lot grew there;
mostly we had to use hinau; long-lasting,
but fibrous – it wouldn't split cleanly.

You'd knock in wedges, and halfway down the log
meet a cross-fibre snagging it together;
hack through that, more wedges, more knots –

it was half splitting and half chopping.
That was my weekend job year after year,
all the time we were bringing in new land.'

1 ton of no 8 gauge plain wire.
Completed 1 mile = 80 chains of fence.
1 cwt makes 26 chains plain.
1 cwt barbed makes 24 chains.

[Staples, nails and tools not included.]

This Lovely Glen

If, as the story went, it was Eva
who first had the yearning for New Zealand,

perhaps the faintest flicker of a hint
can be extracted from her card to Sam

written *whilst walking through this lovely Glen,*
today thursday is grand, you could [two goes,

424

neither of them correct, at '*imagine*']
it was the middle of summer Cyril

send his love and he wonders what you are
doing and who is geting your dinners . . .

The Fairy Glen was at Colwyn Bay, her
favourite resort where she, much alone,

while Sam worked night and day, went with their boy
on holiday. He played with other boys

on the shrubby slopes near their boarding house.
She walked and dreamed, dare we guess, of forests –

with gravel paths and a small bridge, perhaps
(or is that me, tidying up her dream

to match the scene on the postcard? If so
I take it back. Let her dream her own dreams.)

But how much, once they were on their mountain,
she walked in the landscape they had purchased

is hard to guess. A saunter now and then
around the farm on a summer evening

at Sam's persuasion would not surprise me,
but that she might have made her way alone

(the children at school, bread baked, hens fed, and
no urgent tasks pressing for the moment)

into the moist huddle of the bush to
peer and listen: that would be something else.

Migrants

There had been precedents: not just Alice,
adventuring across the globe to cure
the 'ailments' her father quailed from naming,

or Eva's cousins in Auckland, or Sam's
'Bro Joe', stumped in Australia: 'The men
will not work and the horses have fell bad'.

Further back there were Sam's Aunt Mary and
her husband, Mormon converts, embarking
under sail on the first part of their trek

to the Salt Lake Valley, or Promised Land.
The first afternoon out from Liverpool,
in a storm, their five-month-old baby died.

The Saints were all prostrate with seasickness –
not a woman on board able to stand;
the three Elders had to lay the child out

and stitch her into a sack for the deep,
while Mary writhed in her bunk, clutching her
emptied stomach and full-to-bursting breasts.

Nothing would be worse than this. On they went,
landing in New York, crossing the Great Plains
with Captain Homer Duncan's wagon train –

the wagons being to carry the tents
and baggage, the sick and the very young:
Mary and Thomas and their two boys walked,

their feet festering with poisoned blisters,
a thousand and thirty miles; and what with
diarrhoea and mountain fever and

nervous glances at Indians and wolves,
it was as well they had 'Come, come, ye Saints'
(accompanied on the accordion

around smelly fires of buffalo chips
that the women gathered in their aprons)
to ignite their zeal if it grew tepid.

*

Or, for someone duller, Cousin Joseph,
who waited for the age of the steamship,
zipped across the Atlantic in ten days

to the Pennsylvanian textile trade,
and set Polly, aged 10, and Lizzie, 12,
to earn their livings in a woollen mill.

A Manchester Child

I

Eva's father, Cyril's Grandpa, pierced by
some reminiscent look about the boy,
some aching resemblance, warned them that they

'mustn't try his brain too soon'. What nonsense
to us who know the word 'meningitis'
and that it's an infection, not induced

by arithmetic or learning to read;
who didn't watch that other six-year-old,
Eva's brother, boiling with 'brain fever'

through an endless week of August, and on,
on well into September, to die on
that wilted cliché, Friday the 13th.

II

Too delicate for school, was he? He learned
the strength of the meek: kept them hovering
at the table while he inscribed patterns
into squares of cooling mashed potato.

Sunday school they permitted; it was not
thought to excite the brain too much. At home,
hidden from school inspectors, he picked up
such skills as he could in Grandpa's workshop.

He broke his leg once, playing in the street
with some boys who had a pram-wheeled trolley.
'Tell Daddy he must stick it together
with some jam', wrote Alice from New Zealand.

III

The round-faced, round-eyed lad in a lace-edged
travesty of a sailor collar, with
Norfolk jacket, knickerbockers and clogs,

is seven at last, more than ready to
clop along pavements to Lewis Street School
and begin guzzling up education.

In winter the steel segs on toe and heel
freeze to the snow; he has to pause, and knock
clumps of ice from his soles. Five years later

it is his pony that goes out steel-shod.
No one says this child is too delicate
to ride to school barefoot in rain or sleet.

IV

You couldn't go on being called Cyril,
a name designed only to please parents.
At Te Rauamoa School he got 'Squirrel' –

not that such a mammal existed there
where the chief introduced pests were rabbits,
but the curriculum teemed with fauna

wriggling or scuttling through the imported
literature, snorting in a ballad
or growling in a folk tale. (Euro-what?)

A human compatriot of Kipling
was apparently acceptable too,
even before his accent had flattened.

Baggage

Sealed in their heavy luggage in the hold
they'd brought the encapsulated highlights
of their shed lives: Eva's sewing machine
and her Watteau Doulton dinner service;
Sam's tools, of course; the tea urn his father
had made using his skills as a tinsmith,
learnt in the packing-case trade; some books; the
postcard album bulging with eight or nine
years of miniature correspondence;
and the oval portrait, painted in her
sixties, of Sam's apple-cheeked grandmother
Mary Adcock, née Pell (or perhaps Peel),
in her plaid shawl, who came out of nowhere.

As for the books, they ranged in weight down from
the Bible through Sam's other sacred text,
The Amateur Carpenter and Builder,

to a pocketbook-sized sliver: *Hoyle's Games.*
Packed side by side with Sunday school prizes
(*John Cotton . . . A New Temperance Tale of
Lancashire Life*) was something different:
*The Awful Disclosures of Maria
Monk* (convent, nuns, dead babies): a dollop
of bigotry for the new country – which
had its own – and an unexpected read
for a bemused future grandchild to pluck
from the glass-fronted bookcase Sam would build.

Celebrations

*Mr Adcock has just completed his new house, and a few days ago the settlers
tendered him a surprise party. Waipa Post, 19 September 1916.*

The party was set up by the Dayshes
and included a farewell to their son,
home on final leave, Trooper Hector Daysh:
his health, says the report, 'was drunk with cheers'.

And what was it drunk in? The King Country
was a dry area; any liquor
had to be smuggled in, meekly disguised
as cattle medicine or paint thinner.

Not that a drop of it would have entered
Sam's mouth, Son of Temperance as he was.
He liked a party, though, and best of all
a party at which he could make a speech.

This was in that happy category:
he thanked Mr and Mrs Daysh for their
great kindness to a new arrival from
the Old Country, and gave them a present –

or 'made them a presentation', as the
Waipa Post has it; presentations were
big in the reported social doings
of the settlers at Te Rauamoa.

When Mr Bebbington, the carpenter,
and his wife were off to Te Kuiti,
Sam contributed some witticisms
about the Te Kuitian character,

and another presentation occurred.
The next surprise party we hear about
was for the Dasslers, Oscar and Susan,
at their house. A number of songs were sung;

Mrs Murrell had brought her violin.
Mr Adcock (who else?) paid a tribute
to the host and hostess, and all joined in
singing 'For they are jolly good fellows'.

The School

The school was a wooden box on a hill,
surrounded by weather (the day began
with whose turn it was to check the rain gauge
and read the barometer). It contained
twenty or so children – a family –
and Mr Rudolf Honoré, who would
hand you a slate and teach you your letters,
get you through your Proficiency, or find
Latin inside his head, if by some chance
you had higher aims than agriculture.

Nothing wrong with farming – all his pupils
were from farms – but there was more to be learnt
by those who were keen. *Multum in parvo*:
it was all in that one room, and that one

431

consciousness, or he'd direct you to it
and make you want to pass it on: outside
the standard lessons, more books to pursue,
more discoveries to seduce you, and
an occasional spring of pure knowledge –
not all science needs laboratories.

Think of seeing his demonstration with
a magnetised needle pushed through a cork
and floating in a basin of water;
or a strip of newspaper: twist it once,
paste the ends together, and cut along
the centre with scissors, and along, and
along, until there's no more 'along': just
one double-length loop; then cut along the
centre of this – and look at what you get!
It makes your brain wriggle inside your skull.

Mr Honoré

Famous in the district for burying
his piano to save it from the flames
when the bush fire of 1908 came
ravening over Te Rauamoa

(there had been time, clearly, to dig a pit),
he put his dairy farm up for sale and
went off as teacher and (£10 a year
extra) Marine Department signalman

at Marokopa, further down the coast,
a district briefly pullulating with
children after the sawmill opened (though
not a place you hear much about these days),

where he was praised for the 'rapid strides made
especially by the Native children' –
the missionary blood of his Danish
Huguenot grandfather warm in his veins.

In 1913, this time with a wife,
he was back in Te Rauamoa, where
he took over the school from Miss Ashby
and stepped into the role awaiting him.

This too was not without a piano.
After chairing the euchre committee
in support of patriotic wartime
causes (top trophies for the card players:

a handsome palm-stand or a framed picture)
he set about raising funds to buy a
piano for the hall. A nail-driving
contest for ladies was one of his schemes.

This begged-and-nagged-for public piano
was destined, like his own, to be buried,
but permanently and by the long slow
inadvertent smothering of neglect.

District News: Te Rau-a-moa
(*Own Correspondent*)

A successful school concert was held in the hall last Friday. It was known that
for some time past teachers and pupils were actively engaged in preparing
for the annual concert, which proved the event of the year. The programme
consisted of "A Dolly Show" by seven little girls; the mystic drama "Aladdin
and the wonderful lamp", and a musical selection by "ten little nigger boys".

The costumes of the players and the scenery for the four acts of the play were
a credit to the senior pupils and the ladies of the district. Master Arthur
Ormsby personated the Chinese emperor, and caused much merriment. Miss

Gladys Oxenham looked every inch a Princess, quite winning the hearts of the audience, as did also Miss Rene Stewart, the dancing sprite. The difficult role of the wicked magician was cleverly acted by Miss Madge Parkinson.

The leading character and hero of the play was personated by Master Cyril Adcock, whose abilities much impressed the audience. Miss Amy Parkinson, the senior girl of the school, carried out her part as Aladdin's mother with marked confidence and skill, as did also little Dossie Dassler, the maid in waiting to the Princess. Master Bertie Daysh, in a suit of flame, was the second dancing sprite.

The performance was concluded by the ten little nigger boys, whose attire and general appearance amused all and won an encore.

WAIPA POST, 29 December 1916

The School Journal
Children of the Empire, you are brothers all;
children of the Empire, answer to the call!
Let your voices mingle, lift your heads and sing:
'God save dear old Britain, and God save Britain's King.'
      NZ School Journal, Part I, June 1917.

I

There was Empire Day and then Arbor Day,
with a special number of the Journal
for each: you could take it home and file it
in your folder at the end of the year.

'Your teachers will tell you wonderful things
about the British Empire – your Empire,
where children are safe, happy and free.
Some have red skins and live in Canada;

some have black skins and dwell in the land of
the lion and elephant . . .' No room here
for the 'half-starved savages' wandering

in Australia when the white man came.

However, for something closer to home,
in the section aimed at younger children,
you can read a Maoriland Fairy-tale,
learn a new song to welcome the sunshine,

or find suggestions for a charming pet
in the series on baby animals.
But if you fancy a tuatara
for the back garden you'll need a permit.

II

History, geography and civics
in monthly age-related servings, on
wartime paper, with an occasional
garnish of literature or music –

in between 'Great Rivers of the World'
and the latest strand in 'Britain's Sea Story',
a particularly manly portrait
of Byron, with extracts from 'Childe Harold';

or, for the older age-groups, a report
on the February Revolution
(two months after it occurred), followed by
'The Minstrel Boy' in sol-fa notation.

But when it comes to moulding youthful minds
there's nothing like a polar explorer,
and with the Antarctic so close, guess who
impressed the most readers as top hero?

One, at least, assumed him decades later
to be a universal marker for
moral excellence: 'I'm sure Captain Scott
wouldn't have bullied his little sister.'

Fruit

1916. July 25 Fruit trees – £1.10.0, Paid.

Even in Manchester the first thing you'd plant
in the merest apron of soil was a fruit tree.

So here in the land of milk and honey
it went without saying, didn't it? No.

1,200 feet above sea level
on the chillier side of a mountain

was not ideal; and the soil 'bush-sick' –
deficient in cobalt, as later tests

were to reveal (not wonderful, either,
it also emerged, for dairy cattle).

Grace Dassler, who must nevertheless have
thriven there, spoke aged 102

of empty, bladder-like plums that fell off
before they could ripen. The Dayshes' trees

managed an ill-favoured apple or two,
but for Sam it was dearth. He had to wait

a generation to mellow into
the grandfather I knew when I was five,

a deaf man in his sixties, living near
Drury, to be looked for in a greenhouse

pungent with tomato plants, or peering
through sun-warmed lushness from an orchard ladder,

warning us in a Lancashire accent
not to lick the spray off the nectarines.

Mount Pirongia Surveyed

If men in boots had tramped the sacred mountain,
laden with metal implements, compass in hand,
field glasses dangling, puncturing the soil with
the tripod legs of their theodolite stand,
despising the word *tapu* in favour of terms
like 'locked native reserve' and 'second-class land',

deploying their chains to measure slopes of bush
in Anglo-Saxon acres, perches and rods,
reducing ridge and valley to lines on a map,
offering the most perfunctory of nods
to the legal hotch-potch that had been fiddled up
and no respect at all to the ancient gods,

and if then the government had raffled off blocks
and seeded the place with imported farmers, versed
in the wrong kind of animal husbandry,
while spurning the just claimants who were there first,
is it surprising that at least now and then,
here and there, some of it might turn out to be cursed?

The Obvious Solution

A year after the house-warming party
and Sam's off to live in a town again –
or is that a heartless way to put it?

Three words in the diary – 'Came to Dwen' –
commemorate the inadequacy
of the monthly cream cheque to keep them all.

If this is failure, it's temporary
(he hopes), and well-stocked with compensations.
He's packed his kit: razors, razor-strop, comb,

scissors and clippers. He can see himself
reflected in Mr Dwen's tall mirrors
discussing the war as he trims a beard

and clips the back of a customer's neck,
or wielding his less than hilarious
brand of humour while selling tobacco.

He can smell the bay rum he'll spray from his
'ENOTS' plated brass canister. Cyril
has his head screwed on; he'll cope with those cows.

Milk   (*Cyril speaks*)

The thing is to have two milking stools,
one to sit on, the other for your book;

while your hands are busy under a cow,
your eyes and brain can employ themselves elsewhere,

because what is there to think about milk?
The essence of being a mammal, yes

(these four teats), the image of whiteness –
He's set her on his milk white steed.

Now droops the milkwhite peacock like a ghost.
The holly bears a berry as white as the milk –

(although it's not perfectly white until skimmed);
but day after day, month after month,

ping, ping, ping, swish, ping, swish, ping, swish,
and the foam level crawling up the bucket . . .

Mum comes out to turn the separator;
I take the can of cream down to the road

438

for the cream carrier, because the point of it all
is not milk but cream, and not cream, in the end,

but a manufactured product; and in winter
when the cows are dry, all but the house cow,

the dairy company will give us
a 50 lb box of it for ourselves.

The Bush Fire

There was his wife with her eyebrows burnt off
(they never did grow back again properly)
and his barely teenaged son, running round
with wet sacks to batter the flames out –

just what Sam would himself have advised
if he'd been there, instead of standing
miles and miles away, scissors in hand,
outside the barber's at Te Awamutu,

watching the smoke. (They had no telephone.)
Someone had to go and earn money
when the cream-cheque failed, and someone (young Cyril)
had to mind the farm and milk the cows.

So he missed it, poor Sam, the great bush fire –
the striding flames and the filthy black swirls
that choked you even through a wet handkerchief.
Eva was left with a lasting phobia,

Cyril with an intimate knowledge
of how each type of bush timber burns,
and Sam deprived of a first-hand claim
to a first-class story for his customers.

Beryl

They don't mention her much, but there she was:
running around under Eva's feet;
a smudged face in a family snap,
a bundle of pale skirts on someone's knee –

part of the human baggage they all stowed
as kindly as they could, after Alice
met them from the boat: fair shares;
her whole life accidental.

And growing bigger, taking Cyril's place
in the milking shed after he left home;
complaining of the snow on her feet; standing
in the pool where a cow had piddled to warm them.

Cousins

And then if Beryl why not Hazel? –
who came for some schooling when she was six,

there being no school near Okere Falls.
Cyril took her each day on his pony.

Beryl, too young to have it explained
(even if, in that household,

explanations had been on offer),
thought herself Cyril's sister, not Hazel's –

or Clifford's, who arrived aged six
a year later; Bert from up the road

joined Cyril, each of them ferrying
a small passenger on his saddle.

These were the two handsome children
in careful, slightly too large outfits

(her pleated skirt and sailor collar,
his home-tailored jacket and shorts)

with bare feet on a sunlit verandah.
Beryl is not in the photograph.

What variety of pastoral is this?
A temporary one; as are they all.

Telegraphese

Young woman with TB sails to NZ,
finds work up and down both islands until
near Wanaka she lands up on farm
with no other women; worst happens.

Decent young farmer in neighbourhood
marries her, greatly pregnant. She gives birth
in Dunedin, miles from scowling gaze
of his mother and sisters; brings child home.

Has another, a son, with husband.
Conceives a third. Meanwhile, in Manchester,
her widowed father dies. Husband pays
for her to visit surviving kin.

Staying with brother and sister-in-law
while all make plans to start new life
together in South Island, she hears
Charlie, her husband, has died of typhoid.

Rushes back to claim inheritance,
leaving new baby and toddler behind
with Sam and Eva, and taking only
eldest child: not her husband's. Bad choice.

In-laws refuse to honour Charlie's will.
Alice, whom they see as scarlet woman,
must fend for herself. Finds housekeeping job
with kind widower and his small daughter.

Sam and Eva, en route to Dunedin,
must disembark at Wellington, travel
north to meet them, and reassign children
on rational basis. All their lives change.

The Family Bible

This is the Adcock family Bible:
a wedding present, no doubt, to John and
Amelia in 1870.

The Authorised Version, massively bound
in boards and black leather, with gilt edges,
it runs to over 1200 pages

and weighs between ten and eleven pounds:
as much as a thriving two-month-old child
(not the most tactful of analogies).

Annotations and footnotes occupy
roughly two thirds of the page areas;
maps and engravings bulk the volume out.

Between the Old and New Testaments are
pages for 'Children', 'Marriages' and 'Deaths',
interleaved with crisping tissue paper:

Laura, who died aged one year seven months;
Thomas Henry, who died aged eight months; John
who lived for twenty-one years, but damaged;

then Samuel, to whom the book devolved
as the oldest surviving son, although
not, finally, the only survivor –

Polly, Joseph, George and Alice followed
(as well as another short-lived baby)
before Amelia's death was entered.

Sam is reported to have told his wife
he didn't want children. In this he failed:
Eva's parched womb ignored the edict and,

thirsty for insemination after
seven years of chaste betrothal, conceived
Cyril within their first week of marriage.

His is the only name to represent
his generation on the 'Children' page.
(Nieces fostered and then disowned don't count.)

Bush Fairies

What am I permitted to write about Beryl,
a bright child who wandered into darkness?
Among the squalor in her room when she died
were all the poems she'd written since childhood,

from Bush Fairies, 'weeping for their comrades
slain by an axeman's hand', to her lament
for two infant daughters, a stillborn son,
and the young husband she'd nursed for eight years.

If no one quite tells you who you are
how can you decide who you ought to be?
A superfluity of mothers can't prevail
over an Irishman met at a dance.

So: *Mr and Mrs S. Adcock*
announce the engagement of their niece . . .
(previously known, you may recall,
even to herself, as their daughter).

What can you expect if you disgrace yourself
with a consumptive Catholic who drinks?
(Beryl wrote that he took ill from sitting
night after night on his daughter's grave.)

Too much melodrama for Sam and Eva:
need she have lost quite so many babies,
or lain in hospital, coughing and bewailing?
They had seen more than enough TB.

They did their duty: took on the four-year-old
and farmed out the older two; Beryl came home
(streptomycin had been discovered)
and struggled to imitate a mother.

It all dragged on as you might expect:
some lodger, not always the same one,
drinking beer with her in the front room
and listening to the racing commentary;

the sensible daughter coping with the chores
until her turn for a rapid wedding.
And then . . . but all right: it's not my business.
Let me apologise if I've already

bumbled clumsily into the peace
of the living. And might it not have been
more tactful to give Beryl a new name? –
Assuming, that's to say, that I haven't.

Settlers' Museum

The early settlers' museum echoes
to voices chiming 'We had one of those!'
So did we, folks: we all had one of those –
washboard, washing dolly, Reckitt's bluebag,
scrubbing brush, sandstone, bar of Sunlight soap –
or our mother did, or our grandmother.
Surely you've got a wash-house out the back
with a copper in it, and a mangle?
Oh, just the copper; you sold the mangle
on TradeMe or, more likely, wish you had.

The kitchen from a hundred years ago
combines the boringly familiar –
fireguard, hearth brush, poker, shovel, tongs –
with the no longer seen: a butter churn,
that pair of flatirons (one to heat up
on the range while the other's being used),
the black kettle – and is that a trivet?
A side of bacon hanging from a beam;
Willow pattern china brought from England,
and tea-towels made out of flour bags.

In the display the aproned figure posed
amid the props ('Farmhouse Interior')
is visible only in half profile,
busy at the table about some task –
kneading bread, perhaps. It's not possible
to view her from another angle, or
tiptoe around behind the barrier
to ask her name and peer into her face.
The teapot's just like ours. The milk jug has
a bead-fringed net cover (my aunts used those).

Evenings with Mother

As there was only one lamp
they had to spend the winter evenings
at the table, close enough to share
its kerosene-perfumed radiance –

his mother sewing, and he
reading aloud to her the books
he borrowed from Mr Honoré
or the Daysh boys on the next farm:

Buffalo Bill, school yarns from
England (*Talbot something of the Shell*),
and, featuring his own personal
hero, *Deerfoot in the Mountains*.

(Deerfoot rode Whirlwind bareback
without a bridle. His own pony,
Molly, would go anywhere like this,
but Kate, the harness mare, threw him off.)

Their six-volume Walter Scott
absorbed them both for weeks and could then
be swapped with the Dassler family
for Dickens or (why not?) Billy Bunter.

But his mother's attention
may have wandered when his own was gripped,
in a stack of old *Boy's Own Papers*,
by details of wireless telegraphy.

The Buggy   (*Cyril speaks*)

Mum wasn't much of a one for horses.
If she needed to go out anywhere
she had to be taken in the buggy.

Sometimes I drove her, when Dad was away;
otherwise he did, but he wasn't keen:
it had four high wheels, awkward to manage

(we used it for transporting loads); and Kate,
our heavier mare, built like a draught horse,
was such a timid, skittish animal,

a bag of nerves. Well, one day Mum had gone
to Otorohanga with the Dayshes,
and I was to follow in the buggy.

I got Kate harnessed and between the shafts,
the fidgety creature, and all went well
until she saw something she didn't like –

possibly something imaginary.
She reared up, tipped me out into the mud,
jack-knifed the wheels, and trotted off at a

great pace back towards home. There was never
any traffic on that road, thank goodness,
but about a mile and a half downhill

a man working on the verge spotted her,
buggy in tow, and managed to hold her
until I caught up and took her in charge.

We made it in the end – no harm done – but
if Mum had been with me, I dread to think . . .
although at least it would have given her

something to write about in letters home
to friends in Manchester (where there were trams);
if she'd been more of a one for writing.

Eight Things Eva Will Never Do Again

Work in that dressmaking factory,
waiting for Sam to marry her. (He had
duties, and a curious conscience.)

Walk out with him along Peel Green Road
to the Ship Canal bridge, on a May evening
with the hawthorn in flower – if he could snatch time
from his two jobs – or after church, perhaps.
(Seven years of that, walking out together.)

Go home and make clothes for her sisters.
(Someone had to, and you wouldn't catch
Mary lifting a hand around the house.)

Help her mother with whatever (ditto).

Stand in the New Independent Chapel
(a concession by Sam, who is C of E),
sheathed in white, with a pearl choker,
and balancing on her head a cushion
of ostrich feathers, to murmur her vows.

Go to Blackpool. (Everyone loves Blackpool.)
Dear Sam, Sorry you was dispointed . . .
Tell Marion to bring a shall for her head
as we are expecting high tide on Sunday
and give her mine to bring. You will find it
in the bottom draw in the parlor . . .

See Marion, or others of her younger
siblings (names available on request).

Have a baby. (Well, she has Cyril.)

Eva Remembers Her Two Brothers Called James

When she thinks (if she does) of the first James
it is of a six-year-old who died
when she was fourteen, of meningitis.

His spirit, like a trespassing sprite,
flew into his parents' marriage bed
and lurked there as they comforted each other.

A month later, conspiring with the genie
of ovulation and the hormone fairies,
it implanted itself in a fertilised egg,

to be born in July 1890
and loaded with the same eight syllables:
James Arthur Dickson Eggington.

He didn't resemble his first avatar
or any of his incarnate siblings
at Eva's wedding, this gladsome imp

with his long chin. When TB clutched him
'I am still improving', he wrote
from his sanatorium in Devon

on a photograph of six young men
reclining on the grass around a nurse
like petals flopped from a magnolia.

James is the one with the longest legs,
the centre parting, the fetching moustache,
and no intention of dying celibate.

He willed some health back into his lungs,
found work, tacked five years on to his age,
and married an older woman while he could.

How's that for *carpe diem*? Ten months
to bask in matrimony, wisely or not,
before death stalked him to Babbacombe.

Eva Remembers Her Little Sisters

'Alice Maud Mary, Marion Maud Mary,
Ellen Gertrude (the first), Ellen Gertrude Mary –

all us girls got Mary, after our mother,
starting with Mary Ann Elizabeth, then me –

all but one, that is, the first Ellen Gertrude,
and perhaps it was bad luck to have left it off;

she had the shortest life: only nine months old
when she took fits and died (it was pneumonia).

But the first we lost was my playmate Alice:
eight when I was ten. *Tabes mesenterica* –

something internal; a horrible complaint.
It wasn't the way they tell you at Sunday school.

She died ten days after Marion was born.
It was all like that: steps and stairs and overlaps,

birthdays and deathdays and the names given again,
almost as if there was something to cover up.

When Marion took bad our brother Thomas
carried her around the house in his arms . . .

Them pictures they made us pose for, in our mourning,
Nellie and me, before it was too late –

time enough left for me, but not for Nellie,
poor lass, with her shy smile, a bit bucktoothed,

her hair tied back with a black satin bow
in front of the photographer's painted scenery . . .

God forgive me, I'd rather have kept Nellie
than Mary with her snooty ways, or Thomas,

if there was only room left on this earth
for four of us out of the eleven.'

The Germans   (*Cyril speaks*)

I

From our front window we could peer down
at Kawhia Harbour, a quiet place,
ideal for the Germans to land. I indulged
in fantasies, but with an undercurrent.

An unknown farmer moved in next door:
a spy, obviously. The boundary between
us and the spy needed quite a length of fencing.
I don't know when I've worked so hard on a fence.

II

My Uncle Harry, Mum's youngest brother,
was invalided home from the Somme
with something . . . rheumatic fever, they thought –
his heart was enlarged. Or perhaps he had

shellshock. His mother dared not nurse him:
the responsibility unnerved her.
Instead his sister-in-law volunteered,
Thomas's wife. She said he had fits.

Brown Sugar   (*Cyril speaks*)

The teacher's brother, Charlie Honoré,
had a farm close to the school, and also
fingers in other pies from time to time.
He managed the boarding house for a bit,
and even talked of opening a store.

He wouldn't miss an opportunity –
like the day when he distinguished himself
by running three-quarters of a mile to
grab the mail coach, when the horses bolted.
He got himself in the paper for that.

When he hired me to help with his milking
I'd get up in the dark, milk my own cows,
ride two miles to Charlie's place and milk his,
then go to school. But he gave me breakfast,
and boy, was I ready for that porridge!

At Charlie's house it came with brown sugar –
he said raw sugar was better for you.
Everyone had porridge for breakfast,
but I'd never had brown sugar before;
so I persuaded Mum to get some in.

Later, of course, I learned it was better
to have no sugar at all; later still
I gave up cooking the oats, and simply
soaked them overnight in a mug of milk –
a sort of predecessor to muesli.

Supporting Our Boys

I

Syd Ormsby put his stock up for auction,
announcing his departure for the front,
but didn't even get as far as camp
before the armistice overtook him –

bad luck or procrastination? Others
enlisted straight away: 'Anzac hero'
John Linwood did his bit and died at (where
else?) Gallipoli in 1915.

Charlie Honoré, at the farewell for
Trooper Dassler of the Mounted Rifles,
urged all the single men to volunteer
before the arrival of compulsion.

Whatever the impetus, off they marched –
names from the school roll: Smith, Clark, Dearlove, Daysh;
three from the Harris family (only
one survived); two Parkinsons; two Franklins.

In 1917 the *Waipa Post*
bemoaned the shortage of dairy farmers,
noting that fern and other second growths
were creeping into neglected pastures,

and tried to imagine the effects when
the second reserve came to be called up,
since already most of the remaining
settlers were married men with families.

Following his own call to arms, Charlie
Honoré detached himself from his wife,
his businesses, his farm, his committees,
and sailed off with the next reinforcements.

In time it would have gobbled them all up.
It even came snapping at Sam's heels, in
August 1918, with the 16th
ballot, but was just too slow to snatch him.

II

Thirty or thereabouts went; all but five
came back, some in better shape than others –
young Ned Honoré spent two years dying
in Trentham military hospital.

Max Dassler was invalided home from
Egypt after serving scarcely a year,
and settled with other returned soldiers
on the Tapuohonuku block; there,

having something to prove, he was shortly
'bringing his place under in record time'.
His brother Oscar, with no such resource,
turned to the law when accused of stealing

a bag of potatoes; the magistrate,
awarding £10 damages, took note
of the ill feeling caused since war broke out
by his being 'of foreign extraction'.

Meanwhile returned Gunner Stewart, with his
war record and impeccable surname,
continued to act as cheerleader and
auctioneer at the fundraising socials.

Armistice Day

He was fourteen when it ended.
His father gave him a day off
to ride into town for the celebrations.

Ambling along on Molly's back
to Te Awamutu, he whiled away
the miles absorbed in his new treasure:

a textbook on organic chemistry,
saved up for out of his earnings
from doing Charlie Honoré's milking.

After the fireworks, his retina stencilled
with their acidic blaze, he wondered
how easy it would be to make some.

He might have a go, with Bert Daysh,
assuming they could get the ingredients
(or get away with trying to get them;

he could hardly add them to his parents'
next routine order from Laidlaw Leeds
for oatmeal, sugar and fencing wire).

They could celebrate the New Year, perhaps,
or the King's birthday – he'd think of something –
now that there would be no more wars.

The Way Forward   (*Cyril speaks*)

I

Mr Honoré came and spoke to Dad;
I'm not sure how the conversation went,

but the gist of it was that I shouldn't
waste my life being a dairy farmer.

There was no chance of going to high school –
I'd have had to give up work on the farm,

which at that stage could barely totter on.
As for university, forget it.

The path to higher education lay
through training as a teacher, like himself.

First the civil service entrance exam,
then probationer (or pupil teacher,

as they once called it); then training college.
And I'd be paid; I'd be self-supporting.

II

I stayed on at school to Standard 7
and Mr Honoré gave me coaching

in Latin and some other new subjects
for the entrance exam. Not the maths, though –

by then I think I knew about as much
maths as he did; once when he was teaching

contracted multiplication and got
a bit stuck, I helped him from the textbook.

After a few months I left; from then on
packets of correspondence course lessons

would arrive from T.U. Wells in Auckland
for me to complete and post back to him.

I drew up a timetable for myself;
I was a sort of self-governing school.

The Hopeful Author

The professor in 'A Scientific
Capture', with the detective by his side,
effects an entry into the spy's house
by lassooing a chimney, shinning up
the rope and removing a window pane.

He installs his first 'little contrivance'
(a glass-lidded box) behind a mirror,
and another under the wallpaper,
each connected to the telephone wire
and then in turn to a large battery

outside the house. Then (are you still with me?)
back in the professor's lab they can watch
the villain's dastardly doings on a
'cinnamatagraph', but one which can play,
unlike commercial models, a soundtrack.

All very advanced, like the 'flying tank'
of which the prototype has been stolen
by the spy. To ratchet up the tension,
when they are on their way to arrest him
the detective's car runs out of benzine.

It all works out as it should in the end:
more wires, another battery, the spy
electrocuted at his own front door.
On the back of the much-creased final page:
C. Adcock. Remit U.S. Bills & stamps.

A Friend of the New   (*Cyril speaks*)

'One disadvantage of the coherer
is its erratic nature; it's not
a reliable signalling device.'

In Auckland, I had a crystal set,
and made a valve receiver.
But I'm talking about the early days:

to begin with I experimented
with iron filings and nitric acid –
I'd read it all up. Meanwhile Bill Daysh,

Bert's brother, took some wire out of an old
telephone, I bought a little buzzer,
and we made Morse keys, and sent signals

from his house to ours. They were hard to pick up.
We stretched our ears to distinguish them;
there was some imagination involved.

But we got a tremendous kick out of
picking up signals from Awanui –
ZLA Awanui, in Northland;

hadn't a notion of what they were saying.
Of course there was no speech in those days,
only Morse; nothing but Morse in the air.

Shorthand

Might you not have found him a little
exhausting, though? If, for example,
you were his mother, not given

to innovative thinking yourself,
and had this youth (in 1920
the word teenager was not current),

forever coming up with a new
interpretation of Genesis
or sketching plans for a contraption

that must be at least electrical,
if not dangerous. And now this:
a small ad in the *Auckland Star* –

SHORTHAND in three hours. New system,
easily learned. Send 5/- for
course. C. Adcock, Te Rau-a-moa.

That was in June; but on reflection
three hours may have struck him as less than
five shillings' worth. So in December:

SHORTHAND in three days. Write C. Adcock
regarding the Veasy system . . .
Oh, yes, ha ha – Veasy: v. easy.

Did you make any money, Cyril?

The Bible Student   (*Cyril speaks*)

Dad was very thick with the Anglicans
in Te Awamutu. We had no church
at Te Rauamoa, but once or twice a year
a man came to take a church service.

459

There was one time when he couldn't make it
and I volunteered. (Don't look so surprised!)
Dad found someone else for the routine parts
of the service, but I preached the sermon:
my first experience of public speaking.
I was about fifteen, I suppose.

I can't remember what the text was.
I'd been reading a chapter of the Bible
every night, starting with Genesis.
We all had Bibles; Dad's was annotated –
I studied it for the notes – but mine
was the Revised Version; I was adamant
about sticking to the Revised Version.
Then I got the 'Emphatic Diaglott' –
the New Testament in the original Greek
with an interlined English translation.

Also I somehow managed to get hold of
Pastor Russell's six-volume study.
This appealed to my rebellious mind
(I was never happy to take on trust
what I'd been told). He wrote, for example,
that hell was not a place of torment at all:
the Old Testament word meant simply
a place of oblivion, and Gehenna,
the New Testament word, was a place
of disposal: a rubbish tip, you could say.

I was quite voluble on scriptural matters! –
I always enjoyed a good argument.
When they set up a Sunday school,
with me and an older girl as teachers,
the children must have heard some new viewpoints;
I don't imagine it did much damage
to their immortal souls. Later on,
in Auckand, I taught at the Ridgeways' church.
Which denomination? I forget; by then
I'd no time for such petty distinctions.

A Profile

Was he a rather solemn young person?
– There is nothing to contradict that view.
Was he, on the other hand, often filled
with glee at his own schemes and inventions?
– To say that would be equally valid.
Was anything in the nature of fun
mentioned? – He went out shooting now and then:
rabbits, mostly. Once, with Bert and Bill Daysh,
he hunted some feral cats that had been
skulking and marauding around their farm,
raiding the poultry yard. Never got one.
Did the subject of sex ever arise?
– Come on, this was my father talking to
his daughter and grandson. What do you think?

District News: Te Rau-a-moa
(*Own Correspondent*)

Master Cyril Adcock, son of Mr S. Adcock of Te Awamutu, is to be congratulated on having passed the civil service entrance examination.

His success is especially pleasing seeing that the youth has been constantly employed on his father's dairy farm here at Te Rauamoa. It shows what can be done by application. The boy intends to enter one of the learned professions.

Of the two candidates presented for junior national scholarships, Dorothea Dassler, eldest daughter of Mr O. P. Dassler, obtained a free place. She has been a constant pupil at the school here, having been trained throughout by the same teacher.

Some fine crops of Swedes are to be seen on the farms round about, the most promising being those grown on virgin land. Conditions are very favourable for growth, a week's hot weather being invariably followed by copious rains.

WAIPA POST, 8 February 1921

Mr S. Adcock

'Mr Adcock of Te Awamutu'
will have to cease being a hairdresser
of that town, toil back up the hill on his
bicycle, live with his wife and resume

the identity of Mr Adcock,
dairy farmer of Te Rauamoa,
so that his son can freewheel down in the
other direction to be a teacher.

If he could somehow stockpile the milking
by having it done ten times in a row
and then not at all for three or four days . . .
but the cows won't yield until they're ready.

It's time to train Beryl – she's nearly eight,
old enough to start getting her hand in.
He'll have other tasks enough, goodness knows;
it's all coming back to him. So be it,

but he draws the line at cutting firewood.
Cyril will have to cycle home at the
weekends – have a good meal, see his mother.
That's the answer. That's all there is to it.

The Probationer   (*Cyril speaks*)

I

Quite a shock, the switch to a small township
with streets and shops and traffic and strangers.

I was sixteen, and one of three trainees
appointed to Te Awamutu school.

462

The District High School was in a newly
opened building, with the primary school;

it specialised in agriculture and,
for girls, home economics (yes, I know).

My own studies enlarged my horizons –
the topics deemed to be necessary

for a teacher ranged from the close parsing
of a sentence to physiology,

hygiene and diet, the sugar question . . .
It was all very educational.

II

Chemistry was not on my syllabus
but the school science inspector agreed

to let me study it at the high school
one evening a week, designing my own

course of experiments; my friend Bert Fleay
from Te Rahu, a year younger than me

(he was a pupil, I was a teacher)
joined me. Once, for example, we measured

the carbon dioxide in the classroom
after the students had left. I tended

to favour exciting experiments –
lots of burning and electricity,

running fearful wires off the light sockets –
not the routine stuff Bert had done in class.

Te Awamutu Road Rant

You'd see it in your dreams half the night long
afterwards, the road reeling and rolling
in front of you, surging and zigzagging,
hairpin-bending here and there, but slowly –

how could it be fast on a bicycle
except downhill a bit, on the way back,
at Windy Point, for example, where you
might go over if you didn't watch out?

It was twenty-seven miles, which would take
five hours (unless you made the mistake
of going by the back road – that took nine;
once was enough for that experiment).

The first eight miles, from Te Awamutu
to Pirongia, were tolerable;
then came five miles of rough metal – great lumps
this size; you could only ride at the edge.

From there on the rest of it was rough clay,
often waterlogged in the wet season,
which was much of the time: your wheels could glug
through gluey mud as deep as six inches.

It would be raining, as likely as not –
you'd want your oilskin cape, and your leggings
(two and threepence a pair in Laidlaw Leeds'
catalogue, leather or waterproof cloth),

and if you set out late on a Friday
there was also the problem of a light:
a carbide lamp was best, but it wouldn't
last; you'd need an oil lamp as a backup.

(The alternative was to leave early
on Saturday morning, although it might
be just as dark at 4 or 5 a.m.)
Then all weekend the firewood marathon:

hunting down suitable logs, harnessing
Kate to drag them home; then sawing, chopping,
sawing again, splitting, cutting, stacking –
different types of wood for different

cooking, fast or slow: bread in the oven,
stew on the hob, water in the boiler –
and the range to be kept alight all day
for warmth ten months of the year, gobbling trees.

Monotonous, yes, but not hypnotic.
It was the cycling that would haunt your sleep:
all that swinging around seasick curves and
corners, the pedals churning round and round,

the head-down grind; the circularity.
But even if your eyes went round in your
head you'd have to concentrate in case of
tree-roots, loose rocks, deceptively deep ruts.

And back at Te Awamutu you'd still
have three more miles to go to Te Rahu
and your bed in old Hughie Thompson's house;
before the following weekend came round.

The Sensational

I rather suspect there is not enough sex,
murder and cannibalism in these
pages to please such themes' devotees:

no pornographic, priapic or Sapphic
doings on record, no lopping of limbs,
no butchered-out hearts, no roasting of parts,

nothing rococo in the Okoko
Valley, to speak of, as far as I know,
nor within cooee of Ngutunui.

The second and third may well have occurred
a century or two back, in that vast
repository of horrors, the past –

think, after all, of Te Rauparaha
whose first rampages were not very far
down the old coach road, at Kawhia;

and during some war a long time before,
in the days of the moa-hunters, it's said
that after one battle so many dead

were strewn on the ground that they brought to mind
the tumbled mounds of long-legged birds
felled in a moa-hunt; since when the words

'Te Rau-a-Moa' – 'the hundreds like moa' –
have stuck to that place.
                              As for sex, though,
how would we know? It was all so long ago.

The Kea Gun

I

The rifle known to them as the Kea gun
was so named by Cyril's uncle Charlie,
who used to keep it by him to shoot Kea
when those demonic parrots attacked his sheep.

His widow Alice must have snatched it up
with such goods as she could salvage when
'them wretches at Makarora' (Sam's words)
ignored his Will and threw her off the farm.

(Quite soon whatever need she might have felt
for a gun evaporated; Mr Weir –
he was always Mr Weir – protected her
for the rest of their long lives together.)

The rifle featured in an earlier drama
not known to any of them, and to us
only through smart-arse online indexes:
Charlie, in his teens, had embraced

the age-old solace of lonely shepherds,
and was brought before the Chief Justice
convicted of an unnatural offence.
His Honour, in passing sentence, said:

. . . on the other hand, you are only a lad . . .
strongly recommended to mercy . . .
brought up away from many comforts . . .
depraved moral sense . . . better life in future . . .

Six months, with hard labour; and the same,
to be served concurrently, on the charge
of mischievously killing a sheep,
to which he pleaded guilty in the lower court.

Local opinion at Lake Wanaka
was that the charge should never have been brought –
the felony, that is; it was admitted
'that a prosecution in the case

of shooting the ewe with the pea rifle
was unavoidable.' [Semantic interlude:
a pea rifle is a small bore rifle –
a .22. *Pea* rhymes with *key*

but not with *kea*, which has two syllables.
I shan't pronounce on what it might rhyme with.]
The *Otago Witness* was pained to report
that many small children knew all the details –

which is more than we do. Why did Charlie
have to shoot the ewe? *Crime passionel?*
Silencing a witness? – Come on now,
pull yourselves together: we're all grown-ups.

II

'Indelicate' and 'speculate' don't rhyme,
any more than Makarora does
with Te Rauamoa. Often a rifle
is used only for keeping down rabbits.

This was not traditional sheep country.
No kea to shoot, and on this farm no sheep.
A herd of dairy cattle can't compete
with a flock of woolly temptresses.

Glamorous though the front end of a heifer
may be (those eyelashes, those melting eyes)
the bovine frame lacks cuddliness, compared
with the compact snugness of a ewe.

When it comes to interspecies relations
(hardly a matter I'm equipped to judge)
a cow seems not only less alluring
but less well adapted to the purpose.

Fortunately for the young man on this farm
(Charlie's nephew by marriage, let's call him)
by the time he reached 17 (the age
at which Charlie made his appearance in court)

he was working at Te Awamutu
District High School, where there were girls.
He went to at least one jazz concert.
There may even have been jazz with girls.

Sole Charge

If people had said 'Wow' in those days
he might have said it, during a visit
to his aunt Alice, when Mr Weir
left him to run the hydroelectric
power station at Okere Falls
for an afternoon: Rotorua
dependent on a boy for its power!

The needle of his ambition swung
from research chemist to electrical
engineer. But his direction
had been set for him already: he was
going to be a teacher; and not
of physics or chemistry; he was going
to teach primary school children.

At Te Uku, his first posting,
he would live in a tent in the school grounds
on rolled oats, peanuts and raw carrots,
and sleep on a palliasse of hay

with another over him for the cold.
He would teach them everything he knew.
They would think him a freak, of course,

but take to him. His evening lectures
would tickle the parents: music (using
his 'non-tin whistle' and the Walford Davies
gramophone records); poetry; art –
always aglow with the latest. He would stick
in their memories. Decimal currency
(you wait – it will come); steam cars; Esperanto.

The Plain and Fancy Dress Ball

*The evening of Friday last saw the high-water mark of social
entertainment in Te Rau-a-moa raised to a still higher level . . .*
        Waipa Post, 25 October 1924.

The 1920s were in full swing.
Eva and Sam went with the Dayshes,

Mrs Daysh in black silk, 'Mrs S.
Adcock' in a silk net over-dress.

Of the thirty-five ladies listed,
(not counting unnamed 'others'), ten wore

fancy dress, and the rest evening dress.
Mrs Le Prou came as a 'Cheer Germ',

Charlie Honoré's wife as a nurse.
(The gentlemen's clothing was not thought

worthy of journalistic comment.)
Mrs Chase, dressed as 'Evening', received

a presentation. People came from
as far away as Pirongia.

II

Meanwhile Cyril, at Training College
in Auckland, cycled every day from

Point Chevalier, where he was boarding
with his mother's cousins the Ridgeways,

in riding-breeches, leggings and boots
with an oilskin cape in wet weather –

a costume similarly favoured
by the previous year's eccentric,

his fellow-Esperantist, Watson
(a soulmate, had they coincided),

and religiously sent home money,
out of which Eva may have bought the

fabric for her outfit at the ball –
or her update to an older frock.

The Swimmer

(*Cyril speaks*)

Another thing at Teachers' College:
three of us always got in early
to go the length of the swimming bath,
winter or summer, before classes.

On one occasion we got roped in
to a life-saving exhibition.
Yes, I was the victim; I had to
thrash about and pretend to struggle.

I was a fairly small chap, easy
to handle. At that point I hadn't
learnt life-saving – I didn't even
learn to swim till Te Awamutu.

There was a lake at the Thompsons' farm:
they had a bit of bush and a lake
surrounded by raupo: a deep lake –
we never found the bottom of it.

(At Te Rauamoa the only
water was what fell out of the sky,
or the odd stream – nothing to swim in;
the water we used was from our tank.)

Later, of course, I learned life-saving;
I used to teach it to the children
at Rangiwahia – there was a
river nearby – do you remember?

Visiting the Ridgeways

But if they're all in Auckland
standing together in the Ridgeways' garden –
Sam, Eva, Beryl (about ten or eleven)
and grown-up Cyril – then who's milking the cows?

Is the farm over? No, not for a while.
It's Cyril who will unclog them from it,
putting his motorbike down as a deposit
on eight acres in Drury for their rescue.

Meanwhile here they are on a visit:
Eva enduring the camera, Sam tired,
Cyril with his muscular arms folded,
Beryl in a white dress Eva has sewn

as she used to sew for her sisters
in fashions to suit them, during their brief prime.
Likewise this low-belted shift is of its time –
the 1920s – to please Beryl. It's as if

Sam's niece, this unofficial daughter,
were a present for Eva, that might make up
for Nellie and Marion. Oh, too much to hope –
that Eva should enjoy consolation.

Reconstituting Eva

No; I can't get it to knit. Scrunch!
Somewhere on the timeline between
the historical Eva whose
disappointments and retreating
daydreams I so tenderly probe
and our childhood's 'Grandma Adcock'
comes a fracture: Sam's young lady,
eager emigrant, pioneer,
snaps into the dumpy figure

473

telling me off, when I was three,
for proving, at the tea-table,
I could put my toes in my mouth.

The two images crepitate
against each other, and won't graft.
She showed no signs of liking us,
my sister and me, her only
grandchildren, that we can think of.
No reason why she should, except
that it seems to be usual;
but we visited, ate her stew
and washed the dishes afterwards.
Grandpa was jolly enough, and
we had another grandmother
for normal human purposes.

Eva left us out of her will
because of our shocking morals:
no thoughtful little legacies
'to my beloved granddaughter'.
Disapprobation was her norm
and 'aggrieved' her default status.
How baffled she might look to hear
I've kept her prayer book (the one
she used at Drury, parading
as an Anglican to please Sam).
What's more – no thanks to her – I was
given, years ago, her gold brooch.

Ragwort

Senecio jacobaea: bad news,
this pretty weed, this constellation
of tiny suns, this doomful harbinger.

Farmers have walked off their land for less.
Cattle deficient in minerals

develop 'a depraved appetite' for it.

It springs beaming out of the soil
to seduce yet another silly beast
with its fairy gold. Whoa! Keep off!

But no: there they go, pathetic addicts,
mouthing and sucking at its alkaloids
like Laura at fruit in the goblin market

until they stagger with cirrhosis
while the plants, like all drug pushers,
multiply as fast as you cut them down.

Te Rauamoa got it early:
a present from the Seddon government
for the new settlers, smuggled in

with the grass seed. 'The Golden City',
people sneered in 1905
at the ragwort capital of the North Island,

that straggle of bush clearings, jaundicing
the landscape with their urinous tinge.
The authorities marched in a posse of sheep

to munch the invaders to the ground –
for the moment, that is.
                           My own ragwort moment –
my burning bush – on a childhood holiday

in Kent was a clump of dazzle
braided with matching caterpillars
in yellow and black stripes: the Cinnabar moth,

the designated predator. Next morning,
peering from our tent, I saw them felled.
'Poor little things', I wrote in my nature notebook.

Walking Off

Take the Dasslers, for example: even with
a buggy and two horses they were walking –
leaving it all, turning their backs, quitting

for somewhere closer to sea-level
where they needn't top-dress the soil with cobalt
and their young stock didn't wither away.

But the farm just had to sit there, languishing
for anyone who might wander by and want it,
while ragwort sniggered in the long grass;

and the hall couldn't up and walk off: it lay
under its drooping macrocarpas and wilted,
letting the blackberries crawl over its roof –

the piano is still under the wreckage.
No one revived the Post Office
that Susan Dassler had run in her front room;

the butcher's shop in a hut by the roadside
where you helped yourself and recorded your purchase
in a notebook somehow faded away;

a bus took the children to Ngutunui.
And after all, what else had there been but the hall,
the butcher's shop, the post office and the school? –

wrote Susan Dassler with her 'Pioneer's Pen'.

The Roads Again

The *Waipa Post* correspondent frothing,
nonsensical with rage: 'Our settlement . . .
the first to be formed in the King Country . . .
twenty-three years of broken promises –

yet it is without a road'. What he means
is a road better than a muddy track
through the bush; one fit for motor traffic.

The 1890s: ten unemployed men,
one remembered as Old Daddy Hoffman,
another as someone's uncle Dan Coe,
trundled their goods uphill on packhorses
to start clearing two hundred acres each
(donated by Dick Seddon's government)
and build slab huts with doors made of sacking.

Twenty years later it's pit-sawn timber
and windows with proper glass in the frames,
but still no end to the resolutions,
the petitions to the authorities
(in duplicate, the settlement having
the misfortune to straddle two counties),
the jokes about profits for coach-menders;

Mary Scott shuddering her way down the
Pekanui with a two-horse buggy
until her husband has to snatch the reins
to save them both from a gully (she'll learn);
while on the coach road a score of settlers
have made up a party to spread gravel
on the most hazardously washed-out bends.

When the through road no longer grates your bones
or makes your back-seat passengers carsick,
when its crimps and squiggles have been combed out,
angles trimmed off, surface tarsealed, so that
your car glides like butter on a warm knife,
it will have become just that: a through road
with nothing to stop off for on the way.

The Hall: a Requiem

Bill Daysh and the vicar from Kawhia
on cornet, Mrs Chase on piano,
Stan Gilmour making his violin sing,
someone on drums – the joint must have been jumping.
But that was after the tennis club opened
in the 1930s (and before it closed).

The hall began when one of the settlers
gazed at the dairy factory – defunct
now that they all had separators at home –
and was inspired. They laid a wooden floor
over the concrete, turned the engine room
into a stage and transformed the cool-room.

It served for everything: school concerts,
church services, a wedding now and then . . .
Cyril taught Sunday school there, but the only
dances he mentions were at Te Uku,
in his twenties. They went on all night
until it was time for the morning milking –

which, as a teacher, he didn't have to do.
He might have married a farmer's daughter
instead of a music teacher from Drury
where she and her friends in the girls' club
made butterfly cakes and Melting Moments
for the suppers at dances in the Drury Hall,

although even then and certainly later
in Sidcup, when they could snatch time out
from their separate shifts during the Blitz
for the First Aid Post New Year's Eve party,
he was always keener on dancing
than the music teacher turned out to be.

Barton Cottage, 1928

I

There was no mistaking it: this
  white stucco-covered box
two storeys high, planted firmly
  where you'd expect to see
a weatherboard bungalow or
  traditional villa,
on the corner of eight acres
  of manageable land,
and labelled, when Sam had finished,
  with a name imported,
like the building method, from Home.

  The date above the porch
was also on the licences
  for their shotguns – 'Farmer,
Drury', they said firmly (the years
  in Te Rauamoa
barely hinted at on the back) –
  never mind that Cyril
was a teacher at Te Uku;
  this would be Sam, signing
both of them up to the landscape
  his son had found for him.

Having personalised the house
  he began scent-marking
the village (all right, 'the township'):
  opened a hairdressing
kiosk, became a church warden
  at Old St John's, and built
with his own tools and kauri planks
  from the Selwyn cottage
a Sunday school (it stood until
  the road widening); he
was thanked with a barometer.

II

The gloss on this green-streaked apple
  suggests that of a glass
marble, or a healthy eyeball;
  glint is another word,
or gleam, for its wet-look surface.
  It was handed to me
by the present young tenant of
  Barton Cottage, who had
'always wondered about this house'.
  'My grandfather built it,'
I said, 'and planted an orchard . . .'

  Ah, still there. He's walked me
through damp grass to the gnarled trunks, the
  boughs crusty with lichen
but, for the most part, still bearing.
  And the plum trees, he says,
'flood the ground with fruit' in season.
  This waxen globe must be
a Cox's orange pippin, not
  ripe yet; perfect but for
one minute puncture mark that won't
  show in a photograph.

Cyril's Bride

When Cyril brought his bride to live, perforce,
huggermugger with him and his parents,
Eva allowed her new daughter-in-law,
who daily proffered help with the cooking,
daily to make the salad; there was no
other role for her at Barton Cottage –

except, of course, to cosset Cyril from
escaping to an independent life.
(He was not long back from something like that,

camping in the school grounds at Te Uku
with his motorbike and his swotty books –
although guess who got half his salary?)

Aeneas was relieved of Anchises
when Sam and Eva made the big trip Home.
Luck struck: the nearly-local school was closed
and Cyril posted to safely far-flung
Grahams Beach on the Manukau Harbour,
scarcely accessible except by launch.

Freedom set in: baching and making shift,
sleeping out of doors on the verandah
(the uses that man had for a tent-fly!)
rather than smothering in the bedroom
of their rented cottage; reading the minds
of hens that nested half-wild in the bush.

They sold their Austin Seven and bought an
old clinker-built lifeboat, once a whaler's,
which (nobody's fault) stranded them on a
sand bank when they chugged across the harbour
towards Auckland, planning to welcome with
a *fait accompli* their former jailers.

Nostalgia Trip, 1976

He still shared the culture of No. 8 fencing wire
in which, for example, Charlie at Makarora
had cut two lengths from that universal resource
to make a pair of knitting needles for Alice.

So Cyril, or John, as his second wife now called him,
finding himself and her and his daughter (the one from
England) and a teenage grandson locked out of the car,
conjured an entry by means of a noose of fuse wire

attached, with the boy's help, to a rod of No. 8;
and whether he travelled with wire clippers in the boot
is lost. He had parked near the school at Te Rauamoa,
drawn by a mycelium thread of nostalgia

to that fostering parent, a one-roomed box of tricks
once thrumming with rote-learnt grammar and arithmetic,
with singing lessons, geography and Empire Day,
but now muffled, stuffed up to its rafters with hay.

The Education Board carpenter skimped on the timber
in 1897 – kauri would have cost more
than mountain rimu, which nevertheless outlived
the building's function and stood firm until we arrived

to pat its flanks; Cyril/Squirrel examined the porch,
tried the tap (rusty, of course); and then, the car now broached,
continued the pilgrimage, as you'd expect, to his
boyhood home which (but how could it have stayed as it was? –

and it's not as if he'd ever wanted to go back
after all, to the years when he was living there, stuck)
had a new name on the mailbox, one he needn't know,
and a subtly altered silhouette. So be it. So

we gathered pine cones from the trees his father planted
(replacing the specimens nature had provided)
and drove uphill to the Daysh house, a shell now, its trees
ragged with lichen and tufted with perching lilies.

Jubilee Booklet, 1989

The 'Where did you live' map proved to be
quite a tax on people's memories,
remembering just who had lived where,
when. I hope you can find your name.
Bear in mind that a lot of the roads
have been realigned, so your house
may not have been where I have it marked.
For instance Robert Darlow's house
was on the other side of the road
to where I have it marked, just before
the cutting, out on the point. The facts
are as accurate as I have been able
to establish. I am only human too.

The Archive

There were the 'Opa tapes' – interviews
recorded on a reel-to-reel machine
by an anthropologist grandson, copied
to cassettes, and painstakingly transcribed
like Hansard, with interjections: 'How long?'
'Six months.' 'Six *months*!' [Horrified laughter].

There were letters, postcards, photographs –
familiar, or surprising us among
his or his father's papers; there was a box
of glass negatives never printed off
in our lifetimes: remote, secret views
of a log-scattered landscape under snow;

of a boy in long shorts on a horse;
of a harassed Alice, looking plain for once,
clutching at a huddle of under-fives,
with Eva and that same pleasant-faced boy.
There were receipts and firearms licences;
and there was a line called Trespass, not to be crossed.

State Highway 31

The owners of the land round here
haven't spent their time preserving
obsolete structures for potential
grandfather-chasers to post on Facebook.

They don't prop up decaying trees
with splints and crutches like the King's oak
or some contorted trunk proclaiming
where the early settlers landed.

But what did we expect? After all,
we'd viewed the naked course of the road
on Google Earth, and compared it with
the busy splatter of habitations

on the old sketch map. And at least
we've identified the hillock
where the school stood, then and in its
posthumous life as a hay shed.

As for that iconic row of stumps
in front of – yes – the former homestead,
what apter portrait could we ask
of posterity's heartlessness?

So this is the last time I'll say
how, as we sailed past non-stop
on the way back from Kawhia,
my stomach yearned for just one more glimpse.

Notes

The Pioneer

The results of the ballot were announced in the *New Zealand Herald* on 27 August 1915 as follows: 'A ballot was held yesterday for six sections of second-class land . . . there were 120 applications.' Seven people had applied for the section described as Pirongia Survey District. Block IX, Section 17, 150a [acres].

District News

Extracts with this title are from files of the *Waipa Post,* seen in the Alexander Turnbull Library, Wellington. I am also grateful to Catherine Jehly of the Te Awamutu Museum for providing further extracts from this newspaper.

Migrants

Mary Adcock (1825–1899) and her second husband Thomas Hardy, with one son each from their first marriages, travelled from Leicester to Utah in 1862. (Mormon websites are very informative.)

Buffalo chips were bison dung.

The School

The Moebius strip. As my father showed me when I was nine, cutting along the centre of the double-length loop gives you two separate loops, one looped through the other. It was hard to believe.

Evenings with Mother

The title Cyril has in mind is *The Master of the Shell*, by Talbot Baines Reed (1852-1893), first published in book form by the Religious Tract Society, 1901.

The Way Forward

T.U. Wells ran the predecessor to the New Zealand Correspondence School.

Shorthand

Cyril's advertisements were inserted in the *Auckland Star* on 21 and 23 June ('three hours') and 10 December 1920 ('. . . three days. Short, inexpensive, easy correspondence course.'); there was another in the *New Zealand Herald* on 12 July.

The Bible Student

I should like to tell this clever young man, with his contempt for the Authorised Version, that his distinguished ancestor Dr Robert Tighe (of whom he never heard in his lifetime) was one of the translators appointed by King James. On the other hand his enthusiasm for Charles Taze Russell, whose studies gave rise to the Jehovah's Witnesses, was misplaced – as he very soon realised. All the time I knew him Cyril was an agnostic, but with an energetic devotion to idealistic causes and a perhaps reluctant admiration for an occasional good preacher.

The Sensational

See *The Journal of the Polynesian Society*, vol. 28, no. 110, 1919: 'Rangi-hua-moa', by George Graham, pp. 107–110, for the origin of the name Te Rau-a-moa. (Modern maps and other sources tend to use the spelling Te Rauamoa, but I have not attempted to be consistent in my usage.)

The Kea Gun

I am indebted to *Papers Past*, on the National Library of New Zealand website, for extracts from newspapers which provided much of the detail here.

The Roads Again

In *Days That Have Been* (1966), the prolific author Mary Scott (1888–1979) described her early married life as a farmer's wife a few miles further up Mount Pirongia from the Adcocks.

Walking Off

Susan Dassler (1887–1988), wife of Oscar and mother of Grace and seven other children, wrote verses and articles for magazines which were collected in 1983 as *From a Pioneer's Pen*.

Jubilee Booklet, 1989

The words are from John Cleland's 'Editorial' introducing his booklet compiled for the 1989 Ngutunui School 75th Jubilee, which celebrated also Te Rau-a-moa School 1897–1962.

HOARD

(2017)

For my granddaughters – Lily, Julia, Cait, Ella, Rosa –
and my grandson Ollie.

I

Loot

'A COVENTRY HALFE PENNY': a token
minted in 1669
by some trader in that city
to make up for a shortage of small change

and sucked in the mouth of history
for so long that its outer edges
are smoothed away, gone down time's gullet
with a slow wince of dissolving copper.

Fondling it in my early teens,
and too bedazzled by its date to be
logical about geography,
I used to see it in the hand of Pepys.

But then, why shouldn't it have travelled?
After all, it found its way to me.
It could have jingled in the same pocket
as this, from the official coinage:

a hefty farthing, 1675,
half the face value but twice the volume,
with the rugged mug of the second Charles,
'Carolus a Carolo', crowned in laurel.

It could even have met my silver groat –
William and Mary, 1691,
with their unfortunate Stuart profiles
and a hole punched through the top of his wreath.

*

These were gems from a clanking bag
our former evacuee brought me
(looted by her brother from a bombed house)
to make my collection thrice glorious:

worn, a lot of them, or defaced
(that watch-chain puncture); not valuable,
I know now, but I was a-goggle
at their ages. I spread them on the floor

to wallow in: farthings from ten reigns,
cartwheel pennies, every shade of metal
from Europe, strange brass from the East,
and a denarius of Constantine.

I sorted them, listed them, researched them,
and, my subconscious having been misled
into expecting sudden marvels,
dreamed them: I'd be floating along

some hazy beach or a simulacrum
of my local streets and see by my feet
one delicious coin after another,
in archaic, unheard of currencies,

lying there, anyone's for the taking.
Grab them, quick! Stuff them under the pillow;
and this time, if you really concentrate,
they'll still be there when you wake up.

Mnemonic

Nothing I write will be as durable
as the rhyme for remembering the genders
of third declension nouns, stuck in my head
ever since Miss Garai's Latin class.

Masculini generis

I used to fancy I shared it with
generations of English schoolboys,
the colonial servant dispensing justice
under a tree in the African bush,

are the nouns that end in –nis

the wakeful subaltern in the trenches
before the Somme; but now I discover
the rhyme was originally German,
as was Miss Garai. The vision shifts:

and mensis, sanguis, orbis, fons,

the solar topeed official sits
not in Nigeria, but in Kamerun;
the soldier is on the other side of
what looks very much like the same barbed wire,

collis, lapis, piscis, mons,

writing to his girlfriend. I'll call him Kurt,
like the pen-friend Miss Garai found for me
in the Germany she had escaped from
before another world war came round.

sermo, ordo, sol and pons,
dens, sal, as, grex, pulvis.

491

Her Usual Hand

My signature begins with a shape
I never use elsewhere: a relic
of the initial 'F' I was taught
in 'real writing' at my seventh school.

My writing became, if anything,
less real as further schools numbed it,
and the sprinting pace of lecture notes
crushed it into a kind of shorthand.

In my first library job, my boss
thrust a manual on penmanship
at me: the overdue cards I sent
brought shame on the University.

For all the charms of the special nib
and its trellis patterns on the page,
italic script was not the answer:
it was not writing; it was drawing.

So my friends couldn't read my letters?
Very well, I would learn to type them.
My private messages to myself
could remain in their workaday rags.

If handwriting mirrors character
all I can see mine reflecting is
my headlong scramble for the exit,
shouting something over my shoulder.

Six Typewriters

To begin with, my father's reconditioned
German keyboard picked up during the war,
with a spiky Gothic 'o'.
                              Then, I suppose,
when I was married, the use of Alistair's:
details forgotten or repressed.

In Dunedin I answered a small ad
and paid £10 for a museum piece
black and upright as a Model T Ford.

Next, a surprise: Barry Crump's portable
Empire Corona, an honourable
parting substitute for alimony.

It's rusting at the back of a cupboard
in case it should become collectable –
after all, he had his face on a stamp.

Then my Adler Gabriele: brand new,
the machine 'für moderne Menschen' –
handsome and much cherished, until

the last one, a gift from my mother:
electronic with adjustable spacing
and a self-correct facility;

so efficient that for years I spurned
computers. Of them I shall say nothing.

Flat-Warming Party, 1958

It's usual to have guests of both sexes;
but so far I don't know any women –
apart from my professor's wife, of course,
and I don't think it's her kind of party.

Therefore I have invited seven men,
including my self-proclaimed 'fiancé'
(not my title for him) who by the end,
with any luck, won't be speaking to me.

The Anaesthetist

He asked me, 'Would you like to witness something?'
His signature on a document, I thought.
No; an emergency Caesarean.

He was my mother's friend – I hardly knew him;
but grist: yes, he saw I collected that.

The hospital was five minutes away;
he could pass me off as one of his students.
Gowned and masked, I sat in the gallery.

It took seconds: a slash down from the navel,
a transverse cut across the womb, and
they snatched a skinned rabbit out of a hat.

Then there was leisure to stuff wads of gauze
yard after yard into the seeping hollows,

to feather-stitch delicate inner tissues,
haul out the sodden scarlet dishcloths,
and cobble together white walls of fat.

'Wake up,' they said, 'wake up, Mrs Campbell' –
which happened to be my own name at the time.

Even so it was hard to identify
with her (this was like no birth I'd given);
easier, in a way, with the surgeon –

such a neat trick, once you'd been shown how.
If ever I were to find myself stranded
(desert island, snowbound cottage, stuck lift)

with a woman in desperate labour
and a handy scalpel I could have a go.

The Second Wedding

Photographs were by courtesy
of the *Otago Daily Times*:

'Author Weds Poetess' – a shot
of the bride wearing a dazed smile

in her new husband's Land Rover.
Her bruises don't show up at all.

(How easy it is to get cheap
effects with not a word untrue.)

This was after the registrar
had waited for us to put out

our cigarettes, and married us.
It was his job, and we were there.

The Sleeping Bag

But when we rolled him out he didn't move:
curled up like a bud. He'd fallen asleep
snuggled in the back of the Land Rover,

and Barry thought it would be amusing
to tote him up all those endless steps
to wherever we were visiting

like a sack of coal, over his shoulders,
swaddled in impermeable down.
Just hooliganism, really; a joke.

It may have taken seconds, not long minutes,
to shake him and shake him . . .
                                Light of my life
(child of my first marriage – nothing to Barry).

I have some friends who lost a son that way,
smothered in an airless den of feathers;
which, if I'd known . . . But not my son, praise God.

Barry could get away with most things.
Kids thought he was magic. They came flocking.
He was to kill five boys in his time:

by negligence, by booze, by his grievous fault.
They drowned, all five of them together, trapped
in a vehicle, unsupervised.

But my boy wasn't one of them.
(Let me not gloat, Lord. Let me not gloat.)
We'd moved on by then, I and my boy.

A Game of 500

The Muse is a seeker after sensation.
She wants me to tell you about the time
when my second husband offered to play me
at cards for my young lover's life.

Except that it wasn't quite like that:
no death on offer, for example; just
a beating-up. And anyway
he'd left me first, the bastard; and anyway . . .

But enough of that (although yes, I won).
What I'd rather tell you about is how
in this hot summer the little girls
have been chalking on the pavement:

birthday cakes with coloured candles,
and, repeated twice in large letters,
'Horse Queen of the Year' –
whatever they may have meant by that.

La Contessa Scalza

I'm at the bar on the swimming-pool deck,
chatting in German with Giuliano
and drinking Campari. My feet are bare
(hence my nickname) as if to symbolise
the shedding of a few identities –
or is it just a kind of showing off?
My five-year-old is in the cool playroom
two decks down, where the kids hoot and rollick.
Further down, in the hold, my worldly goods:
a large packing-case of household effects,
my sewing machine, Grandpa's cabin trunk
full of our clothes, two cardboard suitcases
splitting with books, and Barry Crump's cast-off
portable Smith Corona typewriter.

North London Polytechnic

Mr Yescombe explains my duties. One
will be to open what he calls 'the post'
(he means the mail). He introduces my
new colleague in the vast pink overall
who will show me around the library.

Then, making conversation, he assumes
I'll 'be wanting to visit Scotland soon'.
I simper politely. (No – why Scotland?
All I want is to wallow in the charms
of England regained after sixteen years.)

Meanwhile if I walk to the next-but-one
bus stop on the way home I'll save enough
to buy either the *Radio Times* (bliss
that it's not the *NZ Listener*) or
a loaf of bread. I'll decide which later.

Election, 1964

Mr Overton, the librarian
of the Commonwealth Relations Office,
came into Cataloguing to bring us
the election result: Labour had won.

'But don't worry,' he added, 'with such a
small majority I don't imagine
they'll be able to nationalise steel.'
I glanced at my colleague, a Sloane Ranger,

and at Mr Overton's kindly face.
These were the English, or samples of them.
How had I got through the vetting system?
This was hardly the moment to confess

it was I who had adorned the mirror
in the Ladies with 'Vote Labour' stickers.
Steel? What did I know about anything?
In New Zealand we had the Welfare State.

Kidnapped

That humming sound you can hear is of bees
feasting on the blossoming cherry tree
outside East Finchley Methodist Church,
into which my little boy was kidnapped
for a year or two of Sunday mornings
to march up and down the County roads
in his navy Boys' Brigade band jersey
and a round sailor-boy hat, yo-ho-ho,
playing whatever instrument he played
and not forgetting his penny for Jesus –
his reward being to appear onstage
at the Sunday school end-of-term gala
in the role of a chrysanthemum petal,
or a letter in the word 'chrysanthemum'.

II

Ann Jane's Husband

Consider for a moment Hugh Devlin,
sail-maker, of Liverpool,
who was married to Ann Jane Eggington
for six weeks before she died.

He must certainly have thought he'd killed her:
fucked her to death, most likely,
clutching her in his arms night after night,
his poor Ann Jane, and pumping

something unforgivable into her
until it erupted in
fever and screaming pain – his fault, surely.
No use to reason with him,

and he could conceivably have been right:
peritonitis can stem
from ectopic pregnancy. For the next
fifty years he bumped around

the dockside alleys, lodging with workmates,
his life lopped off at the root;
a non-ancestor. He would never risk
murdering a second wife.

Mother's Knee

I
If you like stories, here's one to chew on:
a little girl in the street at Cookstown
frightened by something she can't understand –
four men holding the corners of a sheet,
and tossing a body high in the air.

Hustling her away, her mother explained:
the one in the nightshirt had a fever;
that was the only way to bring it down.
Martha was five in 1848;
this must have been the Potato Famine.

II
A generation on, in New Zealand,
we come to Jinnie and the string of beads.
Her teenage sister Lizzie went swimming
at Slippery Creek with Phoebe Godkin,
and little Jinnie was left in their charge.

The only thing was to buy her silence.
Back home, Martha frightened it out of her:
'Where did you get those beads, Jinnie? Jinnie!'
'Phoebe Godkin gave me them, not to tell
about her and Lizzie going swimming.'

III
These are in the pure oral tradition –
mother to daughter to daughter's daughter –
no dates, no writing. It seems almost wrong
to supplement it from outside sources.
Lizzie, for example, married a man

who drove a brewer's dray and smelt of beer;
his last drink was a bottle of Lysol.
You surely can't like knowing that? Better
to leave her in 1880-something
prancing in Slippery Creek in her shift.

Camisoles

Then there was my mother's sister Dorrie
who stitched and trimmed a dozen camisoles
in pastel silk fabrics for her trousseau,
only to discover, as the wedding day loomed,
that the brassiere had made them obsolete.

The March

The Baths Hall

Ellen Wilkinson, in the foam bath at Barnsley,
sees only the road – which, at the moment,
is all I can see myself, being uncertain
as to what exactly the women's foam bath was,

except that she had it all to herself
while two hundred aching men from Jarrow
wallowed and soothed their feet in the men's pool,
also specially heated for their arrival –

the road from Wakefield to Barnsley, that is:
nearly ten miles of it, and she walking in front
until they arrived at Barnsley Town Hall
for a meal of hot potato pie, and the Mayor proclaiming

'Everything that Barnsley can do for you will be done.'
But before too long Ellen's puny shoulders
emerge from the foam, anadyomene.
She may have been a legend; she was not a myth.

Ellen and the Bishops

A two-faced lot, in her experience.
Leicester and his wife were hospitable,
but he was low down in the hierarchy.
Jarrow, that 'saintly man', had blessed the march

as it set out but then had to recant
and call it 'undesirable'. He'd been
got at by Durham, who wrote to *The Times*
of 'revolutionary mob pressure'.

'When the class struggle comes to the surface,'
said Ellen, 'progress is a thin veneer.'
Just as well she wasn't there in person,
to contaminate Durham Cathedral

and waken the misogynistic bones
of St Cuthbert behind the high altar
to a tantrum. A campaigning woman!
He might have kicked the lid right off his tomb.

The Mascot

Then there was the dog: a Labrador, they thought,
or a mongrel, or, someone said, a terrier
(does that look like a terrier to you?)
But certainly a gift to the reporters.

Paddy, its name was, or Jarrow – a stray
that tagged on to the march; or it was called Peter
and belonged to a woman in Hebburn.
Once it nearly pulled Ellen off her feet.

Oh, they liked that, the journalists:
petite Miss Wilkinson, trying to keep up,
tittuping along on her little tootsies,
taking three steps to every stride of the men,

503

hanging on grimly to the mascot's leash
as they formed up to march into a town.
A Labrador will do for the sculpture
posterity is going to erect.

You, Ellen

Heroine

I plucked you out of a group photograph
in our family album: you, composed,
standing in the centre front; my father,
pleased with himself, just behind you, his head,
like yours, tilted slightly back – a habit
learnt from being among taller people.

You chaired the first UNESCO conference
(this wasn't it); you were from Manchester,
you'd been a teacher, you'd served in the Blitz –
you couldn't have been more his cup of tea.
'That's the Minister of Education,'
Mother would boast. So where was it taken?

Three women and fifteen men, all in suits
apart from one ARP uniform
(is that a clue?). Birkbeck suggests itself,
or, more likely, the WEA.
There's no one alive to ask. OK, then:
I shall have to interrogate the dead.

                              *

But the dead are giving nothing away.
They refer me to books. I've read the books:
your books, the books of others, pro and con,
occasional condescending asides

in memoirs by your contemporaries –
all grist, but these are not what I'm after.

I want your personal correspondence
(destroyed by your over-loyal siblings);
I want all the notes and scribbles you burned,
the private diaries you never kept.
Yes, I suppose I could plod through Hansard.
It won't exactly answer my questions.

I want your voice; they advise me to go
to the British Library Sound Archive . . .
Meanwhile, the name of that conference? Ah:
the dead have spoken up; my late father
wrote home about it to my grandparents.
Not madly interesting, it turns out.

The Fiancé

They couldn't work out what you saw in this
'flabby length of pump water' (your aunt's words);
'arrogant; physically revolting'
said your friends; and – oh dear – 'always sniffing'.

You wouldn't have been the first young woman
to get carried away by the wrong chap.
But couldn't they see it was politics
you were in love with? It was the pure flame

of Marxism that soldered you to him –
even so briefly. Years later, after
his *annus* not-very-*mirabilis*
as Westminster's first Communist MP

something still flickered between you, until
you moved unforgivably far ahead;
by which time you had a PPS who
could intercept the hate mail he sent you.

505

The Division Bell Mystery

Well, you were no Dorothy L. Sayers,
but a politician without a seat
needs an avocation that will grip her,
and this was yours in 1932.

Your plot wobbles, your favourite suspect,
sleek and columnar in her haute couture,
leaves us cold; your MP/sleuth is a drip,
and your police a disgrace to the force.

But look, who's this? A young Cockney member
(you in disguise) has joined the cast, to roam
the terraces of your former Eden,
denied to you since you lost Middlesbrough.

Let no one doubt: your true heroine was
the House itself – the sprawling, echoing,
towering Mother of Parliaments;
which in a few years would let you back in.

The Shelter Queen

'Safety, Sanitation and Sleep', meaning
bunk beds and chemical lavatories
for the nightly hordes on the tube platforms
or in air-raid shelters. Twice in your life

the public acknowledged you as a star:
first on the Jarrow March, then in the Blitz,
when having dodged or tired out your minders
you drove your own car wildly through London

(no headlights in the blackout) to offer
what comfort there might be to the bereaved
after the Heavy Rescue men had left,
at the cost of your own sleep and safety.

506

They were less keen when you had to enforce
fire-watching for women as well as men,
but you knew best; you'd been bombed out yourself.
Also there was that severed foot you'd seen.

Herbert Morrison

Not easy for some of us to warm to
a politician who was to become
Peter Mandelson's grandfather – although
a bit of human warmth was what he craved,

his wife having long ago switched hers off,
around the time she banned coal fires (the dust!).
Picture him, then, the Home Secretary,
spending weeknights during the Blitz in his

office basement but country weekends at
his assistant Miss Wilkinson's cottage,
snug by her hearth, one of them on each side,
working on the papers in their boxes;

or ('Caesar's wife' and all that; no scandal)
at some other fireside on his rota:
the Wilmots', Lady Rhondda's; the Frasers';
Lady Allen's – oh yes; Lady Allen . . .

The Hat

What was the 'incongruous' hat they heckled
when you rushed up, flustered, to the dispatch box?
Couldn't they see you hadn't long to live?
(Your fit of asthmatic coughing stilled them.)

I find I have a hankering to view
a parade of your hats, your suits, your dresses:

the black velvet with the broad lace collar
for your 'little waif' act, the apple green

worn with your red hair – and shingled, what's more –
that shook up the House when you first took your seat
('Dress dull,' Nancy Astor advised); the fur coat
you tactfully (or hypocritically)

shed before speaking on a Union platform.
You'd have done better to wear it more often
and to be less valiant about your duties –
going out in all weathers, catching your death.

To Ellen, in the End

I've been procrastinating, edging back
from your pop-star exit – prescription drugs,
a scatter of pills on the floor; the doubts;
the did-she, didn't-she kernel of it.

Except that it wasn't from addiction;
it was asthma yet again, as always.
And it wasn't from love, surely? Not for
Morrison's chubby arms back around you?

His biographer writes baldly: 'Ellen
Wilkinson committed suicide', and
I want to hit him. It wasn't like that –
although it wasn't not like that either.

Perhaps all you longed for was a night's sleep.
There was an inquest: accidental death.
The gossips carry on (here's me, for one).
Your defenders protest. There's always more to say.

III

Hortus

Dreamiest dream for years, this enchanted
amble through cliff-top gardens enamelled
in greens my brain cells have just invented.

Refusing to wake, my fingers fidget
for a mouse to click on Save and store it
among my Favourites, to revisit.

A Spinney

May-Tree

Now that the trees are my family,
the hawthorn is my older sister:
prickly, but to be envied.

Who said she could dress up like that,
in the salty reek of may?
When will it be my turn for white froth?

Crab-Apple

But the adults never understood it:
our co-conspirator at the wood's edge,
climbable, flowering or knobbly with dolls' fruit.

VJ Day came. Drunk with glory,
they chopped it to bits for their victory bonfire.
A streetful of kids howled in desolation.

Elm

Trust me to fall for something doomed! –
the tree in my school grounds I hid in daily,
higher than roof-height, when I was new.

It's gone where all the elm trees go.
I can feel its fissured bark; I can still mourn
the branch Jean Oliver snapped when she tried to be me.

Horse-Chestnut

The squirrels want me to grow a forest.
They plant acorns in my lawn;
I haul them out by the stems, like minims.

They plant a conker. A green hand shoots up,
and lo, I've stabled it in a pot:
a fistful of sticky-buds for next spring.

Yew

Some bird shat out a seed in the alley.
I dug up a stalk of green feathers
and set it in a lighter place to grow.

Summer by summer it fattens and fluffs out –
slow, but wiser than me.
I'm going to let it live for a thousand years.

Fox-Light

Waking out of sleep paralysis
with a back-from-the-brink gulp for breath
and a sudden aversion to bed, I leap
to my feet and hurl the window open.

There is the garden in black and white,
moon-stencilled with shadows; I think of
Erasmus Darwin and his lunar friends
trotting over their lit landscapes to meet.

This is fox-light: illumination
for foxes to go marauding by,
as in the days before they were urban,
and in the days before that; before towns.

Albatross

An albatross chick can weigh ten kilos:
heavier than either of its parents.
In the Albatross Centre they showed us
a saggy fake one in white towelling
to flummox us with its weight when we tried
lifting it. Think of that around your neck –
or even the lanky lattice of bones
it grows into. Imagine earning that.

# #

Walking is the secret of it: alone
or, famously, the three of you setting off
at sunset, Wordsworth laying out his plan
for your ballad and Dorothy noting it down;

walking, that is, and having read 'almost
everything – a library cormorant',
so that when you began there rushed into your brain

helter-skelter as you strode the Quantocks
Mr Philip Quarll on his South Sea island
who destroyed a bird 'as was certainly made for
Nature's Diversion' and the *Arabian Nights*
the merchantmen at the Bristol quays
your friend Cruikshank's dream of a spectre-ship
a menagerie of creatures out of Bartram's *Travels*
the partie-coloured snakes in the Azores
around Hawkins' becalmed ship not to mention
the Bounty mutineers on their rumour-haunted
voyaging Cook's crawling phosphorescence
the dancing fires whatever they were
or the ice-fields from northern latitudes
that could stand so easily for the polar South
lit by celestial phenomena
to wonder at and echoing with spirit voices
plus of course Shelvocke's '*disconsolate black albitross*'
as prescribed by Wordsworth at the beginning.

# #

'*It ate the food it ne'er had eat*' –
biscuit-worms given it by the mariners,
until you edited them out.

This was no spontaneous effusion,
say what they might, but the work of ardent months,

and long after Cottle came from Bristol
to discuss the printing it foamed through your head,
demanding to be tinkered with, modernised, glossed:

a nautical image from your trip to Malta
spliced in, some Chaucerian diction expunged . . .

You didn't need Mr Grouch and his Preface –
'The Poem of my Friend has indeed great defects' –
to keep you going back to fondle it.

Flying fish lay their eggs on floating debris;
hard to avoid slurping them up together.
'It ate the food it ne'er had eat':

toothbrush, golf ball, tampon applicator . . .
What percentage of albatross chicks
have been found with plastic in their stomachs?

All.
        And what about trawl fisheries? Hooks?
No doubt websites can provide some statistics.

# #

But here comes your Old Navigator again,
beginning and beginning and beginning . . .

Cheveux de Lin

This newly scutched and hackled wisp of flax
rescued from the floor of the beetling mill
after the tourist guide's demonstration

matches exactly (in colour although
not quite in texture) the curl clipped from my
son Gregory's head at his first haircut

before his tender squiggles gave way to
thicker strands that darkened to brown, then black,
then, in his fifties, became smudged with grey.

My Erstwhile Fans

Gone are the days when I was all the rage
among the workers at a factory
in Timişoara – or so I was told

by the foreman; not me personally
but Romanian versions of my poems
(perhaps the credit lay with the translator).

Ceauşescu was shot. Poetry gave way
to Western movies and pornography.
I was a victim of the revolution.

The Bookshop

That bookshop where the Longleys and I,
drifting among the levels and chambers
of its peristaltic convolutions
on the last morning of the festival,

were lured in different directions, sucked
and digested in the dreamy caverns,
until we lost sight of each other and
they disappeared – or, as it seemed to them,

I disappeared – (backtrack as we might
there was no reuniting under that roof)
has now itself, apart from its online
phantom, vanished. As they do. As they do.

Maulden Church Meadow

As this is one of the destinations
for my ashes after I'm cremated
perhaps I could start with a trial run:
frizzle up one of my little fingers

while I'm walking here, and scatter it fresh
among the cowslips by the tadpole pond,
or lop one off among the lady's-smocks
on the bridle path as a snack for foxes.

I scoured the hedges around this field once
looking for their den. I could have waited:
what else would you call that excavation
in the north-east corner of my garden,
scooped under the roots of the pissard plum?

You can't really believe they eat children.

Oscar and Henry

If you must have a dog, have a golden retriever
and settle for the lumbering devotion
of one like Oscar, so hugely fixated
that, his master having failed to convey

the concept of 'temporary' or 'back in a month',
he fell into a canine depression
and developed eczema, which mustn't be scratched;
thus causing himself the humiliation

of having to walk around for weeks
with his head in a bucket, or at least stuck through
the base of a bucket, the sides framing
his face like Dog Toby's Punch and Judy frill.

But perhaps it's not a breed for the city
where the temptations can be so corrupting –
think of Henry, who at the faintest sniff
of freedom through a not quite latched front gate

is off towards the High Road, across the traffic lights,
and in at Budgens' automatic doors

to snaffle up another chocolate bar
from the impulse buys at the nearest checkout.

Real Estate

'If you sold this place,' says my neighbour, 'you
could buy a little flat.' A little flat!
One with no room for half my books, no stairs
to keep my knees in flexible order,

one in which on no morning would my eyes
open to next door's silver birch, self-sown
in the days of Marjorie and her cats,
or the house-high pear trees next door but one.

And what would such a deal bring me? Money.
Money with which I could try to buy back –
in vain, the market being what it is –
my garden full of snails and foliage,

my hundred-year-old Codling apple tree,
my self-propagating, sempiternal
primroses, my falling-down lilacs where
the goldfinches pose on their birdfeeders,

my much-repaired and always ailing roof,
my inconvenient, unheatable
indoor spaces, my Victorian bath
just long enough for me to lie down in.

The Lipstick

If I throw it into a bin,
this lipstick I bought by mistake
which wears the same metallic case
as my regular Pink Brandy

but is so shudderingly wrong
that when I use it on my lips
it makes my face look cyanosed,
it will finish up in landfill,
seeping and oozing, leaking fats
through its patiently corroding
armour, wailing invisibly
into the soil with its puce voice.

Hair

Then, fingering my hair, he asks
'What colour would you call it? Mauve?' –

and briefly I'm transformed into
some exotic flibbertigibbet

with rings on her toes, drinking Pernod
and dressed in an assemblage of wisps,

till I remember: he's colour-blind.
'No; just grey. But thank you for asking.'

Pacifiers

They clutch at their phones the way we used to reach for
a packet of Silk Cut: separation anxiety,
a blocky shape to fondle in your pocket.

I had a black cigarette holder, with sparkles,
and a carved ivory one from Singapore.
Smoke fizzed and sang under my breastbone.

                          Them and their apps.

Bender

I can do better than Uri Geller:
I can bend not just forks, and spoons, and knives,
but whole drawers of cutlery at once.

I can bend railings and fence-palings,
vertical stripes on wallpaper,
the spines of books in rows on a shelf,

and, if I rotate the pages
through ninety degrees, lines of type.
I do it with my eyes, at a glance.

– But how bent are they? Curved like a horseshoe,
or rippled as in a distorting glass?
And will they stay bent when you have bent them?

– They are like the waves in a mermaid's hair:
kinked and cranked, not permanently marcelled.
A drench in the vasty deep will uncrimp them.

Kinky eyes are a perversion, surely,
but rectitude returns if I close
my left, my sinister orb – that frail jelly.

Hot Baths

These days when anxious friends confide in me
about their intimate medical problems
it's never that they're afraid they're pregnant
and the situation is complicated
by not being sure whether the father
was that guy from Christchurch at my party
or, two days afterwards, up at Nick's place,
when we all stayed the night sleeping on floors,
our brilliant but unstable student friend –
far too young; and the one from Christchurch, well . . .

plus they've proved that the old wives' remedy –
casseroling yourself in a boiling bath
while drinking gin – serves only to make you drunk,
and not happy-drunk; sickening, really.

Standedge

Let's hear it again for Marsden
with its sudden baking Yorkshire sunshine
and the vicarage-garden-party hat
I scavenged from a charity shop –
immortalised by a kind lady
who clicked us leaning against your car
(look, those are white York roses in the hedge!).

Oh, and the tunnel was open then,
your kind of thing as much as mine.
We joined a good-humoured queue for the boat;
I boasted to the tour guide
about my ancestor's nephew, a legger
(what could be more authentic? I ask you!),
and we chugged entranced into the darkening vaults.

Hic Iacet

'Keep it short and don't talk about yourself.'
But there will be no self to talk about
in that land of the obituary,
in that night of twenty-four hours,
lying on the stones without a stretcher,
weightless, evacuated, no one's dear.

I V

Pakiri

Take me to see the oioi,
which sounds like an Australian marsupial
but is in fact a flowering rush.

Something's eeling about under the lilies.
There are clumps of complicated knitting
constructed of interlocking thorns,

and willow, which can't be stopped from growing –
chopped and stacked for firewood,
the logs are still sprouting green.

Willow, green willow, green willow:
you ran all along the creeks of my youth,
promoting yourself regardless;

but this is an artificial pond;
the willow can stay on the perimeter
with the rest of the non-indigenous –

is that an aye-aye in the oioi?
No: no lemurs allowed, although
Rosa would love a bush-baby.

Paint me an aye-aye, Rosa,
and one for your other grandmother.
Don't forget we saw a huhu.

Helensville

Small-town New Zealand's doing its thing
of channelling the 1930s
with its Plunket Rooms and the adjoining
public toilets (unfortunately shut),
its grand Post Office (now superseded
by a PostShop), and the slightly less grand
historic original Grand Hotel,
in Railway Street (but the station's closed).

Then there's the art deco Regent Cinema,
now an antiques business – owned, it turns out
when we stop the car to take a picture,
by a man whose face is familiar
to our driver – didn't he go to school
with her brother, somewhere altogether else?

Ruakaka
(*For Gillian Whitehead*)

Oystercatchers have flaked out, storm-weary,
on the grass verges down by the beach.
Up here the builders will be back in the New Year;
there's a fridge in a bedroom, an electric jug
on the floor where the kitchen's going to be.

You've made soup and salad; we three have brought
cheese, wine, fruit. The cutlery's borrowed
from Joyce and Ian; this evening, in return,
we'll join them downstairs and you'll cook for us all.
Steamy sunshine's mopping the garden dry.

I'm spelling out what you already know,
for the sake of completing another entry
in our intermittent travelogue:
Newcastle, Ambleside, London, Sydney,
Auckland, the Otago Peninsula

(where I adopted your father's binoculars
and prowled the shoreline, laughing at my first
spoonbill – clearly designed by Walt Disney)
and Northumberland, redolent of Hotspur,
hero of our first collaboration.

After him came a parade of heroines,
from medieval queens to my great-aunt Alice,
to sing their way through their difficult lives.
How they haunted us! KM and Iris,
Elizabeth Percy in Alnwick castle,

and Eleanor; Eleanor. I still have
the green towel I bought in the market
for us to take turns with in that grotty
Paris hotel, when we were on our way
to meet Bill for our tour of Aquitaine.

Blue Stars

To qualify as a New Zealander
I'd have to turn against the agapanthus.
This wasn't mentioned at the passport office,
but my New Zealand nationality
is a part-time thing – a bit of nostalgia.
Genuine applicants don't need to be told.

They drive around in their cars, glaring
at parades of handsome blue stars on stalks
along even the remotest roadside verge,
more abundant than Wordsworth's daffodils.
'Can you believe the size of these roots?' they
pant in their gardens, with spade and mattock.

A country that has no indigenous
wild flowers except those growing on trees
must submit to being colonised again
if it wants ground level decoration.
Too late to complain that you didn't mean it;
that's what they used to say about rabbits.

Yes, yes: not your fault; we know that. The seeds
get carried far and wide by car tyres.
I sit in whoever's back seat cooing
at the floriferous, fluorescent
clusters of miniature sapphire trumpets
carried erect on their marching stems.

I never set eyes on one in my youth
until – when did I visit the Duggans?
But this is the age of garden escapes:
colourful incongruities flourish
incontinently wherever it's mild,
like parrots escaped from an aviary.

Most are accepted – nobody minds
the odd wallflower – but these are villains:
the blue rosette is the booby prize.
Oh, and there's a white variety too,
a luminous constellation of petals
in moon-colouring . . . All right; I'll shut up.

Thank you all for your hospitality.
I'll leave you battling against 'those aggies'
and travel home on my other passport
to – guess what statuesque, architectural,
strap-leaved plants grown years ago from seed
in pots on my outside window-sills?

Fowlds Park

Who does his duty is a question
Too complex to be solved by me;
But he, I venture the suggestion,
Does part of his who plants a tree.
JAMES RUSSELL LOWELL

Or, as the plaque at the entrance has it,
'to complex', with the second 'o' left out
and impossible to insert later,
stone being stone. But thank you, Sir George Fowlds,
for this thirty-acre bowl of greenery
combining sports ground and arboretum.

Here I brought first Ella and then Cait,
as each in turn grew old enough for it,
to identify from *Which New Zealand Bird?*
the kingfisher at his regular station
on the telephone wire; rosellas pasturing
on the grass next to the children's playground.

Everything here matters to someone:
the swings, the coin-in-the-slot barbecue
(when it works), the Rocky Nook Bowling Club,
the perimeter path for the dog walkers,
the elegant sky-high landmark silhouettes
of the gum trees beside Western Springs Road.

The bastards will get their hands on it – sure to;
they will come with their development schemes . . .
But in the meantime here is this ancient
great-great-granny pohutukawa
catching the sun at exactly the right time
for my deep memory to photograph it.

So before the Friends of Fowlds Park line up
with their diagrams and their aerial views
of which historic trees are for the chop –
Norfolk Island hibiscus, Phoenix palm,

Moreton Bay fig, Japanese cedar,
four tulip trees, four maple, one red oak,

and at least six varieties of natives –
let's pay tribute to the stonemason
focussing so hard on the tricky words
that he slipped up just once on a short one,
thus rendering the whole quotation
impossible for a pedant to forget.

Mercer

'The squalid tea of Mercer is not strained.'
A.R.D. FAIRBURN

Brilliant, Rex. And now that's out of the way
two more reflections on Mercer station,
neither including the refreshment room.

I travelled alone on the Limited
up from Wellington, when I was sixteen,
awake all night reading *Faust* in German.

Mercer was the last stop before Auckland
for express trains. Grandma bustled across
and shepherded me by bus to Drury.

Not that Drury hadn't its own station –
her father Richey Brooks, newly arrived
from County Derry, worked for the railways

while the tracks from Auckland were being laid
and stood at Drury to flag the first train
through to the new terminus at Mercer.

(I like to imagine him dressed up in
his old militia sergeant's uniform.)
1875, it was; late May.

Well, *Ave atque Vale*, Main Trunk Line:
you lasted a bare century, before
the tourist industry converted you

into a luxury cruise-line on rails;
the masses may travel by air or road
like us, who've parked somewhere anonymous

on State Highway 1 (is this still Mercer?)
to browse through some bric-a-brac in a shop.
Rejecting teapots, coins, a stuffed monkey,

I yield to half a dozen table knives
with bone-coloured handles, warm in the grip –
you know the ones – still in their tattered box.

Alfriston

It shouldn't be Alfriston at all;
it should be Drury. But Drury went agley,
went off, went bung, turned into shit creek.

No relatives there except underground
in the Presbyterian cemetery –
register kept for years by Uncle Wyc –

where a clump of toetoe, three metres high,
bursts up out of the cracked concrete
over his parents' monumental grave.

What a laugh he had, and the friendliest
false teeth of all the great-uncles!
(Uncle Jim, we thought, was the best looking.)

But now it's Alfriston, a grid of a place,
lines on a map, that we must go to
when we visit my nearest cousin:

Rose; little Rosie, red-haired rosebud,
a toddler when I was five, a basic
ingredient in essence-of-Drury –

Stop that! We're in Alfriston now,
with two more cousins, Shirley and Barbara
(Auntie Flo's girls), and Rose's husband.

The table's adorned for afternoon tea.
Perhaps I'd like a mini-quiche?
(Hang on – isn't that a bit modern?)

Cream cracker with a slice of tomato?
Date loaf? Another of Rose's scones?
And surely someone's knocked up a sponge.

Thames

Rather alternative these days, Thames:
haunted op-shops full of fancy crockery,
tottering canyons of old wardrobes,
a sense of goods for sale that aren't on show.
Hippies cruise by like extras in a film,
togged up in beards and unlikely knitwear.

Most things that happened here happened a while ago:
like the gold rush, with its hundred hotels;
like the locomotive industry
(watch out or you'll turn into a museum);
like staying with Auntie Lizzie and Alma
on our post-war back-from-England tour.

They gave us exotic fruits with real cream
and a crate of nasty American sodas
to make us feel at home in New Zealand.
'That's not fat, it's muscle,' said Auntie Lizzie
when we thwacked her on the bum, enjoying
a new great-aunt we could be cheeky with.

From Pollen Street Auckland to Pollen Street Thames
Alma had come in her middle-aged bridehood,
having married that pillar of rectitude
Mr Belcher of Ezywalkin Shoes.
(You wouldn't dare to wallop Mr Belcher;
we rather doubted if he had a bum.)

Nearly seventy years on, the former
Ezywalkin declines to reveal itself –
how to tell one handsome but faded
shop-front from another? Even this café
has a past. (Whoops! There goes a funeral:
a squad of bikers roaring behind a hearse.)

When we've finished our toasted sandwiches
it's time for the next touristic indulgence.
Andrew offers the bird hide, approached
by a boardwalk over a mangrove swamp:
not quite as long as he'd remembered
but joyously a-flutter with fantails.

By now the chief museum will be open
(and don't worry about that hooter;
it's a call for the Volunteer Fire Brigade –
to which no one seems to be responding).
I thank my clever son for the fantails.
'That's OK – any time,' says the modest.

Raglan

What do you do in Raglan when it's raining?
You sit outside the library, it seems,
under the stone portico, soaking up
the free Wi-Fi. Or you bring your guitar
and huddle among the harmonists, while
the raindrops dance off the Phoenix palms
all along the centre of Bow Street,
de-dah, de-dah. What else can they do?

528

If you're not a raindrop, you could hang out
at the Blacksand Café, or the Shack; or
there's the museum, but when you've seen it
you've seen it – and you've certainly seen it
when you were at school, if you live here.
Or you could dive off the bridge. Be careful.

Miramar Revisited

(*For Marilyn*)

Right: we get off at the stop near Kauri Street,
but at the other end, not the old tram stop –
the airport perimeter encroached on that;
Caledonia Street is the bus route now.

Approaching it from the opposite direction
transfers our house to the wrong side of the road;
and it's gone topsy-turvy – where's the front verandah?
Why has the garage moved to the right-hand side?

We aren't so naive as to ask what happened
to the one our father built from packing cases
for his bargain vintage Model T Ford –
'We're off to see the Wizard . . .' (he knew he was it).

Better check up on the rest of our surroundings.
You think you've identified the old cake shop;
I'm after the newsagent's and the grocer's
where we used to be sent to do the messages.

Knox Church, purveyor of such wholesome pursuits
as table tennis and square dancing, has gone,
swept up like Dorothy's house out of Kansas,
and as for the milk-bar, that could be anywhere.

God knows, my brain's boggled enough already
puzzling out directions with the sun in the north.
Reason doesn't seem to prevail on a sense
lodged as deep as my pituitary gland.

But we're not lost. We've made our expedition.
Sunshine has technicoloured the flat streets;
this three-dimensional wind will be excised
from our memories in a week or two: you'll see.

Carterton

. . . Of which my experience is limited to
the wind-raked station, with Kathleen waiting
to clasp us against her fluffy pink jumper,
and five minutes in a car from there to here:

a former thirty-room hotel, twice burnt out,
so that most of the lower floor is a blank shell
and you have to walk up twenty-six splintery
stairs to the family end of the dining room

where Kathleen's son-in-law, a chimney sweep
in a good way of business, has said a blessing
over our meal (no alcohol, of course –
they're all JWs – but a laden table).

Thirty rooms are a lot, even with most of them
not yet reconstructed: more than enough to store
the entire contents of Kathleen's house, shipped over
from Australia after her husband died,

and still in its containers. Not limitless space,
but even while we've been sitting here eating
ham and potatoes, cauliflower and fish,
passing salads to each other, we've squeezed in

the crab-apple tree from the wood near Kathleen's house
just round the curve in Woodside Way from our own,
more trees, the timber yard where we trespassed,
and our back garden complete with our four ducks.

We've spooled in the track across the common
Kathleen and I used to walk over to school
with our little sisters (mine's here beside me),
rolled up a road or two and stuffed them in somehow,

and compressed a double-decker bus to fit.
There's still the school itself to be folded up,
including the playground and the air raid shelters
under the playground (we're working on those),

and the pub on the green, or at least its back door,
where if you had money you could buy a bag
of Smith's crisps – yes, the ones you've heard about
with a little twist of salt in dark blue paper.

Tinakori Road

A house-sized box of atmosphere, complete
with authentic fittings, repro wallpaper
and the creepy photograph of the dead baby:
the Katherine Mansfield Birthplace, my choice
for an outing in my granddaughter's car
on this drenched morning. OK, Julia? Cool.

Heading back we pass our own family shrine,
the house where your father spent his infancy:
not literally the birthplace – he and Andrew
were born in St Helen's hospital – but
the 'Gregory Campbell Learns-to-walk-and-talk,
rides-a-tricycle, falls-out-of-a-tree-place'.

In between that house, number 245,
and the Birthplace at the far end of the road,
there used to stand the 'Garden-Party' house:
number 75, an even grander
KM residence, background to her teens
and a cherished focus for Mansfield scholars.

I wasn't there when they demolished it
for the motorway, but Prof Gordon was –
eighty years old, fizzing like a rocket,
bouncing in front of the bulldozers, crushing
the impulse to snatch a souvenir plank
(what, after all, could he have done with it?).

The same fate befell her old school – my school:
not the charmless Lego that's replaced it
but the creaky wooden structure where I sat
in what was reputed to have been her classroom,
gazing into the distance, being her . . .
Well, that's it, Julia. If we had more time

we could drive to where you spent your own childhood –
and there she'd be again, preceding us
to Karori, to another of her homes
and her first school. Was it your first school too?
No, yours was Karori West. Still, pretty close.
A kind of phantom stalker, that KM.

High Rise

I spy with my long-seeing eye
a row of rooms in monochrome lighting.
On the largest window someone has scrawled
'P' and 'G' for 'Parking Gallery' –
a sketch of a sign; work in progress.

Behind me in P for pohutukawa,
at something more like street level,
the first tui cranks up the morning.
It is not morning. It is 4am.

This building stands on legs that don't match.

Turn around again. Way below,
at street level minus four or five,
something red and enormous
is reversing into or out of its den;
its indicators ding out the news.

Down to the left, traffic lights are chanting
with a flash, flash and a flash, flash
that boring song you'll never get rid of.

Everything hums: hills, harbour,
hubbub-to-come. But it's not dawn yet.
Look in the sky and Brother, Brother:
twenty floors up, floating in darkness,
fluorescent blue letters mean 'Keep out of my hair'.

The Old Government Buildings

There it sprawls, embodying magnitude –
but also symmetry – not sure whether
to label itself 'buildings' or 'building'.

Dignity would demand the plural, but
'Largest wooden building in the southern
hemisphere' denotes it as singular.

Admittedly it doesn't look wooden:
it could be stone with a thick coat of paint
(decorators' beige, I regret to say) –

which indeed must have been the ambition
of the architect who designed it in
'Italianate, Neo-Renaissance' style.

Stone may look handsomely governmental
but earthquakes crumble it. This wood still stands.
What if certain portions of it are now,

following a safety-conscious update,
bogus – fake wood imitating fake stone
in fibreglass? I still seem to like it.

A couple of thousand times I passed it
on trams, on buses, in taxis or cars,
on foot, in or out of school uniform,

alone, in company, pushing a pram,
very occasionally on a bike,
scarcely glancing to confirm its presence,

before it began staring back at me.
Once, when it was half the age it is now
and still an anthill of civil servants,

I actually set foot inside it
to scan the education department
lists for my School Certificate results.

Now it's architectural royalty.
In front of it, in bronze, Peter Fraser,
clutching his hat, coat and briefcase, trots off

to a meeting, flawlessly brought to life
by my old mate Tony Stones, genius.
He modelled my head, one day in Oxford,

out on his lawn (well, clay gets everywhere).
No one has ever stared with such prolonged
scrutiny right up into my nostrils.

Lotus Land

'This place is unreal, of course.'
JAMES MCNEISH

Walk along Willis Street or Lambton Quay
and you can buy cherries at roadside stalls,
shipped up from the South Island for Christmas,
from Marlborough or the Clutha Valley.

I buy them by the kilo and take them
to all and sundry. Cherries, yes, cherries.

(Did I mention the sunshine? The short stroll
down- or uphill to wherever you want?)

*

This is what they mean when they say *whanau* –
assorted cousins on the trampoline,
blondies and redheads, all Polynesian,
and a new little dark one to pass round.

Beth, aged twelve, big sister *par excellence*,
picks up each baby in turn to snuggle.

(She's my eldest great-granddaughter. I too
am received in this blessed company.)

*

In Unity Books I spot James McNeish –
whenever you go there you meet someone –
beached up reluctantly in his eighties.
We ask each other the standard question.
Oh yes, he says, it's insane – I'm working
on three books at the same time. Publishers . . .

(If it weren't for the wind, rich oligarchs
would surely gobble up this fair city.)

535

*

I've brought my bearded son to midnight mass,
to sing loud carols in the cathedral.

The Bishop of Wellington wears dreadlocks
under his mitre – rather confusing
when viewed from the rear. He fixes me with
an alarming smile: 'The body of Christ.'

THE MERMAID'S PURSE

(2021)

The Mermaid's Purse

        when you pick it up,
is full of squirmy sea-larvae –
she doesn't carry actual money,
but then she's not an actual mermaid
(actuality not being
a possible attribute of mermaids).

Three times I crossed the equator –
by water, that is; flying doesn't count.
The coloured surface is camouflage;
underneath is black; black and heaving.
Rats nest in the diver's helmet.
Why, then they must be sea-rats.

So where do we go from here? Down, down,
where the eels go. Don't wait for me –
I'll be along later. Down, down –
think of me supping at mermaid's milk
as you shrink into your philosophy.
The mermaid's child will be a dogfish.

Island Bay

Bright specks of neverlastingness
float at me out of the blue air,
perhaps constructed by my retina

which these days constructs so much else,
or by the air itself, the limpid sky,
the sea drenched in its turquoise liquors

like the paua shells we used to pick up
seventy years ago, two bays
along from here, under the whale's great jaw.

The Teacher's Wife

Braced on the landing stage in a gale
she will be waiting with her baby.
The ferry will be late, because of the weather.

It will thrash about offshore for a bit,
hurl a few packages at the beach,
and chug away without taking on passengers.

Phyllis and her brother will race up the hill
tripping over themselves with their story
about the teacher's wife – the teacher's wife –

who cried and threw her handbag in the sea.
Their mother will calm them down and tell them
never to speak about it again:

the teacher's wife, poor lady, can't help it.
She isn't used to the solitude here;
she's from the city… and, well…and, um…

But someone will speak about it. Gossip
will say what it hears. Gossip will joke:
'Just as well she didn't throw Fleur in the sea.'

Phyllis will write a story about it
eighty years later, and send it to Fleur,
in the nick of time; the very nick.

Fleur will explain about the dying father
on the other side of the Manukau Harbour
waiting to meet his first grandchild.

Let's have less talk of hysteria
by city people. There's plenty home-grown.
(And anyway, they were from Drury.)

*

Do you remember, asks the teacher's wife,
that woman who drowned herself at Grahams Beach?

No, mother, I was only just born,
if that. You'll have to tell me about it.

She walked into the sea, stood on a rock,
and hit herself on the head with a hammer

to knock herself out.
                    Well, that would do it –
(why are we laughing?) How do they know?

Did they find the hammer in her apron pocket
when she was washed up? Or was that someone else?

And don't call me the teacher's wife.

                              *

Almost irresistible, you'd think,
New Zealand being surrounded by these

emerald/sapphire/leaden waters
waiting to be entered, one way or another.

For example, there was that widowed
second cousin – I don't think we met her –

who slipped out of a care home in her nightie
and toddled across a road into the sea.

We call it the Shirley Brooks solution,
and cling to it for our own futures

(assuming one or other of us is fated
to be bunged into a bungalow facing a beach).

                              *

Naturally I think of Iris, walking
straight down Queen Street and into the harbour

(as soon as two boys had left the wharf),
her *'quite five cold struggling minutes'* before

she *'went deeply down once and again,
and breathed in water as if it were life, not death'.*

She felt her body roll slowly over,
with its face turned away from the sky:

*'peace: no green fields but just a green colour
and the sound of the waters, until they were dumb...'*

But suddenly came a rushing moment,
some sort of vehicle, the police matron...

*

All drowners fight at the end, they say.
No, at those moments close to the end.

At the end another urge takes over:
our brains have a sympathetic lobe

that yearns towards water, intoxicated
with the longing to be absorbed in it,

as if we'd spent our lives in denial
of the substance we're constructed from.

*

Have you noticed they're all women?
I could cite some men if necessary,

but we are the sea for men to drown in,
the ravening tide. No wonder we scare them.

*

Nothing could be easier, in Auckland
or indeed Wellington, than to cross a road
from the city centre and walk on to the wharf.

Green, green swilling under your feet;
seen through the cracks a deep green darkness
inviting you to step up and step down.

What could be easier
                              what could be easier
nothing to stop you
                              nothing to stop you;
nothing could be easier than
                                        nothing.

They'd fish you out, of course; the CCTV
(which was not a thing in the 1930s
for Iris) would have its fish-eye on you.

                              *

No such aqueous yearnings for the teacher's wife;
next time she finds herself aboard an ocean
it will be her care to keep an eye on Fleur

who is after all still a child, even
if she fancies herself as Juliet
and gazes too meltingly over the rail

(don't worry, mother: it's mostly fiction),
while in her sensible daytime mode
she's letting her father teach her to swim

between the strained and bulging canvas sides
of the pool erected on an upper deck
like an upside-down marquee full of water:

a capsule of Atlantic or Pacific
for the sea-deprived from post-war Britain
migrating to where seas are everywhere.

The Islands

Do I still long to go to the islands,
where the mosquitoes are the size of birds,
and rats chew your toothbrush while you're asleep?

Do I yearn for the soughing of palm-leaves
where ghosts are squatting on Bosini's grave?
Or should I leave all that to my children,

and their children, and their children's children? –
descendants of Bosini, every one;
products of my taste for the exotic.

A Bunch of Names
(for Greg)

Gregory Stuart Campbell. But first –
imagine it if you can – a time
before you had a name at all:
the days or weeks when you were 'the baby'
while we, your adamantine parents,
held out against each other's choices.

Your second name was easy: Stuart,
to commemorate your young uncle
killed in the war; but what could precede it?
Your father knew what he wanted; I
knew just as firmly what I didn't want.
How would we ever compromise?

I seem to remember a book of names,
each as impossible as the one before.
Reject, reject, reject, reject:
the rhythm was wrong, or the syllable count,
the associations, the sound of the vowels,
the lack of euphony with 'Campbell'.

We reached a settlement in the end:
Gregory. Nothing to do with a pope,
or Gregory Peck, or Gregorian chant –
just that neither of us hated it,
never having thought about it much.
It would do. This came as a surprise.

Meanwhile, your father had a vivid dream:
he saw you lying in your bassinet,
murmuring to yourself in the night:
'Stupid, clever, genius.'
He walked around repeating it
until I felt I had dreamed it myself.

Our genius child! Before too long
your Auntie Margaret, your lifelong fan,
coached you in your identity:
Gregory Stuart Campbell – or,
as she lovingly parroted after your own
version, 'Bebi Tuti Camel'.

At three you collected names of cars:
Hillman, Vanguard, Ford Popular,
Austin of England – I read them out,
you tucked them into your memory,
to dazzle friends and passers-by.
Your own name continued on its way.

Gregory evolved into Greg
(not easy for some of us). Then came
the mysteriously transferable Rocky,
interchangeable between brothers,
and, rather briefly in another context,
the now long obsolete Snookums.

The soubriquet that charmed me most
is the one I first heard Lily use
to your new grandchild: 'Go to Pops!'
It's been a long journey for you,

but secretly inside my head
you never stop being 'my darling boy'.

The Fur Line

When I was working in the factory,
stitching open-ended zip fasteners
at one of a row of sewing machines,
someone brought in some kittens in a box.

I didn't wait to consult my husband;
I travelled home on the tram after work
with Jonathan snuggled in my bosom.
We had a cat before we had a child.

Sally and Midge, Pussywillow, Ada:
all that fluff got into our synapses,
transmitting itself down generations,
from nerve to nerve, or however it works.

Tiger and Snowflake, Marigold and Prince…
too late to say I've gone off predators
in favour of protecting the birdlife,
when I've bred a tribe of ailurophiles.

It's out of my hands; this is the future:
Brucie, Melba, Sasha, Lady Gaga.
It's no surprise that my great-granddaughters
grow up co-sleeping with their mothers' cats.

A Feline Forage in Auckland

Prince butts in through the cat flap
with a small dark whirligig
that whizzes on the floor like a top:
a bumblebee, you'd think it was.

Not so: when I brace to pick it up
it turns into a cicada.
I set off on a rescue trip
with an empty saucepan full of buzz.

An hour later another scrap
of biodiversity's brought in.
Lopped of the tail it had to drop
it slinks reptilianly away

in the direction of under the sink;
and it's – what do you think? A skink.

House

There was the tiepin-sized guitar
sealed into a shallow indentation
in a bedroom floorboard, as a tease,
forever floating in translucent varnish.

There was the pohutukawa by the gate
planted over the umbilical cord
of the daughter now in her twenties.

There was the patchwork timber floor
constructed out of several smaller floors
(wash-house, lavatory, entry step –
ancient kauri, the lot of them,
and all the levels coordinated)
in that corner of the kitchen
where the sun sets behind high trees.

There was the sunset. There was the view.
There was the horizon of extinct volcanoes.

And then they all melted into money.

Peter's Hat

(for Peter Bland)

Seeing you there, Peter, on the cover
of *broadsheet/19* (your tribute issue),
looking very northern under your hat,
I realise, good God, we're 83
and I've never written you a poem.

Could it be that I took you for granted,
my trans-hemispheric wandering friend?
Every now and then we'd happen to be
both in the same country at the same time,
but it tended not to last very long.

No sooner would you seem to be settled
than you'd get the urge to pack up and move on.
'Well, I've put my house on the market,' you'd
say, having rung the shipping company
(to be greeted as their pet customer).

House after house – glorious, some of them –
heartlessly cleared and vacated and sold
because it had suddenly dawned on you,
probably in the middle of the night,
you and Beryl were in the WRONG COUNTRY.

Looking back, you've told me, you feel guilty
about what you put her through. Don't worry;
I'm sure she forgave you; it was simply
the way you are: home is where your hat is
(which I was sorry to hear you've now lost –

although the replacement looks much the same).

A Small Correction

(i.m. Mike Doyle)

It was a brown coat, Mike, not a blue one
I was wearing when you first caught sight of me,
Alistair's wife, in Philosophy I;
the only coat I owned that year was brown.

Blue was the colour of your little Austin,
at the sight of which, pulling up outside,
Alistair would prepare his excuses,
leaving you to confide again in me

about whatever it was this time:
your dying wife, your platonic ardour
for the one who would be next, or just exactly
how guilty that ought to make you feel.

Gentle, apologetic, vaguely awkward,
good-looking enough to pose in a full page ad
for a tailoring firm, decked out in paper hat
and streamers: I hope they let you keep the suit.

In the Cupboard

Still sneezing from the dust, I uncover
among the souvenir shell necklaces
and the pottery beads from Kathmandu

an oblong satin-lined box cherishing
the pendant I begged my parents to buy
in Queenstown: three ovals of fake amber
lined up along a wispy chain.

The resin, discoloured now, makes the flowers
amazingly suspended inside
harder to distinguish – unless the petals
have themselves been leached of their colours.

What's next? In a cellophane packet, five
diamante and fake pearl buttons
from my wedding dress (not my choice,
either the buttons or the dress itself).

Also a teardrop pearl on a thin gold chain,
the gift of someone who thought, years too late,
that this was the kind of thing I might like.

Giza
(for Cait)

It was in this dress – pink and apricot
glazed cotton in a geometric print
with a draw-string waist, boat neck, small cap sleeves
(home-made from a Simplicity pattern –

we all made our own dresses in those days) –
that I rode a camel in the desert
outside Cairo to the Great Pyramid
of Giza. (Less intrepid than it sounds:

a tourist guide was holding the bridle.)
The skirt was knee-length, and rather too tight –
not suitable for an Arab country;
it rucked right up as I clambered aboard.

Then – a bit of a surprise to me – rain
began to fall. (This was February
1963 – that famous winter.)
Anyway, I thought you might like the dress.

Siena

In retrospect it had been a good move
to fall out with the bibliographer,
(to whom I'd had to explain the bidet
in our room), and catch the train on my own.
I found myself seven centuries back,
in a mirage with a striped cathedral.

On the second night I was picked up by
Antonio, a medical student,
who cruised outside the Pinacoteca
on patrol for arty foreign women.

He took me up to a battered castle,
accommodatingly provided with
unlit architecture to lean into.
We kept in touch by letters for a year.

Realms

Much have I travelled in the realms of gold…
mostly in books, but also in the more
gilded provinces of, while it lasted,
youth, or the willing suspension – heigh-ho,
that willing suspension – assisted by
less than explicit electric lighting.

I refer you to a certain café
notable for the bubble-wrap effect
that cast a golden veil over my eyes –
either an epiretinal membrane
or something we'd pulled down around ourselves
for protection in tumultuous times.

Or was it that fine mesh Vulcan crafted,
smith-work of the slenderest calibre,
to entrap his wife with her fancy man?
Not much good came of that, as I recall,
except the amusement it provided
for the spectators. I'm saying nothing.

In the Cloud

There is flirting
and there is Fleurest;
there is the sweet bye-and-bye
and the sweet never-was,
and a Vera Lynn song over
the white cliffs of nowhere.

Hollyhocks

The hollyhocks at my door needn't have bothered
flaring out in a whirl of roseate skirts.
My guest has been – let's hope the right word is 'delayed'.

Yet still I carry on preparing for her stay:
scrubbing and scouring, smoothing what's already smooth,
primping, prettifying, tweaking; scrubbing some more.

Berries

Spindleberries; you can't eat them.
That gaudy rig is for entertainment.

Outside the camp is *terra ignota*.

Tell me the names of some berries:
what are whortleberries? Can you eat them?

Esurient; etiolated. We have hunger.

Tell me the names of some berries.
Blueberries, colour-berries; black you can eat.
Outside the camp it's…not that kind of jungle.
If it had snakes we'd lure them to our *cucina*.

Those teenage children have lighted on a morsel
and are sharing it between them like the host.
It won't save them – not now.
Last week, maybe; even yesterday; not now.

Mulberry, rowanberry, elderberry.

Outside the camp she is surrounded by briars:
la Belle au Bois Dormant.
Not that kind of jungle. Rosehips might save her,
but not the thorns. The dog rose will bite her.

I am pierced by a needle. By a spindle. Beware.

Those children squatting by the roadside
are picking maggots out of a thing they've found.

In the prison camp in Indonesia
he used to eat flies. He told me.

Amazing Grace

Someone is bawling 'Amazing Grace'
from the vault below St Mary Woolnoth.

It's John Newton, the hymn writer,
reformed slave trader, famous convert,

'once an infidel and libertine…
Rector of these united parishes',

whose mortal remains are deposited,
says the marble tablet, below this church.

But St Mary Woolnoth sold the crypt
to the City and South London Railway.

John Newton, the former incumbent,
is not recumbent under the floor

in the ticket hall of Bank Station,
confused vibrations rattling his coffin.

He's been translated to a better place;
admirers requisitioned his bones

and shipped them back, with Mrs Newton's,
to his old parish of Olney, Bucks.

In which case why is he here, bellowing
from somewhere sepulchral about grace?

If it's grace he wants there's Hawksmoor's ceiling
with its pretty fanlights (buy a postcard).

No, that won't do; that's frivolity.
It's souls he wants, not architecture;

he's here to free them from their snares,
and he's not the kind of man you can shut up.

His mission is to strike the shackles
from the ankles of the City traders

and other worshippers of Mammon –
slaves to flummery, slaves to pelf.

More slaves here than in Olney;
even within earshot, slaves galore.

Käthi Bowden in Bavaria

Käthi is good at looking enigmatic,
but Frau Fischer is not to be discouraged:
'Ah, that is so strange about you English!
You don't enjoy discussing your complaints.'

What is strange about this German spa town
is that it possesses a gully
just like the one in Käthi's Thorndon,
and a harbour, what's more. Käthi is a tease.

Fräulein Sonia and the Herr Professor
have gone off to examine the modern soul.
The Baron is receiving due deference.
The servants are muttering in the kitchen.

Käthi is pleased to have studied German.
They have all found their way into her notes –
the maids, the postman, the posturing guests,
the Advanced Lady, the anxious father –

to be subtly altered, as she alters herself…
But a surge of delegates is approaching,
about to be greeted by the Mayor
in yet another commemoration.

This is a different century.
Käthi slips around the corner,

tucking her notebook into her muff.
If she is quick enough she may dodge them.

Divining

What you do, he said,
to make divining-rods:
take a metal coat-hanger, like this,
and pliers; clip it into an L-shape –
you won't need the bit with the hook;
bend the angle to 90°.
Make another one the same: two L-shapes,
one for each hand, matching.

Right: the long side is the divining-rod,
the short side is the handle.
Curl your fist round it – loose like this –
softly; no pressure;
looser: you're holding a baby bird,
it's timid, it needs to breathe.

Now: one step at a time
steady as you can, slowly, slowly,
glide forward, both rods parallel,
pointing ahead, level with the ground.
No, no; don't clutch – let them flutter
when they want to. Not everyone can do it.

The first time I tried, he said,
I was visiting an infants' school:
rows of little kids cross-legged on the floor.
A teacher was giving a demonstration
and she let me have a go.
When the rods are aware of water
they swing slowly towards each other
and cross over. It's a powerful sensation,
like living things writhing in your hands.

We took turns walking round the hall,
divining the radiators for a start –
you couldn't fail to notice it.

And of course people are just bags of water;
all those kids down at knee-level
triggered the divining-rods –
got them criss-crossing as I walked through.
There I was with these wire antennae
flexing and flipping over all the little heads.

Welsh

If all else fails you could learn Welsh:
such an exacting discipline –

surely they'd have faith in you then?
I've heard of good online tutors.

Tip-top health is not essential
if you remain articulate

and your fingers still obey you,
whatever else may be astray.

A person who has mastered Welsh,
or grasped more than the fringe of it,

is not to be dismissed lightly.
What an example to us all! –

except of course to Welsh people,
who have an unfair advantage.

Yes, it could well be the answer:
Welsh. Or perhaps hieroglyphics.

This Fountain

Hats are all very well, but the best shade
is an umbrella of leaves, high up, to
sit under catching words from passers-by –

'But then what if you're making a salad;
do you wash it in bottled water? Or
what do you do?' And they move out of range.

I amble along the path. 'This fountain
is being repaired and has been turned off.'
(Like the sky, you could say, these last long weeks.)

The stone receptacle built into the base
for dogs to drink water from is empty –
or was, until a family arrived

with anxious children and relief supplies.
That's the dogs attended to, just for now.
When is the sky going to be repaired?

Tiny flies position themselves under
my hat brim and dance in front of my eyes,
trying to drink the moisture from my breath.

Magnolia Seed Pods

Among the wonders vouchsafed to me
during my suburban wanderings
in two countries, this one and that one,

were these exotic excrescences,
each a miniature pineapple,
framed in petals the size of saucers.

The first I saw were strewn underfoot,
with no magnolia bloom in sight:
a mystification until I asked.

It was late in life when I found them.
Who would have thought I'd still be allowed
to walk out freely where there were trees

and carry on as I've always done:
picking things up and looking at them?

Bats

Once again the low scoop over my shoulder
by the lilacs, the dipped-wing fly-past,
the reversal in mid-thought, the sudden soar; but

imagined this time, and always something else:
a late-flying bird, a wavering twig,
a trick of the eyesight at dusk.

Scoop, swoop, loop the loop.

Your small elderly faces, gaping

If I could but see

Spooks

Again and again, and never again,
Spooks

Beloved.

*   *

That particular area of sky,
in the lee of the bulkiest sycamore
(because you don't like the wind)

waits for your entry on to the scene,
your merry aerial patterns against
the post-sunset – a greenish-yellow backdrop.

Look at all the insects
my foliage has bred for you,
if you would only come back.

I can't eat them myself;
the foxes don't want them.
No one but you can dance after them.

*   *

You were established; you were a colony
for a dozen years or more before the crash –

a colony of one, to begin with,
strayed here from some wood or other

straining our credulity –
no one else around here had bats.

And then, *mirabile dictu*, you were
plural, truly, whenever I counted.

Flittermouse; flattermouse –
I felt so honoured to have bats.

Better than television,
all those evenings, in the long dusk –

Come and look, visitors;
grandchildren, kneel at the window –

until a derelict bird box, forgotten
for years, crashed out of my tallest tree.

You know the one about the Bluebird of Happiness –
all the time in your own backyard?

*　　*

Gone, stuck in the past, blocked.
Gone beyond the back of beyond,
back of the rainbow, back of the black stump.

This new scientifically designed
National Trust approved bat box
won't lure you back. You won't see it.

You liked the old one, mounded with droppings,
rotting away from whatever clamped
its crumbling panels fast to the tree.

Let me prevail on you to relent –
wherever you are, and whichever wood,
Coldfall or Highgate, has received you

If you're alive.

Come and spook me; come and dazzle me
with your darkness when I least expect you,
early on a May morning or at sunset,

zooming out into your high patrol.
When I'm finally convinced you're over,
strike me senseless with astonishment.

Novice Flyer

What was the use of these brisk new wing-blades
or these legs like springy twigs, young robin,
if they couldn't lift you just a bit higher
than the jaws that snatched and punctured you
and then dropped you on my flower bed,
right here, beside the antirrhinums?

It's far too early for a rosy breast,
but I see the advance markers of it:
two shreds of orange fluff on your bosom,
nestled among the tweedy russet.

You loll on my hand as I pick you up,
surprisingly heavy, surprisingly warm –
just getting the knack of being dead.
The reddest thing is the splash on my palm.

Wood Mice

They'd better stop doing that, though,
if they want to go on living here –
running up the stairs in kangaroo hops
(a big leap for mouse-kind),

nibbling at everything from stationery
to paracetamol, shinning up
the striped ladder of the tradescantia
to chew on its translucent stem-joints

as if they were celery (the cheek of it)
and playing hide and seek under the bureau;
then galloping down again, a sight to see,
their little bandy legs viewed from behind –

otherwise it's into a box with them –
a humane one, of course –
and down to the woods for a new life;
but it has been known to go wrong,

alas, O alas,
which tends to make the householder
more sentimental
than might otherwise be.

So in the meantime, pending reform,
a discreet crumble of toast
or a few peanuts under the cooker
for Big-ears in the night.

Sparrowhawk

That day Storm Ciara brought a sparrowhawk
to hunch on my wind-wobbled buddleia
dazzling me with her brown and white barred front,
the stripiest thing since Bridget Riley.

She sat full on, a witch from the woodlands,
immobile apart from her swivel-head,
trying to cast the evil eye on me
through the glass of my dining-room window.

Her gold-ringed orbs were hypnotic, all right;
the small birds had deserted their feeders.
I quaked for them, and for our battered globe.
It took days until my robin dared come
to chat with me in his throaty subsong,
before the next weekend and Storm Dennis.

Election 1945

The first election I can remember
is the one in which my father and mother
voted Winston Churchill out of office,
and we got the National Health Service –

which gave me an exaggerated view
of what democracy can actually do.

The Little Theatre Club

1945: the Principal Boy
(Ninette, *née* Edith, seventy this year)
hauls out her costume trunk again: it's time
to shroud her bony shanks in the green tights
that have served her well since before the war.

Now there's no blackout more children will come
to watch this thing they'll call a 'pantomine'.
No, they won't think of it as magical;
it can't out-magic *The Wizard of Oz*
or other films they've seen at the Regal.

But they'll cotton on to the convention
of gender-swapping, loving its daftness
(who's the Dame? It will have to be Anton,
Ninette's husband, parading his bosom),
and they'll giggle at the grown-ups having fun.

And what will you remember, my young dears?
Will it be the lights, the smell of make-up,
the topical jokes about coal rationing
and Mr Attlee? It will be those tights:
apple-green, and wrinkled about the knees.

The Other Christmas Poem

Or you might prefer to read about the Christmas
when after all the hosting and feasting

we finally got the kids off to bed
and the rest of us, the grown-ups
(if that's an accurate designation),

opened up another case of wine
and put on some Rolling Stones records.

I think it was Ruth, a friend of a friend,
who found the room a bit overheated
and made the decision to take her top off –

something it seemed she was given to doing
at the slightest provocation.

Her husband greeted this with tolerance,
and before too long had removed his shirt;
several other people shed theirs.

One of the women undid her dress,
with a vaguely absent-minded air.

The dancing hotted up; Ruth took off her bra;
someone stepped casually out of his trousers.
You can see the way this is going.

By the time Alex tiptoed upstairs
for more wine from the stash in his study

(the children, thank God, were sleeping soundly)
he was the only adult in the house
wearing so much as his underpants.

Ah, what a memorable party,
we'd reminisce in the years that followed,

thinking of the camaraderie –
and of how our necks had been stiff with the strain
of never glancing below anyone's waist.

Anadyomene

Talking about Greek words reminds me:
if you were to strip off the layers
of emulsion on that stretch of wall
beside the window in the spare bedroom

you might find microscopic flecks
of golden paint: traces, you could say,
of the tresses of Botticelli's Venus,
copied studiously from a postcard
a teenage fan bought at the Uffizi.
It was all an education to him.

After a year or two, he rollered over her.
The magazine shot of Liza Minnelli
(with clothes on) inside his wardrobe door
survived his occupation of the room.

Victoria Road

I'm saying to Meg and Alex
'I came past your street this afternoon.
I wanted to visit you but you're dead.'
And Meg is saying, in her sensible way,
'Can't be helped. Next time check up first',

while Alex gives a sort of rueful smile
mouthing 'Sorry!' as if through a window
(I can't hear him), and flinging his hands out
in apology, as when they met me
at Kathmandu airport in a thunderstorm:

'Sorry about the rain!'

Sorry about the deaths. But let's not start.

Anyway, now that we've established that
we can get on with the conversation.
I'll show them the pictures I took
of Meg beside the two saplings
on a riverside walk in Stony Stratford
where we planted Alex's ashes;
we used to visit the swans around there.

Alex will embark on a story
about spotting his hero Graham Greene
in the south of France, and trying
to pluck up courage…
I think I may have heard it before,
but I was never sure of the ending.

To Stephenie at 11 PM

One last crumb of family history,
dear cousin, all these months after your death:
our great-grandmother Martha used to say
'Night brings home all sorrows.' So I find it.

Lightning Conductor

On the eighteenth anniversary of
my mother's death, I've been watching a man
in a vertiginous cherry-picker

attaching copper wire to the finials
on the church roof. I'm pleased with myself
for remembering the word 'finial',

which I associate with a poem
by Amy Clampitt, but madly searching
for the name of my mother's neighbour

who kindly let me lodge in her house
on one of my visits to Wellington.
When I was leaving it for the airport

the taxi, swinging around two corners,
startled me with a glimpse of my mother,
to whom I'd already said goodbye,

walking firmly and with concentration
in her familiar red dressing gown
up the outside staircase to her flat.

It was not my last view of her,
but the last on that particular trip,
and likely to outlive several others.

Finial. It sounds like a fancy,
over-decorated word for 'final'.
Lightning is the least of my worries.

The Annual Party

They have wheeled in the famous novelist,
the sacred monster; we thought he was dead,
after that biography… We saunter past
his chariot, pretending not to look.

In fact we are rather more concerned
with the actual dead whose obituaries
we've read – or written – during the year
(less wittily than they'd have written ours),

or with the barely living but absent.
We can point to the spot in this very room
where we last tried to find encouraging
words for our friend who had heard them all.

Then there are the inexplicably
missing (has anyone recent news
of that not-always-patient editor?
Has his workload finally crushed him?)

– And of course the explicably missing:
the poet who for as long as his term
on the Council lasted felt it his duty
to show his face here, but shows it no more,

and the older poet confined to views
of the bird-feeders outside his windows
or, when his carers turn him around,
of the bleak peaks he refuses to leave –

unlike his near contemporary
from a gentler brand of rural landscape
who trotted about with her little trolley
year after year until – when was the last time?

Instead we find ourselves among
a sprinkling of the pseudo-senior –
writing for *The Oldie* at 53
(bah! We've got children older than that) –

and a phalanx of the under-40s,
lured in by the new initiative
(we know what that was all about). Well,
just one more circuit of the room, perhaps.

Letting Them Know

(for Connie Bensley)

We need to find a way of telling them,
those of us addicted to living alone;

if we lose the power of speech, and all the rest,
we need a non-vocal way to make it known:

not to call for help – it's too late for that –
but simply to inform them that the bird has flown.

No particular advantage is gained
by having someone there on the spot

when all you need is a messenger
to convey the information, posthumous or not;

you could leave the front door open, perhaps,
for some passerby to figure out the plot.

The thing is – how can we put this gently? –
we just want to be found before we rot.

Blackberries

1
Soft with last Thursday's deluge, blackberries
melt into my hands as I pick them.
My polythene bag oozes, catching
on bramble thorns. This is the best place,
this boggy, shaggy heath-in-the-making
neglected behind the tennis-courts.

2
An old man pads along on his son's arm.
I overtake them, to check the profile
of my probable contemporary
between the cloth cap and the jacket collar
in case it belongs to an acquaintance:
grey moustache, drooping underlip… No.

3
'Have you got the time?' 'Sorry, what?' 'The time!' –
a lad practising basketball shots.
Avoiding my sleeve, I tilt my watch-face
with one sticky, garnet-stained finger.
'Six o'clock.' The park is emptying.
I have a watch. He has the time.

Tatters

A wind from all directions
is harrying fits and scraps of snow
as I scramble out of bed
to look up the origins
of the word 'tatterdemalion'.

I wonder if Shakespeare made it up.
But no: it's post-Shakespearean,
1622 and later –
derived from 'tatter' or 'tattered',
with a 'factitious element'.

Clearly somebody made it up,
and other jokers fiddled with it.
It can have a double 'l' –
Tatterdemallion. Rhymes with Italian.
Or so they say.

And look – wouldn't you know –
someone has named a band after it.
Meanwhile the snow… Also the wind…
It feels pretty Shakespearean to me.
I bet he knew it anyway –

even if it isn't in a play.

The Old Road

I meet some sheep and pause to laugh at them.
They stare at me and turn to each other:
'What does she mean?' they ask. 'What does she mean?'

I mean them no harm: I'm bubbling over
with goodwill. I've come here empty-handed,
but I can see the funny side of sheep.

A hand-painted sign: 'Caution. Nesting birds.'
Lapwings, probably, or curlews. The sheep
with their risky hooves are across the road,

on the downward slope, towards the river,
behind a gate. There's been some thought in this:
no offspring are going to be trampled.

Ah, I can guess where all this is heading:
the nature notes, the forced optimism,
the upland landscape with its bleakish tinge,

even these kingcups blazing with light in
the ditch, and a lapwing clattering up
into the sky. Don't tell me. Don't tell me.

POEMS FOR ROY

i.m. Roy Fisher, 1930–2017

Dead Poets' Society

Yet once more, O ye laurels, and once more,
myrtles and suchlike, I come to complain –
though not to you, innocent shrubs. My target
is mouldy old Death, who keeps grabbing my friends.
I have some words for you, Skeletonguts:
You've snatched more than your share of poets,
crammed them in your long pack and carried them off
to munch at leisure in your den.
Why couldn't you have used some judgement?
To you we may all seem much the same,
but I tell you, Boneface, today
the life you had the gall to pluck
(not untimely – he was old enough,
but gifted with wits, with wit, with a brain
that these witless times can't easily spare)
was exceptional. It was Roy you took.
Think about that, if you can, for a moment,
Gogglesockets, and repent!
Yes, Roy, dear friend and matchless poet;
Roy, who has not left his peer.
He and I kept a running correspondence
to note each colleague who became your prey –
endless mailings headed 'Another one'.
We were against you, as he managed to say
to your face when you came fumbling for him.
His last word, I'm proud to report, was 'Fuck'.

Jade Plant

This one's called *The Pathetic Fallacy*:
The 'money tree' you gave me in the form of

a bulbous, finger-length twig to bring home
on the train in a margarine container,

pot up in gritty compost, and watch
expanding through slow reliable decades,

has spent these last few weeks bending over,
limb by stiff limb, trunk turning pliable,

fat green oval jade coins dropping off
in twiggy clusters of three and four

as if it 'knew something'; as if
(what nonsense) it had 'decided' to die.

Do not resuscitate, you said once
in another context. I shan't.

Double Haiku

On the other hand
choosing the spring equinox
as a date to be

blighted for ever
could have been called irony,
if you had chosen.

Elm

As I stumble around among
words like 'outlive' and 'survivor'
in connection with the grand elm
just up the lane from your house – or
your former house, as it is now –
in the Peak District (too high up,
you said, for the elm bark beetle)
the scenario's clear enough.

When I allow myself to plunge
into my file of your letters
from our pre-electronic days
and your annual birthday cards,
each one inscribed with a poem,
it won't surprise me if I find
(secreted where I can't lose it)
a cellophane pack of pressed leaves.

Four Poems and a Funeral

I've kept this red rubber band;
it's the one I took off

the flowers from my garden –
wallflowers, drooping lilac

(you know how cut lilac droops),
forget-me-nots, rosemary –

before I laid them down
on your wicker coffin.

Maundy Thursday 2017

The priest, no longer a young man, creaks down
on to his knees, washes and dries my foot,
wrenches himself upright with his stick, and
moves on to the next prewashed foot.

Listen: those must be the hosts of heaven;
why else would they be singing in Latin?
They are Nick and Marian and the rest
up in the choir gallery. Same thing.

Incense. Candles. Hymns, for God's sake!
How you would have hated all this;
and how you despised your younger self
for having once fallen for it.

One day in a church in Romania
you caught me trying the elaborate
hand gestures of the Orthodox blessing,
so much fancier than the Roman one.

I was copying a peasant woman.
I was, I have to admit, showing off.
But to whom? To her? To God? Not to you.
Your face was without any expression,

yet you were always tolerant of me,
with my role-play and my little dramas,
enmired in my fallen state. There are
friends, you said, and there are intimates.

The priest kissed my foot; it was his duty.
I thought how they wash the feet of the dead.
I thought of your feet yesterday, under
your coffin lid, and now nowhere at all.

An April Bat

From the place where you are now
you've sent me a bat. Thank you.
I looked out of the pantry window
to catch a glimpse of the sunset

(rosy-pink with pollution as it was)
and there, circling and flipping low
above my flowering trees,
apple and lilac, was this bat.

Birds, we used to send each other:
a woodpecker, a jay. But this
is for the dark time.
Don't think I value it less

for being a cliché. You know
I haven't a very original mind.
You were generous enough
to send me a thing I'd understand.

Porridge

I was thinking about that saucepan of yours:
the Pyrex one, so improbable, made of
amber glass, the colour of barley sugar.

Not a utensil to be used on gas, I
imagined; but on your electric cooker
it squatted contentedly in its glory.

Everything about it looked precarious –
liable to melt into golden syrup
as soon as it encountered heat, or explode

into a shrapnel blitz of orange splinters.
But of course it was tougher than that: solid,
quaint with survival from an earlier age.

All you had to do was not drop it too hard.
I almost felt I was demeaning it by
stirring mere porridge in it. But oh, the glow!

Now that the house is cleared it must be somewhere –
safe in a crate, perhaps, or a cardboard box –
until whatever happens to it happens.

Annual Tribute

I needn't think that just because you're dead
I'm absolved from my annual duty
of writing a poem for your birthday;

it's just that this one won't come on a card
like its predecessors in our sequence
of reciprocal yearly well-wishings.

In the old days it might have reflected
on the weather, or something topical –
your latest book of poems, your new cat –

or some mathematical property
of your age: 'tetrahedral' went down well
on your eighty-fourth (a magic number).

Usually we tried to be funny.
This year there's an election to gawp at;
plenty of scope there for satire, ho, ho.

Also, being greetings card doggerel,
it had to rhyme. You had a knack for that.
One year you wrote a virtuoso riff

circling around without ever naming
a rude word I'd used when playing Scrabble
with friends who were slightly prim (that's a clue).

All those ditties fluttering between us!
I'm sure I can come up with another;
it's just rather tricky to gauge the tone

in this new situation. Still, here goes,
even if I can't expect a response
on my own birthday, or ever again

(unless you've prepared a massive surprise);
even if – yes, I know the 'even ifs'.
I'd better think of a joke to end with.

Winter Solstice

Nine months on from the spring equinox
when that 'Are you sitting down?' phone call
implanted the unshiftable fact.

Nine months, as if it were a full term
pregnancy, with a birth almost due.
But what shall I hug to my bosom

when the time comes? All I can predict
will be something small, dark and smothered:
a lump of knowledge, wrapped in a shawl.

Snowman

You were my snow contact, my on-the-phone
link to a vicarious fairyland.
'Are you snowed in?' I'd ask. Yes, you'd confirm,
as the Tesco van got stuck in the lane
again on its stoic route from Buxton.
'Ah!' – (trying to make my sigh of envy
sound a bit more like sympathy) – 'Oh dear.
Just boring old rain down here.' That was then.

Now that London has managed a blizzard
and what it brings – the hypnotic light, the
self-important coping with frozen pipes –
I've no one in the Peak District to tell.
On my lawn a blackbird is peck-shredding
the orange-peel grin from next door's snowman.

Mayonnaise

'Could I prevail upon you,' said Lorna,
'to make me some more of that mayonnaise?' –
with garlic, for dipping *crudités* in:
a small thank-you-for-having-me gesture
after my stay in her Newcastle house.

She had another guest on my last night.
He sat with us next morning at breakfast,
drinking his coffee as I stirred and whisked
and added this or that and whisked some more,
while Lorna made notes. He said there should be

a genre painting recording the scene
(this being in the days before Facebook)
in case the three of us became famous,
called 'Roy Fisher watching Lorna Tracy
watching Fleur Adcock making mayonnaise.'

Quite soon he dropped me off at the station,
and drove to Durham for his assignment.
'A most entertaining man, Roy', I wrote
in my journal on the train going home,
'with a nice line in pedantic phrases.'

He was fifty-two, which I then supposed
to be quite old, but as it came about
we had something like thirty-five years more,
on and off, to entertain each other
one way or the next, as our lives allowed.

Notes

The Teacher's Wife

In May 2013 I was signing books after a reading in Auckland when a woman asked me to sign one for a 90-year-old relative, Phyllis, who had been my father's star pupil when he was teaching in a tiny, one-teacher school at Grahams Beach on the Manukau Harbour, a place then scarcely accessible except by boat. During his second year there, 1934, I was born and my mother's father entered his final illness. She took me across the harbour to visit him before his death, but her first attempt to do so was thwarted in a dramatic way. I learned this from a little story Phyllis sent me about an episode in her childhood that had puzzled her; fortunately there was just time for me to explain it to her before she died. I began this poem in February 2017, struck by the contrast between Phyllis's account of the incident at Grahams Beach and my mother's reminiscences of her time there. It grew into a wider meditation on ways in which New Zealand women, including Iris Wilkinson (the poet and novelist Robin Hyde), have been drawn to the sea or to drowning. It became an excuse for playing games with tenses, registers and viewpoints. I refer to myself in the third person – as a baby, as a teenager on board ship – and to my mother (who in her confused old age sometimes thought me a contemporary) under a stylised label. I hope she'd have forgiven me.

Käthi Bowden in Bavaria

In 1909 Katherine Mansfield was hiding out in Wörishofen, Bavaria, because she was pregnant and had run away from her husband George Bowden, not the father of the child, after one night. The pregnancy came to nothing, but she began writing the stories that eventually made up her first collection, *In a German Pension*. She based several of the German characters on people she had known in Wellington, and the landscape also underwent confusing changes in her imagination.

Bats

They responded: the following year (2019), to my astonishment, they or another pair of bats moved into the new NT bat box. But the miracle was too good to last, and before too long they dis-appeared one by one, perhaps the victims of predators. My appeal for their return must stand.

NEW POEMS

(2024)

Stint

Who was it who hung up
the Sibyl in a bottle,
and when they asked 'What do you want?'
she said 'ἀποθανεῖν θέλω'?

Small and shrunken, she was,
the thousand-year-old Sibyl,
trapped in her echoey cave,
wailing that she had done her stint;

her voice a whisper: 'ἐθέλω'
it lisped inside her skull, a faint
three-note whistle, thin as a breath
exhaled from her glassy bubble.

'Ἀποθανεῖν,' it piped, pleading
to burst free, prophesy no more,
scuttle off, less than a shadow,
into the armpit of death.

Sorry!

Don't expect the dead to be forgiving.
They lie there sulking in their chilly bed,
not in the least concerned for your conscience,
growling at what you wish you hadn't said.

Priam

(*for Michael Longley*)

Let me donate an extra portrait
for your Homeric father's album.
I never met him, but I met his clothes;
a tweed jacket and a striped shirt (blue,
I think it was), with you inside them
sitting on a floor among poets
at the launch of an anthology
in a room shaded with a grapevine.

You tell me you've forgotten the grapevine –
and the party too, I shouldn't wonder.
Picture your young head on the shoulders
of your father's jacket; remember how,
unwilling to let him go so soon,
you dressed up in his clothes as a tribute.

Thaw

Drip, squelch, ooze, a subdued pitter-patter,
a background hum that is scarcely there.
Mostly silence. Faint creaking. Drip, drip:
a twig bows to unleash a flop of snow.

The washing-line is hung with shapeless
rags of ice, on the verge of transforming
into aerial sheets of water.
What do they taste like? Like nothing at all.

The wood pigeon complains, complains, complains.

Smaller birds venture to the branches
around their feeders, displacing now and then
a puff of white from over-laden twigs
as they tweak out half-defrosted seeds.

The wood pigeon returns to its moan.

Optimistic Poem

It's been a while. Let me get used to it.
I knew about the widows, of course,
but hadn't quite expected the crutches,
the walking frames, or that poor agitated
soul endlessly pacing at the front.
On the other hand, the baby chirruping
during the one minute's silence
could hardly have given any offence.

It's been a late, cold spring; last year's was
also cold and late, but it happened.
Normal operations are being resumed.
Someone has died, at nearly a hundred,
of natural causes. Weep, but not too much.
That white shower was not snow, but petals.

Notice to Foxes

Take back your big green foam rubber ball
and the red one with teeth marks, and the shuttlecock.

Take the leather sandal kidnapped from next door.
Take your chewed KFC packaging,

plus the sachet of sauce, the paper napkin
and the surgical mask you scavenged from the pavement.

Replace the mountain of earth you dug out
from under the roots of our sycamores,

and the panel of fencing you knocked over
on the way to trampling my bedding plants,

snapping off tall foxgloves at the root,
and dragging down my Rosa Mundi.

Go squealing and scrapping in some other garden,
with all your trappings. You have ceased to be cute.

Goliath

Ooh, look, two severed heads in the same room.
No problem recognising Goliath:
never mind the features, regard the size
of the face with its – ah, yes, fuzzy hair.
If the artist wasn't entirely sure
how a Philistine looked, he searched his files
and picked a convenient foreigner.

An instructive image, if it's needed,
for possible targets in Mud Gully:
Shutterstock from the Book of Samuel,
in case young David should roister along,
ruddy with triumph, slingshot at his belt,
arm in arm, nearly, with his new best friend,
and lugging…you know what he was lugging.

The other head was served on a platter:
by Judith perhaps, unless you favour
the Salome identification.
A woman, in any case, parading
the fruit, greyish-green and a bit floppy,
sprawling on a dish to catch the juices,
of what has been an unwomanly deed.

She glares at us accusingly over
one shoulder: 'Now look what you made me do!'
is what she appears not to be saying,
whoever she is. This can't be Judith,
hero, icon, saviour of her people,
nobody's tool. And she hasn't the style
of that flashy, venal bitch Salome.

For a true Judith, let me direct you
to Artemisia Gentileschi.
This woman's a model, bored with posing
for Sebastiano del Piombo,
who's more concerned to achieve the exact
skin tone for the contents of the platter.
A good head, though. Better than Goliath.

A Woodlouse for Kevin

My eyesight is just about up to reading
the insect fauna that colonise my kitchen,

but the small black speckles of lettering
on anything printed are less distinct.

So when I sit downstairs at 3 a.m.,
at a loss for soporific entertainment,

I'd be better served by a page of ants,
paired up in couples to chant '88',

as a reminder of your new birthday,
than the latest issue of the *TLS*.

And that draft of a poem from a year ago,
mysteriously entitled 'Woodlark',

is nothing so Keatsian after all,
but a typo for the Kiwi 'slater'.

Conditional

If I still remember the terms
protasis and *apodosis*
from Latin grammar days at school,

why can't I exchange this knowledge
with its minimal relevance
to my subsequent life, in which

sentences trot along quite well
unparsed and without their clauses
needing precise designations,

for instant access to the names
of acquaintances approaching,
all smiles, at social gatherings?

The Lift Shaft

In the days of our bohemian youth
a friend much given to adultery
found himself caught by an angry husband
who, discovering in his Chelsea flat
a classic tableau of *in flagrante*,
avenged himself on this Casanova
by hurling all his clothes down a lift shaft.

Rather than trudge barefoot across London
without so much as his own front door key
to cover his nakedness, let alone
money to pay for a taxi, my friend
weighed up his options (visualising
the Medea-like fury of his wife),
and rang 999 from a street call box.

Rewarded by the sniggering mercy
of the police, who wielding their powers
dredged up from the subterranean depths
his now perhaps dust-besmirched possessions,
he resumed his dignity with his clothes;
though whether or not they found both his shoes
may depend on what you think he deserved.

Between the Toes

When he was a young reporter, writing
for the *Straits Times* on the Korean War,
my brother-in-law was based in Japan.

His girlfriend, Itsuko by name, taught him
certain refinements concerning hygiene
that had not been part of his upbringing:

for example, to dry between his toes.
Sometimes I embarrass friends by asking
if they include this in their own routine –

although that implies a further question:
do they, in the first place, wash between them?
Apparently not everybody does.

O Westport in the Light of Paul Durcan
(for Tim Cunningham)

A memorable title is a name full of names
as in the title of Paul Durcan's poem,
which was also the title of his first book –
O Westport in the light of Asia Minor –
and incorporated the name of an Irish town

which otherwise I might never have heard of
before you and your family settled there
after all those years in Billericay.

O Westport, welcome to my mantelpiece!
O townscape photographed by Tim's daughter Eve
and turned into a card by his wife Alex
(whose names tinkle among the strung beads
of our history together with the names of poets
and festivals), I greet your roofs and steeples!
Welcome into a long concatenation
of accidents I can only call friendship.

Monica

Today I reminded Monica of
a Sunday in the 1970s
when she arrived at church in a nightdress
(primrose floral cotton with lace trimmings)

because it was too hot to wear a dress.
I looked at her with secret approval,
too cowardly to wear my own version
of the very same garment (in pale blue).

Marks & Spencer made durable clothing
in those days, and church, or frugality,
makes durable women. Both nightdresses
have survived. Shall we wear them next Sunday?

But have I the style to carry it off?
I think not. Over to you, Monica.

Saint Brigid

Do you remember my St Brigid's cross,
woven from grass and bought somewhere sacred
as a present? One of several from
someone whose heart had room for multitudes.

It hung benignly on my bedroom wall
till the narrow-hearted, narrow-gutted
likes of a two-year-old in a tantrum
ripped it down and shredded it with his teeth:

jealous of the donor, needless to say.
No matter: that particular wall-space,
to which my breath floats up when I'm asleep,
has another occupant: my mother's
painting of the view across her garden.
I like to think St Brigid might approve.

Saint Christopher

The nearest thing to a graven image
that I carried with me over the years
was the St Christopher medal brought back
by my ten-year-old son from a school trip

to Canterbury. Something persisted
of the Cathedral's numen. Alas, though,
the saints we call on to protect us are
less powerful at protecting themselves.

My purse with the medal in it was snatched
on a London Transport escalator
by some denizen of the Underground.
But, as my instinct (or the saint) advised,
I'd kept the much-folded sheet of paper
it came in, inscribed 'Dear Mum, Your present'.

Mildred's House

'NO SCRABBLE HERE' says the invisible
notice on the downstairs window, behind
the visible one in the form of a
house agent's board among shoulder-high sedge.

No Scrabble, no tea, no competitive
cake around the Scrabble table, after
too much went wrong: one fall too many,
a bewildering series of scam calls,

the relentless paramedics. Even
the cat sensed the mood and found a new home,
because there seems to have been no answer –
least of all tears, that self-wounding weapon –

and eventually the sort-of-niece
or distant cousin would sort it all out.

Poor Jenny is a-weeping
(*in memory of Jenny Gould*)

I

It was what the blackbird sang in the garden,
making a sentence of it, as they do:
turning it into blackbird rhythms.

Poor Jenny is a-weeping, it sang.
chanting at me urgently to find out
about the weeping, about the news.

And when I did, poor Jenny, the tears
were mine; you could scarcely speak at all
in whatever time was left to you.

It's I who was weeping, on a bright Easter day.

II

For years we must have shared the same blackbird,
when you had the next but one garden –
you who were so given to planting trees.

I can still see them from my bedroom window:
lilac and viburnum, knitted together
with honeysuckle and climbing roses,

and your signature New Zealand Pittosporum
grown high enough to dodge the attacks
of the foliage-hating neighbour between us.

They must have lodged generations of blackbirds.

III

The joys of resuscitating an old house!
I remember you, after you first moved in,
washing your long hair in the kitchen sink,

then continuing with the transformations.
Tony lopped rogue branches with his kukri
while you, one day, pruning the jasmine

by the front door, were intrigued to discover
its stems were multicoloured inside…
Oh no – telephone wires! Never mind.

All things pass, dear Jenny. Rest in peace.
I shall think of you in a Paradise Garden.

In the Desert

As the Taliban surged back into Kabul
and the international correspondents
looked more exhausted with every broadcast
but not as exhausted as the refugees

I thought of my young second cousin Matthew,
one of the four hundred and fifty-seven
flown back from Afghanistan in sealed coffins
to Wootton Bassett and then, in Matthew's case,

to York for his military funeral
in the Minster, after which the gun-carriage
paraded him on a tour of the packed streets
before beginning its sedate procession

to the cemetery while we, the mourners,
plus vanloads of soldiery sped off ahead
at a pace Matthew would surely have preferred,
with sirens and flashing lights, to get there first;

all of which might have been designed to persuade
his parents that being blown up by a bomb
at twenty-three was a worthy destiny –
an opinion they are perhaps revising.

Jacky
(i.m. Jacqueline Simms, 1940-2021)

Let's go back in time, Jacky,
now that the present is not much fun,
to the menagerie you proposed,
entitled *The Oxford Book of Creatures*.

The range would be from whale to amoeba,
we agreed: Moby Dick to Cell DNA.
The whole of literature was eligible,
although with a limit on dogs and cats.

I was to find the poems, you the prose.
I plodded through alphabetical shelves
in libraries. You consulted friends,
and turned the project into a party.

Our final editorial meeting
was like a horizontal version of
varnishing day at the Academy,
with photocopies as the exhibits;

they spread all over the floor of my study
in loops and chains and winding circuits,
overlapping, sparking connections,
wandering in and out of categories.

We crawled among them, tweaking the order,
introducing them to each other:
Darwin and Pliny and D.H. Lawrence,
Beatrix Potter in bed with some fleas,

Richmal Crompton's William leading
a posse of rats; one of Drake's mariners
dining on 'a fowl whose flesh is like
a fat goose'. (We call it a penguin.)

I'll sit with your checked rug over my knees
(who else would think of arriving for lunch
with a rug instead of flowers?). Thank you,
dear Jacky, for inviting me aboard your ark.

Being Ninety

(for Karl Stead, Kevin Ireland and Peter Bland, on the eve of my 89th birthday)

Auckland's the place for reunions with
the poets of my sparse generation:
not war babies – when the war came
we were already little scholars,
printing our names, conning our infant books,
one of us as old as seven.

We were all children of the Depression,
born in the thirties. Karl, the first of us,
crossed the bar to nonagenarian
with a high jump or a high dive
into the seas of the Auckland region.
All that swimming kept him alive.

Next in the calendar came Kevin,
who transplanted his new identity
for twenty-five years to a base in London
whence Kiwi-accented poems marched back
loyally to their place of origin
until he followed (the fishing was better).

I came third, an Antipodean
by birth but another wanderer,
hooked on my English childhood, and given
to writing about my ancestors,
but also tugged to the land of my children
and these poetic contemporaries.

The last was Peter, born the same year
as me, although a few months younger
and in the opposite hemisphere –
from which he galumphed into Wellington
to sweep his way through the poetry scene
and stage a raid on the acting profession.

Now we've reached a level of stasis,
but there are thresholds yet to be crossed,
and I'm too cowardly to examine
what lurks ahead for any of us.
So rather than hope for a reunion,
when surely our travelling days are done,

I'll tot up the years by ordinal
rather than cardinal computation,
and opt right now for a practice run –
tiptoeing or tightrope-walking,
along with my fellow funambulists,
into the storms of my ninetieth season.

Notes

Stint

The Greek words spoken by the Sybil mean 'I want to die' ('Apothanein thelo'.) The version here is from Petronius, as quoted by Eliot in the epigraph to *The Waste Land*, but the wording of my Sibyl's plea is the one that has stuck in my head since my student days, ready to be muttered on suitable occasions. The word 'Stint' is also another name for the lesser sandpiper, which has found its way into the poem.

Goliath

The painting of David and Jonathan (?) [sic] is by Giovanni Battista Cima da Conegliano, about 1459 to about 1517-18, known as Cima.

INDEX

INDEX OF TITLES

INDEX OF FIRST LINES

617

ACKNOWLEDGEMENTS

This book includes all the poems from Fleur Adcock's *Poems 1960–2000* (Bloodaxe Books, 2000), *Dragon Talk* (Bloodaxe Books, 2010), *Glass Wings* (Bloodaxe Books and Victoria University Press, 2013), *The Land Ballot* (Bloodaxe Books and Victoria University Press, 2014), *Hoard* (Bloodaxe Books and Victoria University Press, 2017) and *The Mermaid's Purse* (Bloodaxe Books, 2021, and Victoria University Press, 2020), as well as a collection of *New Poems* (2024) first collected in this edition. Several of the new poems have appeared in the following publications or websites: *New Zealand Poetry Shelf, PN Review, Pennine Platform* and *The Spectator*.

It is also an expanded edition of Fleur Adcock's *Collected Poems* (Victoria University Press, 2019) published in New Zealand in hardback only under licence from Bloodaxe Books not including the later poems from *The Mermaid's Purse* nor the *New Poems*. This expanded edition of *Collected Poems* is published in the UK by Bloodaxe Books in hardback and paperback editions and in New Zealand in paperback by Te Herenga Waka University Press (formerly Victoria University Press of Wellington).